Joe. Peter,

C000278393

Blackstone's G.

TRANSPORT & WORKS ACT 1992

Planning for Infrastructure Developments

To our colleagues and our friends
in the transport industry

Blackstone's Guide to the

TRANSPORT & WORKS ACT 1992
Planning for Infrastructure Developments

Joe Durkin, LLB

Peter Lane, MA, LLM

Monica Peto, LLB, LLM

Solicitors and Parliamentary Agents
Partner, Rees & Freres, Westminster

BLACKSTONE
PRESS LIMITED

First published in Great Britain 1992 by Blackstone Press Limited,
9-15 Aldine Street, London W12 8AW. Telephone 081-740 1173

© J. Durkin, P. Lane and M. Peto, 1992

ISBN: 1 85431 241 3

British Library Cataloguing in Publication Data
A CIP catalogue record for this book is available from the British Library

Typeset by Style Photosetting Ltd, Mayfield, East Sussex
Printed by BPCC Wheatons Ltd, Exeter

Contents

1   Background to the Act   1
1.1 Introduction 1.2 Nature and function of private Acts 1.3 Necessity for
statutory authorisation in case of certain infrastructure projects 1.4 Problems
with the private Bill system 1.5 Private Bills or public local inquiries 1.6 Private
Bills and the planning system 1.7 The movement from private Acts to ministerial
orders 1.8 The Joint Committee on Private Bill procedure 1.9 The Government's
response 1.10 The Transport and Works Bill 1.11 An outline of the Act.

2   The new authorisation system in outline   16
2.1 Section 1 and section 3 orders 2.2 Orders initiated by the Secretary of State
2.3 Scottish transport systems 2.4 Schemes of national significance 2.5 Commencement of the new system.

3   The new authorising orders   20
3.1 Transport systems to which the new procedure relates 3.2 Contents of orders
under section 1 or section 3 3.3 Applications for orders 3.4 Alterations to
applications 3.5 Objections to orders 3.6 Decisions on applications 3.7 Challenging the validity of orders 3.8 Special parliamentary procedure 3.9 Model clauses
3.10 Power to apply for, or object to, orders 3.11 Transport Consultative
Committees 3.12 Delegation of Secretary of State's functions to appointed
persons 3.13 Crown land.

4   Schemes of national significance   49
4.1 The background 4.2 What schemes are 'schemes of national significance'? 4.3
The procedure for dealing with schemes of national significance 4.4 The effect of
Parliamentary approval 4.5 Schemes of national significance initiated by the
Secretary of State 4.6 Hybrid Bills.

5   Planning permission, other statutory consents and blight notices   60
5.1 Introduction 5.2 Planning permission 5.3 Listed buildings and conservation
areas 5.4 Hazardous substances 5.5 Coast protection consent 5.6 Assimilation of
procedures 5.7 Blight notices.

6 The authorisation of Scottish transport systems 76
6.1 Scottish private legislation procedure 6.2 The Joint Committee's recommendations and the Government's response 6.3 Railway authorisations after the Act 6.4 Harbour orders.

7 Harbours 80
7.1 Introduction 7.2 Harbour revision orders and harbour empowerment orders 7.3 Harbour orders and private Acts 7.4 Marinas and other recreational facilities 7.5 Reduction of harbour facilities 7.6 Harbour authorities having several harbours 7.7 Footpaths and maps 7.8 Works in the harbour 7.9 Harbour businesses, development of land and delegation of functions 7.10 Conservation and the environment 7.11 Special parliamentary procedure 7.12 Fees, costs and technical changes.

8 Inland waterways and works affecting rights of navigation 96
8.1 Introduction 8.2 The new s. 3 orders.

9 Tramways (light rail rapid transit systems) 99
9.1 Introduction 9.2 Leasing of tramways in operation at Royal Assent 9.3 Application of public service vehicles legislation 9.4 Exclusion of hackney carriage legislation.

10 Rail crossings 103
10.1 Stopping up and diversion of footpaths and bridleways crossing railways 10.2 Tunnels and bridges for footpaths and bridleways crossing railways 10.3 Safety at private crossings in England, Wales and Scotland.

11 Safety on transport systems 112
11.1 Introduction 11.2 Approval of works, plant and equipment 11.3 Extension of powers of HM Railway Inspectors 11.4 Reporting of accidents 11.5 Insurance and limits on speed and loads.

12 Control of drink and drugs on transport systems 118
12.1 Introduction 12.2 Transport systems to which the new controls apply 12.3 Principal offences 12.4 Police powers 12.5 Evidence in proceedings for offences under s. 27.

13 Private Bills after the Transport and Works Act 1992 126

Text of the Transport and Works Act 1992 128

Index 179

ONE
BACKGROUND TO THE ACT

1.1 INTRODUCTION

The Transport and Works Act 1992 ('TAWA') represents Parliament's response to two distinct problems involving rail and sea transport which were identified in the 1980s. The first concerns the way in which approval is given for certain infrastructure projects such as railways, tramways (and other 'guided' systems), ports and harbours. The second arose out of the realisation, following railway accidents at Clapham Junction, Cannon Street and Morpeth, and the fire at King's Cross underground station, that additional controls were needed to ensure safety upon railways and other forms of guided transport.

Although the safety provisions (largely contained in Part II of TAWA) are far-reaching and important, it is not necessary at this stage to say anything further by way of background. On the other hand, the question of how to give approval for certain infrastructure projects requires some understanding of the form of authorisation which Part I of TAWA replaces, namely private Acts of Parliament. This chapter is intended to give a short description of the previous system and the reasons why a fundamental change came to be regarded as necessary.

1.2 NATURE AND FUNCTION OF PRIVATE ACTS

1.2.1 Forms of legislation

Acts of the United Kingdom Parliament can take one of three forms. First, and most important, is the public Act. Such Acts are general in their effects, and deal with matters of public policy. Most Government legislation takes this form, although it should be noted that backbench MPs (and peers who are not Ministers) can introduce public Bills. (In the House of Commons, such Bills are known as private Members' Bills, and are not to be confused with private Bills).

The second form is the private Act, and it is this with which we are concerned. Private Acts are particular, rather than general, in their effects. They confer particular powers or benefits on a person or body of persons, in excess of or in conflict with the general law. Bills for private Acts are not introduced by a member of the legislature, but are sought by the person or body promoting them, who must deposit a petition for the Bill in Parliament, together with a copy of the Bill itself. Private Acts may be local or personal in nature but this chapter is concerned solely with the former.

The third form is the hybrid Act which, as its name suggests, is a combination of both a public and a private Act. It is public in that it raises questions of public policy; its private element derives from the fact that it treats a particular private interest in a different way from the interests of other persons or bodies in the same category or class. Hybrid Bills are introduced by the Government in the same way as other public Bills. Recent examples include the Channel Tunnel Act 1987 and the Severn Bridges Act 1992.

1.2.2 Importance of private Acts

Although there is little general public awareness of private Acts, their importance in the legislative history of the United Kingdom has been considerable. Indeed, until the early-twentieth century, the number of private Acts passed in each session of Parliament commonly exceeded (often to a substantial degree) the number of public Acts. Nor were the scope and importance of private Acts in any way insignificant. Britain's canal systems were constructed in the late-eighteenth and early-nineteenth centuries under powers conferred by private Acts, as were Britain's railways in the nineteenth century. Around the turn of the present century, many hundreds of private Acts facilitated the creation of public utilities for the provision of electricity, gas and water. The achievements of private Acts were well (if somewhat colourfully) summed up by Cyprian Williams in 1945 when, in his history of private Bill procedure, he wrote that every citizen:

> wherever he mounts an omnibus or tram or gets into a railway train, whenever he turns on a water tap supplied from a company's main, ignites a gas burner or switches on a company's electric current, wherever he walks in a well-paved and lighted street, saunters on an esplanade or listens to a band playing in a municipal bandstand, and in many other actions of his daily life, is profiting from the results of private bill legislation. (Williams, O.C., *The Historical Development of Private Bill Procedure and Standing Orders in the House of Commons*, London: HMSO, 1948, vol. I, p.1.)

1.3 NECESSITY FOR STATUTORY AUTHORISATION IN CASE OF CERTAIN INFRASTRUCTURE PROJECTS

As has already been mentioned, the reason for seeking a private Act is to obtain powers over and above those enjoyed under the general law. In the case of railways, tramways and similar transport systems, promoters were mainly concerned to achieve two things by means of an Act, namely powers of compulsory acquisition and immunity from liability in nuisance.

1.3.1 Railways, etc.

In the case of any significant railway, tramway, etc., it is necessary to ensure that the promoters have power to acquire compulsorily any land not already in their ownership which is needed for the construction and operation of the system. It is perhaps one of the major achievements of the private legislation of the nineteenth century that ways were found of reconciling the interests of the private landowner with the public interest of securing the creation of new transport systems, which not only brought the country general economic benefits but also for the first time provided ordinary people with opportunities to travel beyond the confines of their immediate neighbourhoods.

In 1845, Parliament enacted two so-called 'clauses' Acts (the Railways Clauses Consolidation Act and the Lands Clauses Consolidation Act) which standardised the procedure for acquiring land compulsorily and compensating those having interests in the land. These Acts (or relevant portions of them) were incorporated by reference in individual private Acts, whose promoters henceforth largely could confine themselves to the task of establishing to Parliament's satisfaction the desirability of taking the particular piece or parcels of land in question. By and large this remains the position today, although private Bills now often apply the Compulsory Purchase Act 1965, instead of the Lands Clauses Consolidation Act 1845.

The second reason for seeking private Act powers in the case of works projects was to obtain immunity from claims in nuisance (and related torts such as that of the rule in *Rylands* v *Fletcher* (1868) LR 3 HL 330). The very nature of a railway is such as to give rise to liability in nuisance by, for example, the emission of noise and fumes. If the system is run under statutory powers, however, the operator will, as a general rule, be liable only where an action is carried out in a way which the court considers to be negligent. (See *Halsbury's Laws*, 4th edn, London: Butterworths, 1980, vol. 34, paras. 345, 375 and 380; *Allen* v *Gulf Oil Refining Ltd* [1981] AC 1001; *Tate and Lyle Food Distribution Ltd* v *London Council* [1983] 2 AC 509.)

1.3.2 Ports and harbours

In the case of ports and harbours, the reasons for seeking powers under a private Act are similar, except that, in most cases, the immunity which the promoter is seeking will be immunity from liability for interfering with public rights of navigation. Under common law these rights extend over all navigable tidal waters and any interference with them is actionable as a public nuisance (see Hobday, S.R., *Coulson & Forbes on Waters and Land Drainage*, 6th edn, London: Sweet & Maxwell, 1952, pp. 506–19). For this reason, any structure placed below high-water mark (e.g., a jetty or pier) will constitute an interference with public rights of navigation and so must be authorised by statute.

Promoters of railway, harbour and related projects will often have other reasons for seeking statutory powers by means of a private Act. A proposed railway may, for example, involve closing or diverting or otherwise interfering with public rights of way, or the promoter may consider it necessary to seek power to make byelaws regulating the use of the proposed facilities.

1.4   PROBLEMS WITH THE PRIVATE BILL SYSTEM

Many of the reasons why Parliament decided, in effect, to abolish private Bills
for most works schemes lie in the procedure which those Bills must follow in
Parliament. Like public Bills, a private Bill must be read a First, Second and
Third time, and have a Committee stage, in each House of Parliament. However,
the Committee stage of a private Bill differs drastically from that of a public Bill.
Because a private Bill seeks to confer special rights or powers upon a person or
body, anyone whose rights or interests would be adversely affected by the
exercise of the promoters' rights or powers can ask to be heard at the Committee
stage, in order to seek to persuade the Committee either to reject the Bill
altogether, or to amend it in a way which will protect that person's interests.
Such a person is entitled to be heard before the Committee if he deposits a
petition against the Bill before the date set or determined by the Standing Orders
of the House in which the Bill is pending. In these circumstances, proceedings
before the Committee are of a quasi-judicial nature. The Committee hears
evidence from promoters and petitioners, each of whom is entitled to be
represented by counsel.

1.4.1   Increase in number and length of Opposed Committees

Such contested, or, as they are called, 'Opposed' Committee proceedings are by
no means a recent phenomenon. Many of the major railway Bills of the
nineteenth century were opposed in this way, often fiercely (see e.g., Vaughan,
Adrian, *Isambard Kingdom Brunel — Engineering Knight Errant*, London: John
Murray, 1991). Nevertheless, it is fair to say that, until the mid-1980s,
Parliament (and especially the House of Commons) had not considered itself to
be unduly burdened by the private Bill system. This was due partly to the fact
that there were no railway or tramway schemes of any significance, and partly to
the creation of alternative procedures for dealing with various matters which
would otherwise have been the subject of private Bills. The situation started to
change, however, in the mid-1980s.

There were several reasons for this. For the first time in many years, major
railway and tramway schemes began to be developed and put to Parliament in
the form of private Bills. These schemes included light rapid transit systems for
Avon, Birmingham, Manchester and Leeds. Not all of these schemes were
politically controversial, or contested in principle, but they nevertheless generated substantial opposition from those whose properties were to be compulsorily acquired, or injuriously affected, by the proposed works. At about the same
time several major port schemes were introduced as private Bills, including two
which were particularly controversial. The Felixstowe Dock and Railway Bill
(which began life in 1984) sought to authorise a large expansion of dock facilities
at Felixstowe. It was heavily opposed, both by those who resented Felixstowe's
status as a port which was not subject to the National Dock Labour Scheme, and
by those who considered that the project represented a threat to bird habitats.
The Opposed Committee in the House of Commons sat for a total of 24 days
over a period of five months, a modern record. In 1987, the petition for the
Associated British Ports (No. 2) Bill was deposited in Parliament. The aim of

this Bill was to enable Associated British Ports to construct a major coal importation facility at Immingham. This Bill was strongly opposed at its Committee stages by those who feared that the new facility would result in a serious loss of employment at English coal mines.

1.4.2 Opposition on floor of House

As a result of the number of significant and/or controversial private 'works' Bills, Parliament found itself having to provide members to sit on more Opposed Committees, for increasing periods of time. However, this was not the only matter which Parliament began to view with concern. It became common for MPs who were opposed to a particular private Bill (whether on political grounds or because of a more limited reason such as the desire to seek protection for a particular property owner) to object to the Bill on the floor of the House of Commons, at its Second and Third Reading stages (and also on Consideration (or report) stage for those Bills which had been amended in Committee). The 'blocking' of a Bill (as it is commonly known) can be achieved by a single MP shouting 'Object', when the title of the Bill is read out, and then putting down an appropriate motion. The MP is not obliged to give any reasons for taking such action. If a private Bill is unable to pass its stage without objection, then, if the Bill is to make any further progress the promoters must ask the Chairman of Ways and Means to have time allocated for a debate on the stage in question. Normally such debates occur between 7 p.m. and 10 p.m. on a particular evening. The growing number of private Bills seeking to authorise significant works projects, sometimes of a politically controversial nature, coupled with the increased use of delaying tactics – or outright opposition – to private Bills on the floor of the House of Commons, led to complaints from the legislators that Parliament was devoting too large a proportion of its time to private legislation.

1.5 PRIVATE BILLS OR PUBLIC LOCAL INQUIRIES

Criticism of the private Bill system was not, however, confined to what some saw as the excessive demands it was placing upon Parliament's time. From both inside and outside the Palace of Westminster there came complaints that the system itself was flawed, and that private Acts were not the best means of dealing with works schemes such as those involving railways, light rail transit systems and harbour developments.

In the nineteenth century – the hey-day of private Bills – there was no general system of town and country planning, and hence no concept of local authorities having statutory powers of what we now call development control in respect of building and other works of construction in their areas. Although Parliament had legislated on certain planning matters before the Second World War, it was not until the enactment of the Town and Country Planning Act 1947 that a comprehensive system of development control was established.

1.5.1 Planning inquiries

In its present form – contained in the Town and Country Planning Act 1990 (or, in Scotland, the Town and Country Planning (Scotland) Act 1972) together with numerous related statutory instruments and Departmental circulars – local authorities are (broadly speaking) given powers to determine whether development (as defined in the Act) should be given planning permission. In the case of refusal, an applicant for planning permission has a right of appeal to the Secretary of State. Unless the applicant chooses to proceed by way of written representation, such an appeal involves the holding of a public local inquiry before an inspector appointed by the Secretary of State. In certain cases, where the matter is particularly controversial or complex, the Secretary of State may himself 'call in' the application and determine it himself, again following a public inquiry. Over the past 40 years or so the planning system has achieved widespread acceptance, and there can be few members of the public who are unaware of the basic nature and purpose of a planning inquiry, even though they themselves may never have had occasion to attend one.

1.5.2 Comparisons with Opposed Committees

Critics of the private Bill system for works projects pointed to the differences between public local inquiries and the system of Opposed Committees for private Bills, claiming that such Committees are inherently less satisfactory than the inquiry system, at least from the point of view of an objector. An inquiry will be held locally, making it easier for interested persons to attend than is the case with an Opposed Committee held within the confines of the Palace of Westminster. Public inquiries were also seen as less intimidating than Opposed Committees, with a more familiar procedure and more predictable timetable. One particular aspect of private Bill procedure which frequently annoyed objectors is the rule of *locus standi* , under which only those directly and specially affected by the Bill have the right to be heard before an Opposed Committee. At a public inquiry, it is rare for an inspector to deny anyone the right to be heard, although the inspector may seek to cut short any representations which he considers to be irrelevant to the subject matter of the inquiry. Critics of private Bills also argued that the MPs or peers sitting on an Opposed Committee would be unlikely to have any special expertise in what would often be highly technical matters raised by the Bill, whereas inspectors tend to be selected for particular inquiries on the grounds of their having the relevant professional expertise. The final comparison between inquiries and Opposed Committees was that inspectors must give written reasons either for their decisions, where they are appointed by the Secretary of State to decide the matter, or for their recommendations to the Secretary of State, who in such cases must himself give reasons for his decision. Furthermore, all such decisions are subject to review in the High Court on points of law. In the case of a private Bill, the Committee need give no reasons, and neither its decision nor anything which happens to the Bill on the floor of the House is reviewable by the courts.

1.5.3 Advantages of Opposed Committees

It is interesting to observe that those who compared Opposed Committees unfavourably with public local inquiries tended to do so from the point of view of the opponent of a works scheme. By contrast, many promoters of private works Bills saw the private Bill procedure, in particular the Opposed Committee system, in a positive light. They pointed to the fact that there is more discipline in the timetable of an Opposed Committee than in that of an inquiry, which can take several years to complete its task. No doubt in their minds also was the fear that a public inquiry, often held in the heart of the area to be affected by the proposals, is more susceptible to disruption of the kind which occurred at the inquiry into new road proposals at Archway in north London, than is a Committee in Parliament. Furthermore, the corollary of the requirement that both inspectors and the Secretary of State must give reasons for their decisions is the inevitable and often lengthy delay whilst their reports or findings are formulated. This contrasts unfavourably with Opposed Committees which are able to give their decisions speedily, often within minutes of the conclusion of the proceedings. Unlike the objectors to a scheme, promoters viewed with concern the prospect that the decision to go ahead with the scheme would be susceptible to challenge in the High Court and thereafter on appeal, with all the delay and uncertainty which that would bring.

1.6 PRIVATE BILLS AND THE PLANNING SYSTEM

It was not merely the difference in procedure between private Bills and the planning system which disturbed the critics of such Bills. The actual relationship of the two regimes was a further cause for concern, which found expression in the complaint, frequently heard during the late-1980s, that promoters of works schemes were seeking to use private Bills in order to override or avoid planning controls.

The relationship between private Acts and the general planning law is currently governed by the Local Government (Miscellaneous Provisions) Act 1976, s. 42, which provides that any local (i.e., private) Act passed after or in the same Session as the 1976 Act is to have effect subject to the provisions of the enactments relating to town and country planning, except so far as the local Act expressly provides otherwise. Instances of a private Act expressly overriding the general planning law are rare (but see e.g., the London Underground (Safety Measures) Act 1991, s. 33, in respect of listed buildings). Of much greater significance, however, is the Town and Country Planning General Development Order 1988 (SI 1988/1813), art. 3 and sch. 2, Part II, which provides that (subject to certain restrictions) development carried out under a private Act, which designates specifically the nature of the development authorised and the land upon which it may be carried out, is permitted development for which planning permission is automatically deemed to have been granted. In a very real sense, therefore, Opposed Committees on private works Bills were being asked to determine questions of development control, since the promoters, if successful, would often be able to implement their schemes without having to seek any further planning consent from the local planning authority.

Some objectors went so far as to claim that in certain cases promoters were seeking powers through a private Act solely in order to avoid having to go through the planning or some other process involving local decision-making or public local inquiries. In fact, a promoter of a private Bill has to swear on oath in each House that the purposes of the Bill cannot be effected without the authority of Parliament, with the result that it would not have been possible to obtain a private Act to carry out a project which merely required planning permission. Nevertheless, more informed critics of the system believed that they had detected in certain cases attempts by promoters, who required Parliamentary powers for certain limited aspects of their projects, to include in their private Bills a complete package of authorisations, including those which could in fact be obtained under the general law.

One measure which attracted criticism of this kind was the Hampshire (Lyndhurst Bypass) Bill, which sought to authorise the building of a bypass around the New Forest town. Powers already existed under the Highways Act 1980 to carry such a scheme into effect, but the promoters justified the Bill on the basis that certain aspects, such as the fencing of the road within the New Forest, could not be achieved without a private Act. The Bill was heavily opposed in Parliament and it never reached the statute book.

By the late-1980s many in Parliament had become so anxious to avoid conflict between private Bills and the planning system that (except in the case of linear developments such as railways) promoters often felt compelled to include provisions in their Bills disapplying the provisions of the Town and Country Planning General Development Order 1988 referred to earlier, so that planning consent for the scheme had to be sought from the local planning authority irrespective of statutory authorisation. Even then, however, Opposed Committees were often reluctant to approve the proposed powers until the relevant planning permission had actually been granted.

1.7 THE MOVEMENT FROM PRIVATE ACTS TO MINISTERIAL ORDERS

Those who advocated the introduction of a public inquiry system for scrutinising works schemes, instead of the private Bill procedure, could rely upon a substantial number of precedents, stretching back to the nineteenth century, whereby matters previously the subject of private Acts were removed from Parliament's responsibility, to a greater or lesser extent, and transferred into the hands of the Executive, to which an application for special powers has to be made and which is able to give the necessary authorisation (usually in the form of an order), after holding a public inquiry in case of objections.

1.7.1 Provisional orders

This process can be traced back to the 1840s, when the idea arose of holding a preliminary local inquiry into certain proposals before the introduction of a private Bill implementing those proposals. The Public Health Act 1848 went a stage further, in that, following an inquiry by its inspector, the General Board of Health (which was established by the Act) could make a provisional order applying parts of the Act to the district in respect of which the inquiry had been held. The Local Government Act 1858 established local boards who could apply to the Secretary of State for a provisional order. The Secretary of State had to institute a local inquiry into the proposals which, if found to be justified, were then contained in a provisional order, which was itself brought before

Parliament in the form of a confirmation Bill. The main advantage of such Bills lies in the fact that a number of different orders can be scheduled to a single confirmation Bill. Procedurally, however, there is little difference between them and private Bills, and, with the important exception of Scotland, where different considerations apply, they are now little used (the last occasion being in 1980).

1.7.2 Special parliamentary procedure

Another form of procedure evolved which placed more power with the Executive and less with Parliament. This form is known as special parliamentary procedure and the system which governs it is largely contained in the Statutory Orders (Special Procedure) Act 1945. The 1945 Act arose from a desire on the part of Parliament to lessen the burden of private legislation and was given the necessary impetus by the massive legislative demands which the post-war Attlee Government was placing upon the legislature. The most important of the provisional order-making powers were converted by the 1945 Act to special procedure order-making powers, and s. 1 provided that the new procedure was to apply to all future powers to make orders in respect of which provision is made requiring any such order to be subject to special parliamentary procedure.

In essence the 1945 Act enables an order to be challenged on the floor of each House, while also making provision for those particularly affected by it to be heard by Parliament. In each case, however, the process is much more limited than in the case of a private Bill. Challenge to an order on the floor of the House is achieved by making the order subject to a form of 'negative resolution' procedure, whereby any member of either House may move that the order be annulled. As is the case with any other form of statutory instrument which is subject to negative resolution procedure, the chances of securing a debate on such a motion before the requisite period has elapsed are very slight. Meanwhile, persons adversely affected by the order may (subject to certain conditions) be heard in Parliament by depositing a petition after the order has been laid before each House. If the petition meets the necessary requirements it is referred to a Joint Committee of Lords and Commons (three from each House) who, after hearing from the petitioner and the Minister who made the order (or, if the latter allows, the applicant for the order), may report that the order be not approved, or that it be approved either with or without amendment.

The 1945 Act system was an ingenious compromise between the need to save valuable Parliamentary time and effort upon matters of essentially local importance, and retaining the ability of MPs and peers both to challenge the measure on the floor of the House and to consider objections to it in a quasi-judicial capacity.

The scope of special procedure orders is in theory very wide, but they are perhaps best known in connection with the compulsory purchase of land. Certain compulsory purchase orders are subject to special parliamentary procedure, with the result that those adversely affected can seek to have the Minister's decision to make the order overturned by a Joint Committee. The types of compulsory purchase order which are subject to this procedure depend upon various factors such as the nature of the acquiring authority, the landowner or the land itself. For example, under various enactments, where the acquiring authority is not a local authority (or analogous body), or a statutory undertaker or a Minister, the landowner affected will be entitled to special parliamentary procedure. Statutory undertakers (such as harbour authorities and public utilities) themselves have such a right in certain circumstances, as does the National Trust, whilst land which is a common or open space is also subject to the procedure.

1.7.3   Problems with special parliamentary procedure

Support for the 1945 Act system has, however, waned in recent years, both inside and outside Parliament. Although Joint Committees under the 1945 Act sit much less frequently than Opposed Committees in the case of private Bills, there were still those who believed that legislators should not be asked to devote time to matters of local, as opposed to national, or even regional, interest. Furthermore, special parliamentary procedure has a curious sting in its tail, which in one celebrated case of the 1980s caused amenity bodies and other objectors considerable alarm and anger. Section 6 of the 1945 Act provides that, where a Joint Committee has reported against an order, or amended it, the Minister concerned may bring the original order before Parliament in the form of a confirmation Bill which then follows an expedited procedure, under which it is deemed in each House to have passed through all its stages (including Committee). The only occasion on which a Minister has introduced a Bill to confirm an order which has been rejected by a Joint Committee occurred in 1985 in the case of two compulsory purchase orders relating to a proposed new bypass of Okehampton, Devon. The Government's action in overturning the Joint Committee in the Okehampton case met with a barrage of criticism, especially from those, such as the Open Spaces Society, who felt that they should not have been allowed to go to the trouble and expense of presenting their case to the Joint Committee if the Government never had intended to accept a decision in the petitioner's favour.

The weakness of the 1945 Act is, therefore, essentially a political one in permitting a parliamentary Committee to overturn what is at that stage a Government order, only to allow the Government to overturn that Committee's decision by means of an expedited Bill. Those advocating the enhancement of the importance of local inquiries and the removal of essentially local matters from Parliament were able, after the Okehampton case, to point to this weakness as a further reason for curtailing the ambit of special parliamentary procedure.

1.8   THE JOINT COMMITTEE ON PRIVATE BILL PROCEDURE

In January 1987, pressure for change to the private Bill system led to the establishment of a Joint Committee on Private Bill Procedure. That Committee's work came to an end when Parliament was dissolved prior to the general election of June 1987, but in October of that year a new Joint Committee was established. Its main terms of reference were to consider whether:

(a)   there were matters of a kind currently dealt with by private Bill which could more appropriately be dealt with in some other way, taking account of the interests both of promoters and other affected parties;

(b)　any changes were desirable in private Bill procedure; and
(c)　any amendments were desirable to the Statutory Orders (Special Procedure) Act 1945.

The Joint Committee received evidence from a wide variety of sources, including major promoting bodies such as the British Railways Board and London Regional Transport, amenity bodies such as the Nature Conservancy Council, the Open Spaces Society and the Ramblers' Association, MPs, peers and Government departments. Those bodies who found themselves opposing private Bills for works schemes tended in the main to favour a non-parliamentary means of authorisation, involving a public local inquiry, citing the reasons set out earlier in this chapter, as well as what they saw as the anomalous position of private Bills within the town and country planning process. Those involved in the promotion of private Bills, on the other hand, were broadly supportive of the system, which they felt could be streamlined by procedural changes to House of Commons Standing Orders, designed to reduce the amount of time spent on private Bills on the floor of that House (e.g., by making it more difficult to 'block' Bills). Some witnesses suggested that use could be made of a Joint Committee (along the lines of the 1945 Act) to hear petitions against opposed Bills, thereby avoiding the possibility of Opposed Committees in both Houses.

1.8.1　Recommendations on railways

The Report of the Joint Committee was published in October 1988 (Joint Committee on Private Bill Procedure, *Report*, HL Paper 97/HC 625, London: HMSO, 1988). The Committee recommended various changes in the way private Bills are handled in Parliament, but its most radical proposals concerned the way in which statutory authorisation should be given to railway and related transport schemes. The Joint Committee broadly accepted the criticism of private Bill procedure for works schemes as described earlier in this chapter, and was also swayed by the arguments of those MPs who considered that an excessive amount of Parliamentary time and effort was being expended upon private legislation. The Committee accordingly recommended that British Rail, or any private rail operator, should be able to apply to the Secretary of State for an order authorising proposed railway works. If objections to the draft order were received, the Secretary of State would be able to make the order only after causing a public local inquiry to be held and considering the inspector's report. The order would have effect to authorise the carrying out of works as if it were an Act of Parliament, thereby conferring the necessary immunity from actions in nuisance.

Another reason which the British Railways Board had advanced for seeking powers by way of private Act was for matters related to railway works which involve the interference with or extinguishment of rights of way, for example by stopping up level crossings. The Committee accordingly recommended that the Highways Act 1980 should be extended so as to permit stopping-up orders to be made on safety grounds, in appropriate cases, through the usual Highways Act procedures, including confirmation by the Secretary of State following, if necessary, a public local inquiry. An order-making procedure for trams was also recommended, to be in similar form to that proposed for railways.

1.8.2 Constitutional questions

As can be seen from the brief historical description contained earlier in this chapter, the Joint Committee's recommendation that railway and tramway matters be removed from the realm of private Bills to an order-making procedure represents a further significant step in a process which began in the mid-nineteenth century, and which considerably quickened in the twentieth. The Report makes it clear that the Committee considered its main recommendations to be wholly consistent with this process, the previous instances of which in the Committee's view negated any argument that the proposed transfer of power from Parliament to the Executive was constitutionally improper. Moreover, the Committee was able to point to an existing order-making power for the authorisation of railways, contained in the Light Railways Acts 1896 to 1912. Under this procedure an order may be made by the Secretary of State in respect of the construction or alteration of a light railway following a public local inquiry in the case of objections, except where he is of the opinion that it is necessary to refer the scheme to Parliament by reason of the magnitude of the proposed undertaking or of its effect on the undertaking of any existing railway company, or for any other special reason. Such a referral takes the form of a confirmation Bill. As the Department of Transport told the Joint Committee, the light railways order procedure is inadequate as a general substitute for private Acts because most of British Rail's lines are not light railways (this expression being in fact undefined in the Light Railways Acts). The procedure's main usefulness today lies in providing a form of authorisation for 'leisure' railways, often running along former British Rail routes, such as the Bluebell line in Sussex. However, the light railways procedure will continue to be available in Scotland, notwithstanding TAWA, and is therefore dealt with in more detail in chapter 6.

The Joint Committee considered that the Light Railways Acts:

> are proof that in 1896 there was no reason in principle why railway works should require to be authorised by Parliament, even if in practice the Acts failed to render the railway private bill redundant; and the Committee find no more reason today why railways should be an exception to the general rule . . . that works proposals should be authorised by non-parliamentary procedures.

The Committee concluded that it was 'satisfied that a comparatively straightforward procedure could be devised drawing on existing models contained in the Light Railways Acts and the Highways Act 1980, adapting them to meet modern requirements' (para. 46).

1.8.3 Recommendations on ports and harbours

In the case of works schemes involving ports or harbours, the Joint Committee again recommended a move from private Acts to orders, but here, unlike the position with railways, relatively modern order-making powers already existed, in the form of ss. 14 and 16 of the Harbours Act 1964. These sections (read with schs. 2 and 3) provide respectively for the making of harbour revision orders and harbour empowerment orders. Many significant harbour works have, since 1964, been authorised by such orders, but the Committee found that the scope of the powers themselves was such that certain types of harbour works, such as marinas, and works-related projects such as footpath diversion, would not (or arguably might not) be covered, with the result that such works or projects could be authorised only by way of private Bill or, in Scotland, a provisional order. Moreover, s. 62 of the 1964 Act in effect provided that a private Bill or provisional order could still be promoted even though its objects might be obtained by means of a harbour revision or empowerment order, thus overriding the requirement previously mentioned, that a promoter must prove that the objects of the private Bill or provisional order cannot be obtained except with the authority of Parliament.

The Committee recommended that the permitted scope of orders under the Harbours Act 1964 should be broadened, and that s. 62 of the Act should be repealed. A detailed description of these orders, and the changes made by the TAWA, is contained in chapter 7.

1.9   THE GOVERNMENT'S RESPONSE

The Report of the Joint Committee was debated in both Houses of Parliament in the spring of 1989, and the Government's own response to that Report came in June 1990, with the publication of a Consultation Document (*Private Bills and New Procedures – A Consultation Document*, Cm 1110, London: HMSO, 1990).

In their joint Foreword to this document the Lord President of the Council and the Secretaries of State for Transport and Environment encapsulated the arguments for change described in this chapter, and concluded that the thrust of the Joint Committee's proposals for both new and extended order-making powers was right. The Government agreed with the Joint Committee that there was no reason why the authorisation of most private works and land schemes needed to remain with Parliament, referring to the apparent anomaly whereby the only way in which British Rail could secure approval for the construction of even short stretches of track was by Act of Parliament, when much more significant development is authorised by local authorities or central Government.

With one exception, the Government's proposals for new railway order-making powers closely followed the system recommended by the Joint Committee which, in turn, was based upon the Light Railways Acts. That exception concerned the identity of the person who would make the orders. The Joint Committee assumed that all orders would be made by Ministers, but instead the Government envisaged a 'three-tier' approach, whereby certain schemes would be considered and approved locally, whilst others would be the responsibility of Ministers, with a small minority being referred to Parliament.

The Consultation Document stated that if first-tier schemes could be authorised by local planning authorities there were likely to be time savings. However, it seems that, even at this early stage, the Government appreciated the difficulty of differentiating between the first and second tiers, particularly where aspects of the particular scheme would in every event need to go to central Government for approval, for example because they involved the compulsory purchase of land. As for third-tier schemes, the Government considered that the Secretary of State should have power to refer to Parliament those schemes which he considered to be of national importance, once any public local inquiry had taken place. Any such order would be subject to affirmative resolution procedure, with the result that Parliament would have specifically to approve it (following a single debate on the floor of each House). Second-tier orders would not, however, be subject to any parliamentary procedure, unless they contained provisions repealing or amending earlier private Acts (other than those relating to works or lands), or powers to take certain types of land or the land of particular persons or bodies. In both such cases, orders would normally be subject to the negative resolution procedure, in the latter case as part of the special parliamentary procedure under the 1945 Act.

On the question of harbour powers, the Government broadly accepted the Joint Committee's recommendations regarding the expansion of the existing powers in the Harbours Act 1964 to make harbour revision and empowerment orders, but it was not attracted by the Joint Committee's idea that general works projects, not related to railway, light rail rapid transit or harbour schemes, should still come to Parliament for authorisation as private Acts, shorn of any provisions which could be dealt with by other means. Instead, the Government proposed a more radical solution, whereby the new order-making procedure for rail and light rail rapid transit schemes would be extendable (by subordinate legislation) to cover other works projects which would otherwise require authorisation by private Act. Such projects might include tidal barrages (like those proposed at Cardiff, Stockton-on-Tees and – on a larger scale – the electricity generating barrage on the River Severn), artificial islands for oil exploration (as in the Hook Island (Poole Bay) Bill, 1990), as well as canals and other inland waterways.

1.10   THE TRANSPORT AND WORKS BILL

The Transport and Works Bill was published on 12 November 1991. The provisions relating to works schemes differed in two significant respects from the proposals contained in the Government's consultation document. Having considered the responses to that document from a wide range of bodies, the Government chose to abandon the local authority first tier of decision-making for railway and light rail rapid transit orders, while, in the case of schemes of national significance, it was decided that Parliament should have the opportunity of debating (and voting on) the policy and principle of the scheme before rather than after the public local inquiry had been held.

The first change proved popular with those promoters who had regarded the direct involvement of local authorities as both inappropriate and impracticable in the context of linear developments such as railways, but it was not welcomed by those most committed to the principle of local participation in development control. The second change was, on the other hand, generally welcomed, particularly since it would avoid the risk of protracted local hearings and the subsequent ministerial decision being rendered abortive, if the scheme itself could not command the support of Parliament. Interesting questions of policy and procedure are, nevertheless, raised by having Parliament decide on the matter at an early stage in the procedure, and those questions are considered in chapter 4.

1.11 AN OUTLINE OF THE ACT

The Transport and Works Bill, which was introduced into the House of Commons, was amended both in Standing Committee and on Report. It completed its substantive House of Lords stage in a single day – courtesy of the impending general election – and received Royal Assent on 16 March 1992.

Part I of TAWA contains the new order-making powers for railway, tramway and other guided transport schemes, and makes provision for the extension of the new procedures so as to cover inland waterways and other works which interfere with navigation.

Part II deals with various safety matters:

(a)   Chapter I contains provisions for controlling the use of drink or drugs by workers on railways and related systems such as trams.

(b)   Chapter II contains various other safety provisions, including those implementing the Joint Committee's recommendations regarding the stopping up or diversion for safety purposes of footpaths and bridleways crossing railways.

(c)   Chapter III deals with consultation by the Secretary of State on various matters in Part II including regulations about alcohol limits, as well as dealing with matters relating to offences created by Part II.

Part III deals with the leasing of tramways and the conduct of their staff and passengers. It also extends the purposes for which harbour revision and empowerment orders may be made under the Harbours Act 1964, in response to the recommendations of the Joint Committee.

TWO
THE NEW AUTHORISATION SYSTEM IN OUTLINE

2.1 SECTION 1 AND SECTION 3 ORDERS

The Transport and Works Act introduces two types of authorising orders. Orders under s. 1 authorise the construction or operation of transport systems on dry land, such as railways, tramways, trolley vehicle systems and other systems using a prescribed mode of guided transport. Orders under s. 3 authorise the construction or use of an inland waterway in England and Wales, or the carrying out of works which interfere with rights of navigation. Because there is a close relationship between works which continue to be authorised by harbour revision or empowerment orders under the Harbours Act 1964 and those which are to be authorised under s. 3 of TAWA, works over inland waterways and below high-water mark are dealt with separately in chapters 7 and 8.

Sections 6 to 14 of TAWA set out the outline of the procedure by which applications may be made and will be dealt with. These provisions, which apply equally to applications for s. 1 orders and for s. 3 orders, are explained in chapter 3.

2.2 ORDERS INITIATED BY THE SECRETARY OF STATE

In special circumstances, the Secretary of State is empowered by s. 7 of TAWA to make a s. 1 or s. 3 order on his own initiative. These fall into two categories – defence transport systems and orders made in the interests of safety.

2.2.1 Defence transport systems

The Secretary of State may initiate orders for the construction or operation of, or which relate to, a railway tramway or other transport system within s. 1(1) for naval, military, airforce or other defence purposes (see s. 7(1)(a)).

Up to the coming into force of TAWA, the Secretary of State for Defence had powers under the Military Tramways Act 1887 to apply to the Secretary of State for Transport for provisional orders authorising the construction or operation of tramways for military purposes. The 1887 Act was due for revision. Amongst its disadvantages were that it applied only to tramways and that orders under the Act required to be confirmed by Parliament. The 1887 Act is now repealed and replaced by the new order-making power under s. 7.

2.2.2 Orders in the interests of safety

The Secretary of State may by order under s. 1 or s. 3 make any provision which appears to him to be necessary or expedient in the interests of safety, either for the suspension or discontinuance of any operations or in consequence of the abandonment or neglect of any work (see s. 7(1)(b)).

Under this power, the Secretary of State can prevent a transport system being operated dangerously by suspending its operation or, in the last resort, closing it down completely. The power provides a simple mechanism for dealing with abandoned or neglected transport works. With the possible future proliferation of transport operators, the chances increase that some of them may become insolvent or that schemes may be abandoned for financial reasons. The power provided by s. 7 will enable the Secretary of State to remove works such as discontinued railway lines which would otherwise be left to scar the environment.

2.3 SCOTTISH TRANSPORT SYSTEMS

The new authorising orders apply only to transport systems in England and Wales. The present system for private legislation in Scotland, which is laid down in the Private Legislation Procedure (Scotland) Act 1936, is to continue since the Government determined not to make any radical changes in the Scottish procedures beyond certain of the purely administrative improvements suggested by the Joint Committee in their Report (Private Bills and New Procedures – A Consultation Document, Cm 1110, London: HMSO, 1990, para. 53). The Scottish system is discussed further in chapter 6.

2.4 SCHEMES OF NATIONAL SIGNIFICANCE

Section 9 of the Act provides a special procedure for the authorisation of schemes which, in the opinion of the Secretary of State, are of national significance. There is no attempt in the Act to define what is meant by a 'scheme of national significance' nor to provide any guidance to the Secretary of State. The Secretary of State's decision that proposals are of national significance must be made within eight weeks of the date on which the application under s. 6 is received. Once the decision is made, no order may be made on the application unless each House of Parliament passes a resolution approving the proposals of national significance on a motion moved by a Minister of the Crown. An order on the application may not include any provision that is inconsistent with a proposal approved by Parliament. If modifications to the proposals are considered desirable, the Secretary of State may go back to Parliament with a motion that the modifications be approved.

This procedure gives Parliament the opportunity to veto a scheme of national importance at an early stage. If the Secretary of State decides to make an order on the application, the order must give effect to the outline proposals approved by Parliament. On the other hand, Parliamentary approval does not ensure that the scheme will go ahead, since the Secretary of State retains the option not to make an order at all.

Schemes of national significance are discussed in more detail in chapter 4.

2.5   COMMENCEMENT OF THE NEW SYSTEM

The Act provides for its provisions, including the provisions of Part I, to come into force by commencement order. Different days may be appointed for different provisions and for different purposes (s. 70(1)). It is likely that the new order-making procedures will be introduced for railway and tramway schemes and for inland waterway schemes before they are brought into force for schemes interfering with public rights of navigation.

The Act itself provides only the framework for the new system, leaving a number of procedural matters to be dealt with by subordinate legislation before any part of the new system can come into force. These are:

(a)   Rules under s. 6 prescribing procedures for making applications (see 3.3 below).

(b)   Rules under s. 10 which will lay down procedures for the making and hearing of objections to applications (see 3.3 below).

(c)   Orders under s. 8 prescribing model clauses for incorporation into the draft orders to be submitted with applications (see 3.9 below).

(d)   Regulations under s. 15 which will provide an interface between procedures under the Act to authorise works and parallel procedures for obtaining various other consents or licences required under other Acts for the works (see chapter 5).

The task of preparing the necessary subordinate legislation is well on the way. In determining the timetable, account had to be taken of the process of consultation on the proposed subordinate legislation (which started well before Royal Assent) and the fact that rules under ss. 6 and 10 and regulations under s. 15 are to be made by statutory instrument subject to negative resolution procedure, that is to say that they must be laid before Parliament and are for a period of 40 days subject to annulment by a resolution of either House of Parliament. Statutory instruments have to be laid when the House is sitting but the period of 40 days may run while the House is in recess.

The Department of Transport has therefore indicated that Part I of TAWA will be brought into force on 1 January 1993 for transport schemes under s. 1 and for inland waterway schemes under s. 3(1)(a). Section 3(1)(b), which relates to the authorisation of schemes for the carrying out of works interfering with the rights of navigation, cannot be brought into force until an order has been made under s. 4 prescribing descriptions of works to which s. 3(1)(b) is to apply. At the time of writing, it is expected that an order under s. 4 will be made by mid-1993. There has been considerable pressure on the Department of Transport to bring the new procedures into force as soon as possible after November 1992, at least for railway and tramway orders. This is because promoters of private Bills are required to deposit the bills and related plans in Parliament in November in each year. Various new railways and tramway schemes are under discussion. The proposed Thameslink railway line is one example. Had the Act not been passed, private bills seeking authorisation for some of these proposals would be deposited in November 1992. Promoters would be reluctant to risk Parliamentary disapproval by depositing bills in November 1992 even if the new procedures were not yet in force. It would obviously cause concern if any hiatus delayed the authorisation of important new infrastructure schemes.

The new procedures will replace the existing system for obtaining light railway orders under the Light Railways Acts. The Department of Transport has indicated that transitional provision will be made under which applications pending under the old system will continue to be dealt with under the old system.

THREE
THE NEW AUTHORISING ORDERS

3.1 TRANSPORT SYSTEMS TO WHICH THE NEW PROCEDURE RELATES

As has already been explained in chapter 2, there are two sorts of orders under the Act – orders under s. 3 authorising the construction or operation of an inland waterway or the carrying on of prescribed works which interfere with rights of navigation (discussed in chapter 8), and orders under s. 1 authorising the construction or operation of transport systems. In both cases the procedures laid down in Part I of the Act apply only to schemes in England and Wales. Scottish systems are discussed in chapter 6.

The new order-making power under s. 1 applies initially to schemes for the construction or operation of railways, tramways or trolley vehicle systems. The Act breaks new ground in distinguishing between these three systems of transport by defining them in s. 67(1). Despite the existence of a considerable body of legislation relating to railways, tramways and light railways, thus far no attempt had been made to define these expressions. It was probably considered that a railway, like an elephant, is too well known to require explanation. Nor was a definition of 'tramway' included in the Tramways Act 1870. With the decline in the popularity of tramways there has not, up to now, been any need to build on the 1870 Act, and the omission of a definition has not given rise to any problems. However, the demarcation between the different sorts of transport systems has assumed greater significance with the contemporary revival of interest in light rail rapid transit systems. Each mode of transport needs different provisions to deal with the special issues peculiar to each. Tramway orders, for example, need to balance the interests of the highways authority, the transport operator and the other users of the highway. The model clauses under s. 8 will not only include clauses common to most transport systems (such as provisions relating to the compulsory acquisition of the land) but also clauses relevant only to a particular mode of transport.

3.1.1 Railways

A 'railway' is defined in s. 67(1) as a system of transport, not being a tramway,

   . . . employing parallel rails which—

(a)   provide support and guidance for vehicles carried on flanged wheels, and

(b)   form a track which either is of a gauge of at least 350 millimetres or crosses a carriageway (whether or not on the same level) . . .

The definition picks out, as the key feature of the railway, the employment of parallel lines for flanged wheeled vehicles. The definition is wide enough to include ordinary overground and underground railways, steam railways, pier or mineral lines, funiculars, cliff lifts and mountain lines.

Narrow gauge railways (i.e., systems using a track having a gauge of less than 350mm) are excluded unless they cross a carriageway. The effect is to exclude certain very small railways from the order-making procedures in Part I of the Act and the safety provisions relating to railways contained in Part II. The exempted railways include miniature railways built on private land as part of leisure complexes and fun fairs. If miniature railways cross the carriageway of a road it is appropriate to make a special provision for their regulation under the Act. But otherwise they have less in common with ordinary railways than with other fairground entertainments such as big-dippers and, like them, are better regulated under the Health and Safety at Work, etc. Act 1974.

3.1.2   Tramways

A 'tramway' is defined (also in s. 67(1)) as: . . .

a system of transport used wholly or mainly for the carriage of passengers and employing parallel rails which—

(a)   provide support and guidance for vehicles carried on flanged wheels, and

(b)   are laid wholly or mainly along a street or in any other place to which the public has access (including a place to which the public has access only on making a payment).

As in the case of railways, a tramway system uses parallel rails to guide vehicles with flanged wheels, but there are two additional elements in the definition. First, the system must be used wholly or mainly for the carriage of passengers and, secondly, the rails must be laid wholly or mainly along a street or other place to which the public has access (whether or not on payment). The definition is wide enough to include systems such as the Great Orme Tramway, much of which is not laid in the street, and the line at the National Tramway Museum at Crich, which is constructed on private land.

Any overlap between a tramway and a railway is avoided because a railway is specifically defined so as to exclude a tramway. If a system employs parallel lines to guide vehicles with flanged wheels but does not fall within the definition of 'tramway' because, for example, it is not used wholly or mainly for the carriage of passengers, it will (unless it is narrow gauge) come within the definition of 'railway'.

Narrow gauge tramways are not excluded from the definition of 'tramway'. The statutory regulation provided by Parts I and II of the Act is appropriate for all tramways however small because, by definition, they operate in close vicinity to pedestrians and other road users.

The definition covers all sections of a tramway in a public place, whether laid in parts of the highway which are shared by cars and other road users, in specially allocated parts of the highway such as verges or strips between dual carriageways or in areas which, like parks, are used only by pedestrians. If most of a tramway system is laid along a street or in a place to which the public have access, any parts of the system situated in locations used only by the tramway, such as tunnels or flyovers, will also come within the definition.

3.1.3 Trolley vehicle systems

A 'trolley vehicle system' is defined (also in s. 67(1)) as: . . .

a system of transport by vehicles constructed or adapted for use on roads without rails under electric power transmitted to them by overhead wires (whether or not there is in addition a source of power on board the vehicles).

Systems which use rails as well as overhead wires come within the definition of a tramway rather than the definition of a trolley vehicle system. There is no requirement that a trolley vehicle system shall be used wholly or mainly for the carriage of passengers.

3.1.4 Vehicles

The term 'vehicle' features in the definitions of 'railway', 'tramway', and 'trolley vehicle system'. Section 67(1) provides that a 'vehicle' for these purposes includes a mobile traction unit. 'Vehicle' is often statutorily defined as including a locomotive but, without express provision, it would not be clear that in TAWA vehicles include mobile traction units such as are used in the operation of mono-rails. The expression 'mobile' makes it clear that the kind of static unit used on a funicular railway is not intended to fall within the definition.

3.1.5 Other guided transport systems

The Secretary of State is given power under s. 2 to extend the order-making power in s. 1 to systems using modes of guided transport other than railways, tramways and trolley vehicle systems. The power is exercisable by statutory instrument and would be subject to the affirmative resolution procedure, that is to say, no order extending s. 1 could be made unless a draft of it had been laid before and approved by resolution of each House of Parliament.

Section 67(1) defines 'guided transport' as 'transport by vehicles guided by means external to the vehicles (whether or not the vehicles are also capable of being operated in some other way)'. Railways, tramways and trolley vehicle systems are therefore all forms of guided transport. An order extending the order-making power in s. 1 to a new mode of guided transport will need to identify the mode of transport by defining it as has been done by s. 67 in the case of railways, tramways and trolley vehicle systems.

Section 2 ensures that it remains open to the Secretary of State to extend s. 1 to cover any additional system which becomes popular, whether it uses an existing form of guided transport or a form yet to be invented. The Department of Transport has announced that it is proposing to prescribe eight modes of guided transport under s. 2. They are aerial cableway, lift, magnetic levitation, monorail, road-based with cable guidance, road-based with rail guidance, road-based with side guidance and track-based with side guidance. These modes were chosen because they cover the various types of 'unconventional transport' which are either in use in England and Wales already or have been seriously proposed. If statutory authorisation is required for a system using a mode of guided transport because, for example, it is proposed that the system should cross a highway, the necessary authority would need to be conferred by private Act, unless it is prescribed under s. 2.

3.2 CONTENTS OF ORDERS UNDER SECTION 1 OR SECTION 3

3.2.1 General

Sections 1 and 3 are drafted in very general terms. The terms of the power, in each case, are to make an order *relating to, or to matters ancillary to*, the construction or operation of a transport system, in the case of s. 1, or, in the case of s. 3, the construction or operation of an inland waterway system or the carrying out of relevant tidal works. Section 5 elaborates the terms of the power, both by providing that certain matters may be dealt with in the order and, expressly or by implication, restricting the ambit of the power in certain respects. Schedule 1, introduced by s. 5(1), sets out (for illustrative purposes only) a list of matters as to which provision may be made in the order. The scheduled matters are discussed in 3.2.4 below.

The intention is to provide promoters with powers which are sufficiently wide to enable the new orders to deal with all the matters relating to the construction or operation of transport schemes or schemes falling within s. 3 which have up to now been contained in private Bills.

Orders under s. 1 may make provision in relation to more than one scheme, system or mode of transport (s. 5(2)). This will enable promoters to apply for multi-purpose orders similar to the general powers Bills hitherto promoted by the British Railways Board. The British Railways Act 1990, to take a typical case, contains miscellaneous proposals, including the construction or diversion of railways at Birmingham, Doncaster, Ashfield, Bristol, Warrington, Stockton-on-Tees, Newport and Port Talbot. In future, the British Railways Board will instead be able to apply for omnibus orders under s. 1. It will also be possible for a single order to relate to more than one mode of transport. So only one application will be needed for a rapid transit system which, like the proposed Croydon Tramlink, encompasses both tramways and railways. Orders under s. 3 may similarly relate to more than one inland waterway or to the carrying out of more than one project falling within s. 3(1)(b).

3.2.2 Supplementary provisions

Section 5(3) authorises the order to apply, modify or exclude any statutory provision (defined as including both a provision of an Act of Parliament and a provision of an instrument made under an Act), but only to amend, repeal or revoke a statutory provision if it is of local application. This enables orders to follow private Bills in incorporating general provisions such as sections of the Railways Clauses Consolidation Act 1845 or provisions of the model clauses to be introduced under s. 8. This power is required since the essence of private Bills, on which the new orders are based, is to confer on promoters particular powers or benefits in excess of, or in conflict with, the general law. It follows, as was recognised by the Joint Committee, that it should be possible for the general law to be modified or disapplied for the purposes of particular schemes being authorised by the new orders.

In the Transport and Works Bill, as introduced, power was given to the Secretary of State to amend, repeal or revoke any statutory provision if the amendment, repeal or revocation appeared to him to be necessary or expedient in consequence of any provision of the order or otherwise in connection with the order. Opposition to the proposal was expressed by members of the Standing Committee in the House of Commons who labelled it a 'Henry VIII clause', that is to say, a clause which, by empowering the Secretary of State to amend or repeal primary legislation, may be said to usurp the legislative functions of Parliament. In response to this concern, the power was amended at the Report Stage in the House of Commons so as to restrict its application to statutory provisions (whether of primary or secondary legislation) of local application. It was said by the Minister that, as originally drafted, the provision would have allowed the Secretary of State permanently to alter legislation of general application. In fact, no amendment or repeal of general application could have been effected because the power would only have been exercisable for the purposes of the particular transport scheme in question.

Under the provision as enacted, a scheme may, for example, alter transport schemes authorised by previous private or hybrid Acts of Parliament. The amendment, repeal or revocation of a statutory provision of local application will be authorised only if the Secretary of State considers this to be 'necessary or expedient in consequence of any provision of the order or otherwise in connection with the order'. In other words, the powers may be exercised only if the repeal or amendment is ancillary to the main authorising provisions of the order.

An order may contain any provision that appears to the Secretary of State to be necessary or expedient for giving full effect to any other provision of the order, or any supplemental or transitional provision which appears to him to be necessary or expedient (s. 5(4)). This authorises the inclusion in orders of ancillary provisions such as the making of byelaws for the operation of a transport system or the submission of disputes to arbitration. Further, it is provided in s. 5(4) that an order may make provision that appears to the Secretary of State to be necessary or expedient for giving full effect to any provision of an earlier order under s. 1 or s. 3 or any provision contained in, or in an instrument made under, an Act of Parliament passed before Part I of the

TAWA is in force. This enables orders under s. 1 to amend or supplement private or hybrid Acts passed before Part I is in force which relate to particular transport schemes. For example, any further refinements required to the Midland Metro Acts 1989 to 1992 could be authorised by an order under s. 1.

3.2.3 Restrictions on provisions to be included in orders

There are three express restrictions on what provisions may be included in orders. First, an order may itself create a summary offence or authorise the making of byelaws creating summary offences but, under s. 5(5), no term of imprisonment may be imposed and the maximum penalty relating to the new offences is a fine of level 3 on the standard scale (within the meaning of s. 37 of the Criminal Justice Act 1982).

Secondly, under s. 5(6), no public right of way may be extinguished by an order unless the Secretary of State is satisfied either that an alternative right of way has been or will be provided or that the provision of an alternative right of way is not required. This was inserted into the Act at the Report Stage in the House of Commons to meet concerns expressed on behalf of the Rights of Way Review Committee, which includes representatives of the Ramblers Association and other bodies concerned with access to the countryside. Section 5(6) is similar to s. 251(1) of the Town and Country Planning Act 1990, which deals with the extinguishment of public rights of way over land held by a local authority for planning purposes.

Thirdly, s. 5(7) makes it clear that orders under s. 1 or s. 3 may not override ss. 104(3), 105(3) and 112 of the Transport Act 1968, which lay down special procedures for changing the classification or maintenance requirements of inland waterways. Thus, changes in the classification or maintenance requirements of an inland waterway of the British Waterways Board, or the extinguishment of statutory rights and obligations which relate to other inland waterways, must still be authorised under the relevant procedures in the Transport Act 1968. This provision was inserted into the Act by an amendment at the Report Stage in the House of Commons instigated by concerns expressed on behalf of the Inland Waterways Amenity Advisory Council and the Inland Waterways Association.

3.2.4 Matters in sch. 1

The list of matters in sch. 1 for which provision may be made in orders under s. 1 or s. 3 is not exhaustive. The usefulness of sch. 1 lies in the fact that it removes any doubt over whether any of the specified matters can be included in the orders. The list is intended to include most provisions which are typically to be found in private Acts authorising transport schemes.

The list contains the following matters:

(a) The construction, alteration, repair, maintenance, demolition and removal of railways, tramways, trolley vehicle systems and other transport systems within s. 1(1) of the Act, waterways, roads, watercourses, buildings and other structures (sch. 1, para. 1), and the carrying out of any other civil engineering or other works (sch. 1, para. 2). The authorisation of transport works will often be the principal purpose of a s. 1 or s. 3 order. So far as other works are concerned, these must relate to or be ancillary to the construction of works falling within s. 3, or to the construction or operation of a transport system within s. 1 or an inland waterway in England and Wales.

(b)   The acquisition of land, whether compulsorily or by agreement (sch. 1, para. 3), the creation and extinguishment of rights over land (including rights of navigation over water), whether compulsorily or by agreement (sch. 1, para. 4) and the payment of compensation (sch. 1, para. 11). In many cases the promoter will require powers compulsorily to acquire land (which by virtue of the Interpretation Act 1978 includes 'buildings and other structures, land covered with water and any estate, interest, easement, servitude or right in or over land') or to take rights over land, such as rights of way or drainage, or temporary possession of land for use as a work site. Orders relating to the construction of works of any magnitude will generally need to authorise the temporary or permanent stopping up of streets or footpaths to enable the works to be executed. The power to extinguish public rights of way is subject to the restriction in s. 5(6) discussed in 3.2.3.

Orders authorising the compulsory acquisition of land or the compulsory taking of rights over land will also have to make provision to ensure that those affected are properly compensated. It is envisaged that the provisions of the compensation code contained in the Land Compensation Act 1961, the Compulsory Purchase Act 1965 and the Acts supplementing them will be applied. The model clauses to be prescribed under s. 8 will include a clause applying these provisions to which promoters will be expected to adhere rather than devising provisions of their own.

Paragraphs 3 and 4 of sch. 1 refer to provisions authorising the acquisition of land, or the taking of rights, by agreement. Such provisions will only be necessary where the promoter is a body constituted by or under an Act of Parliament which does not have powers to acquire land by agreement for the particular project in question. No special provision would be required where the promoter is a company registered under the Companies Act 1985. Most companies have wide powers to acquire land and enter into similar transactions; and, if the powers of any company are inadequate, they can be extended by altering the company's memorandum of association under s. 4 of the Companies Act 1985.

(c)   The abrogation and modification of agreements relating to land (sch. 1, para. 5). This power will be required where the proposed works impinge on private contractual arrangements such as private accommodation level crossings and private bridges. Section 1 orders authorising the abandonment of railways and other tramway systems will be able to abrogate contractual rights. The extinction of statutory obligations is authorised by para. 4 of sch. 1 (see (b) above). These powers are similar to those which have hitherto been exercisable as ancillary to orders for the abandonment of railways under s. 83 of the Transport Act 1962 (the relevant part of which is repealed by TAWA).

(d)   The conferring on persons providing transport services of rights to use systems belonging to others (sch. 1, para. 6). This provision, which appeared in pre-nationalisation private railway Acts, will come into its own if the British

Railways undertaking is privatised. It would then become necessary to ensure that rival railway operators are able to use each other's systems so as to facilitate the provision of a comprehensive network of train services.

On the privatisation of other utilities, the public need for a nationwide system has produced various devices to require competing operators to cooperate with each other. In the case of telecommunications, for example, a licence granted by the Secretary of State for the running of a telecommunication system may authorise the connection of the system to another telecommunication system, or may include conditions requiring the licensee to permit the connection to the system of other telecommunication systems or apparatus (see ss. 7(4) and 8(1)(b) of the Telecommunications Act 1984).

(e) The protection of the property or interests of any person (sch. 1, para. 7). This enables orders to include protective provisions for the benefit of third parties. Up to now it has been common form for private Bills authorising the construction of works to include provisions for the protection of statutory undertakers and their apparatus. However, many protective provisions relating to street works have been rendered unnecessary by Part III of the New Roads and Street Works Act 1991 and the subordinate legislation made under it. Together, these provide a code of general application for the execution of street works by statutory undertakers and the protection of highway authorities and public utilities whose apparatus may be affected by the works.

(f) The imposition and exclusion of obligations or of liability in respect of any acts or omissions (sch. 1, para. 8). Section 1 or s. 3 orders may lay down special obligations with respect to acts or omissions relating to the construction or operation of the transport system. Taken with s. 5(3)(a), which provides that an order may apply, modify or exclude any statutory provision which relates to any matter to which an order may be made, this power is very wide. It is as yet unclear to what extent it would be considered appropriate for orders to exclude statutory obligations or liabilities under other enactments.

(g) The carrying out of surveys and the taking of soil samples (sch. 1, para. 10). Provisions to this effect have commonly been included in British Railway and London Regional Transport Bills to enable promoters to carry out surveys, etc. without first having to acquire the land compulsorily. The power is particularly important in the case of underground railways.

(h) The charging of tolls, fares (including penalty fares) and other charges, and the creation of summary offences in connection with non-payment (or in connection with a person's failure to give his name or address in accordance with the provisions relating to penalty fares) (sch. 1, para. 12); the making of byelaws by any person and their enforcement, including the creation of summary offences (sch. 1, para. 13); the making of agreements to secure the provision of police services (sch. 1, para. 9).

The power to charge passengers for conveyance on a transport system is essential to its operation. The British Railways Board and London Regional Transport already have statutory powers to charge fares, evasion of which constitutes a summary offence. Under the British Railways (Penalty Fares) Act 1989, British Rail also have power to impose penalty fares (instant fines for fare evasion) as an alternative to summary prosecution. London Regional Transport are currently promoting a private Bill seeking similar powers. Principles for penalty fare schemes have been formulated by the Working Group on Penalty Fares which included representatives of the Home Office and the Lord Chancellor's Department. It is likely that powers to impose penalty fares to be included in s. 1 or s. 3 orders will be required to adhere to those principles.

Both the British Railways Board and London Regional Transport currently control the conduct of their passengers by the making of byelaws (breach of which constitutes an offence) which are enforced by the British Transport Commission Police established under s. 53 of the British Transport Commission Act 1949. The British Transport Commission Police were transferred to the British Railways Board under the Transport Act 1962 and their services are provided to, amongst others, London Regional Transport under powers conferred by the Transport Act 1968 and the London Regional Transport Act 1984. Paragraph 9 of sch. 1 to TAWA will enable other transport operators to make similar arrangements.

By s. 5(5) no penalty greater than a fine of level 3 on the standard scale may be imposed for an offence created by an order under s. 1 or s. 3 or by byelaws made under such an order.

(i)   The payment of rates (sch. 1, para. 14). Private Acts for light rail rapid transit systems have included provision for the rating of the system authorised by the Act. Typically these provisions empowered the Secretary of State to determine the rateable value of any hereditament forming part of premises occupied as part of the transport system. (See, for example, s. 39 of the Avon Light Rail Transit Act 1989.) This was rendered necessary because the special provisions for the rating of premises occupied by transport undertakers, contained in the General Rate Act 1967, applied only to premises occupied by the British Railways Board, the British Waterways Board and London Regional Transport. Because of the changes made by the Local Government Finance Act 1988 which, with effect from 1 April 1990, replaced the General Rate Act 1967, it is no longer appropriate for similar provision to be included in s. 1 or s. 3 orders.

(j)   The transfer, leasing, discontinuance and revival of undertakings (sch. 1, para. 15). This provision will assume particular significance if railway services are privatised. With the emergence of competing railway and tramway undertakings, it will become more likely that transport systems will be operated under successive managements and will be discontinued or revived as their profitability fluctuates.

(k)   The submission of disputes to arbitration (sch. 1, para. 16). This provision will be necessary in most orders to resolve disputes arising, for example, under protective provisions giving rights to third parties. Private Acts often provide for disputes over compensation to be determined by the Lands Tribunal and for disputes involving an assessment of the impact of works on property to be determined by an arbitrator appointed, in default of agreement, by the Institute of Civil Engineers.

(l)   The imposition of requirements to obtain the consent of the Secretary of State (sch. 1, para. 17). It is likely that such requirements will be imposed where transport operators are given wide powers in relation to the operation of systems. Any power, for instance, to lease or to dispose of a transport undertaking will be subject to the Secretary of State's consent.

As introduced, the Transport and Works Bill contained a further paragraph in sch. 1 referring to 'the alteration of the powers of any body established by or under an Act of Parliament'. This was removed from the Bill by an amendment made in the House of Lords. Since the list of matters in sch.1 is not intended to be exhaustive, the effect of the amendment is not clear. The provision would have applied only to a body established by or under an Act of Parliament. Section 5(3) enables statutory provisions of local application to be amended or repealed if it appears to the Secretary of State to be necessary or expedient in consequence of any provision of the order or otherwise in connection with the order. It appears that the powers of a statutory body could be amended under s. 5(3)(b) so as to enable the body to perform functions relating to a transport system provided the amendment related only to statutory provisions of local application. If, on the other hand, the statutory provision were contained in a public Act, it is now doubtful whether the amendment could be made by the order. The impact of the Lords' amendment is, however, lessened by the fact that under s. 20, a body which has power to promote or to oppose Bills in Parliament is automatically given power to apply for, or to object to, orders under s. 1 or s. 3.

3.3 APPLICATIONS FOR ORDERS

Section 6 provides that, except for orders made on the initiative of the Secretary of State under s. 7, an order under s. 1 or s. 3 may only be made on an application made in accordance with procedural requirements to be prescribed by rules. A prescribed fee will be payable on the application. Rules made under s. 6 will be subject to negative resolution procedure.

At the time of writing, the Department of Transport had circulated draft rules to consultees. It is expected that the rules will be made and laid before Parliament in October 1992. The following comments are based on the draft rules and can therefore only give a broad indication of the likely procedure.

It appears that the procedure will be similar to that now applicable to private Bills under the Standing Orders for private legislation of each House of Parliament. The main features of the draft rules, which reflect similar requirements in Standing Orders, are as follows:

(a) The application will require to be accompanied by a draft of the proposed order, an explanatory memorandum, a location plan, plans and sections of proposed works and, in some cases, ordnance survey maps.

(b) The application will require to be submitted with an environmental statement unless the Secretary of State directs otherwise. A waiver may not be given if the development project in question falls within any of the classes listed in Annex I to the Council Directive 85/337/EEC or any of the classes listed in Annex II to the Directive where the project by virtue of its nature, size or location is likely to have significant effects on the environment. These provisions are the minimum required to meet obligations under the Council Directive (85/337/EEC). The Secretary of State will consult local authorities and others before giving a waiver.

(c) Where it is proposed that the order should authorise the compulsory acquisition or use of land, or the compulsory creation or extinguishment of rights, the application will have to be accompanied by a book of reference containing the names of the owners and occupiers of the land in question.

(d) Where consent, permissions or licences under other enactments have been applied for or obtained in connection with the project, particulars must be given. The position with regard to these concurrent consents is affected by ss. 15–21 of TAWA which are discussed in 3.10 and 3.11 below and chapter 5.

(e) Copies of the application and the accompanying documents will, in all cases, have to be deposited with every local authority in whose area the transport system or inland waterway (or part of it) is situated and, depending on the type of application being made, with a number of other public bodies. For example, if the works affect the bed or banks of a river, it will be necessary to deposit the documents with the National Rivers Authority. 'Local authority' here includes a county council, a district council, a London borough council, the Common Council of the City of London, the Council of the Isles of Scilly and a Passenger Transport Executive.

(f) Where authority is sought for the compulsory acquisition of land, or the creation or extinguishment of rights over land, notice of the application containing prescribed particulars must be served on every owner and occupier of the land in question. In addition, it will be necessary to serve notice on other classes of persons, depending on the type of project being authorised.

(g) Notice of the application containing the prescribed particulars must be published in the *London Gazette* and in at least one newspaper circulating in each area to which the draft Order relates.

(h) In some cases, for instance when a highway is to be stopped up, a notice containing the prescribed particulars will be required to be displayed at the highway in question.

The draft rules also contain other, more controversial, requirements. It was originally proposed that applicants should be required to consult local planning authorities where the order would authorise works constituting development, Her Majesty's Railway Inspectorate where authority is sought to carry out works on transport systems, and other bodies to be specified by the Secretary of State. That requirement had no equivalent in the Standing Orders of Parliament relating to private legislation and was open to criticism on several grounds. Most importantly, a difficulty would have arisen in the application of s. 6(1) of TAWA. This provision imposes a duty on the Secretary of State not to make an order under s. 1 or s. 3 except on an application made in accordance with rules made under s. 6. If the rules included a requirement to consult, it would follow that the Secretary of State would be obliged under s. 6 to satisfy himself that the requirement had been complied with before making the order; and that would raise the question of exactly what is meant by consultation. Following representations to that effect, the Department of Transport decided to include only a limited requirement to consult local planning authorities for the purpose of obtaining the view of those authorities on specified planning matters. Other statutory bodies will be required to be notified of the intended application.

The draft rules would require promoters to furnish an estimate of the cost of the project and concise details of proposals for funding the cost of implementing the order and, in particular, of acquiring blighted land. The first requirement is precedented in Standing Orders, but the second has no equivalent in Standing Orders or planning procedures. Many projects are now financed by a combination of public and private investment and it may well prove unhelpful for a promoter to be obliged to publicise particulars of such arrangements.

3.4 ALTERATIONS TO APPLICATIONS

One of the greatest disadvantages of the private Bill procedure from the promoter's point of view is that once a Bill is deposited no amendment can readily be made to it if the effect of the amendment would be to extend the powers of the promoter. So the promoter of a private works Bill who wished to modify the proposed works, even to a slight extent, was often obliged to seek leave of the Standing Orders Committee to promote 'an additional provision', which is in effect very similar to promoting a further amending Bill. This procedure is lengthy and cumbersome, and to obtain the leave of the Standing Orders Committee is by no means a foregone conclusion.

It may well prove to be easier to make minor adjustments to schemes under the new procedure. The draft rules indicate that it will be possible for an applicant for a s. 1 or s. 3 order to amend the terms of the proposed order or the documents accompanying the application, subject to the applicant complying again with the requirements in the rules as to the deposit of documents and the service of notices. However, where amendments would extend compulsory purchase powers or, in the opinion of the Secretary of State, would materially alter the character of the matters for which provision is made in the draft order, it will be necessary for the promoters to make a fresh application rather than to amend the existing application.

3.5 OBJECTIONS TO ORDERS

3.5.1 Who may object?

Any person may object to a proposed Order under s. 1 or s. 3 whether or not he can show that he has a special interest to protect – for example that he is the owner of property which is proposed to be compulsorily acquired. This constitutes a significant departure from private or hybrid Bill procedure. Only an individual, a group of individuals or an organisation directly and specially affected by the provisions of a Bill may petition against it. If the promoters consider that a petitioner is not directly and specially affected they may challenge his *locus standi*, that is to say his right to be heard against the Bill by the Select Committee considering it on the grounds that he is injuriously affected by its provisions. The rules of *locus standi* have been expanded over the years to allow Select Committees discretion to hear local authorities, societies or associations sufficiently representing a trade, business or interest alleged to be injuriously affected by the Bill, and societies, associations or bodies sufficiently representing amenity, educational, travel or recreational interests which they allege would be adversely affected to a material extent by the Bill. By cutting down on the numbers of persons entitled to be heard, the rules of *locus standi* substantially shorten Select Committee proceedings. Strictly speaking, petitioners are entitled to be heard by the Select Committee only on matters raised in their petition, though, in practice, they are often given considerable latitude.

Promoters of transport schemes had hoped to persuade the Department of Transport that the right to object under the new procedure should be subject to restrictions somewhat similar to the *locus standi* rules. It was feared that public local inquiries would be overburdened and proceedings unnecessarily extended if everyone were to be entitled to be heard as of right, regardless of his interest, whether the objection had been lodged within the prescribed time limit or whether proper notice had been given of the substance of the objection. The Government, however, decided that to impose such restrictions on the making of objections would be counter-productive and might be thought to infringe the principles of natural justice.

The result appears to be that anyone may object to a proposed order under s. 1 or s. 3, whether or not he can show that he is directly and adversely affected by the proposals. Furthermore, objectors may be heard at public local inquiries even if they have failed to comply with the rules relating to objections to be prescribed under s. 10(1).

3.5.2   The making of objections

The making of objections is to be covered by rules to be made under s. 10(1). The draft rules circulated for consultation envisage that objections will be required to be made in writing within 42 days of the date of the application, and to state the grounds of objection and the objector's name and address. The Secretary of State will have the discretion to waive these requirements in any particular case.

Non-compliance with these rules will not necessarily mean that no account will be taken of the objection. The position depends on whether or not a public local inquiry or a public hearing under s. 11(2) is to be held (see 3.5.3 below). If neither is to be held, the Secretary of State is required by s. 10(2) to take into consideration the grounds of any subsisting objection made in accordance with the rules (unless it is frivolous or trivial, or is wholly concerned with compensation). Though he is not required to consider other objections (for example late objections), he is not precluded from doing so. Where a public inquiry or a public hearing is to be held, the Secretary of State is under no direct duty to consider objections but is instead under an obligation to take into consideration the report of the person holding the public inquiry or hearing (s. 10(4)).

A key question is therefore whether a person who has failed to lodge his objection in accordance with the rules will be permitted to be heard at the public inquiry or hearing. In the case of a public inquiry, the answer to this question will depend on rules to be made under the Tribunals and Inquiries Act 1992 which will regulate the conduct of the proceedings. The draft rules indicate that an objector who notifies the Secretary of State of his wish to appear at the inquiry will be entitled to do so if he serves a statement of case in accordance with the rules and others will be permitted to appear at the inquiry at the discretion of the person holding the inquiry. (See the Town and Country Planning (Inquiries Procedure) Rules 1988 (SI 1988/944), r. 11, which rules apply to public inquiries investigating applications for planning permission referred to the Secretary of State under s. 35 or s. 36 of the Town and Country Planning Act 1990.) In the case of a public hearing under s. 11(2), the matter may well be left to the person holding the hearing subject to any guidance given by the Secretary of State.

3.5.3 Public local inquiries and public hearings

Section 11 provides two ways in which arguments for and against the making of a proposed order may be heard – a public local inquiry or a public hearing.

Public local inquiries are a well-established procedure used in related areas such as the consideration of applications for planning permission, harbour revision or empowerment orders and highways schemes. Proceedings at the inquiries will be governed by rules made under s. 9 of the Tribunals and Inquiries Act 1992. The draft rules which have been circulated to consultees are based on the Compulsory Purchase by non-Ministerial Acquiring Authorities (Inquiries Procedure) Rules 1990 (SI 1990/512), with amendments to reflect the current view of the Department of the Environment of the Town and Country Planning (Inquiries Procedure) Rules 1988.

A public hearing, a procedure used particularly in the case of planning appeals, is a less formal forum for the hearing of oral representations both by those promoting and those opposing the application. It is expected that the procedure for public hearings, like the public hearings of planning appeals, will not be formally regulated by rules under s. 9 of the Tribunals and Inquiries Act 1992 but rather by a code of practice. A public hearing is appropriate only where the issues to be considered are few and relatively simple and do not give rise to widespread public concern. In the case of a complex or controversial project, a public local inquiry is more suitable.

The Secretary of State *may* refer any application under s. 1 or s. 3 for consideration by a public local inquiry. The task of the person holding the inquiry is to investigate fully the proposals concerned and to report to the Secretary of State. This includes the consideration of evidence put forward by the promoters, the probing of that evidence by cross-examination of witnesses and the hearing of objections. The Secretary of State is free to refer proposals to a public local inquiry even if the application is unopposed. This power may, for instance, be exercised if he considers that the proposals raise issues of public importance. The purpose of a public hearing under s. 11(2), on the other hand, is to consider arguments put forward by objectors. The existence of at least one objection made in accordance with the rules is a pre-condition to a public hearing being ordered under s. 11(2).

Under s. 11(3), in certain circumstances, consideration of an opposed application *must* either be referred to a public local inquiry or to a public hearing under s. 11(2). This is the case where an objection to the proposed order has been made by a person who has a special interest defined in s. 11(4) and who has notified the Secretary of State in writing that he wishes the objection to be referred to a public local inquiry or to be dealt with at a public hearing. The obligation under s. 11(3) does not arise if the objection is withdrawn, or if it appears to the Secretary of State to be frivolous or trivial, or to relate to matters which fall to be determined by a tribunal concerned with the assessment of compensation. Whether a public local inquiry is held or such an objection is dealt with at a public hearing under s. 11(2) is in the discretion of the Secretary of State.

Section 11(3), which is similar to s. 13 of the Acquisition of Land Act 1981, ensures that persons with special interests are given the opportunity to make oral representations and to probe the promoter's case. In addition to the right to call for a public local inquiry or a public hearing, these persons have the right to be notified under s. 9(3) of any determination by the Secretary of State that the proposals in question are of national significance (see further chapter 4) and to be notified under s. 14(1)(a) of the Secretary of State's final decision.

The persons whose interests are given this special protection are:

(a) any local authority for an area in which any works authorised by the proposed order are to be carried out. 'Local authority' here means a county council, a district council, a London borough council, the Common Council of the City of London, the Council of the Isles of Scilly and a Passenger Transport Executive.

(b) Where the proposals include the compulsory acquisition of land, any person who, if Part II of the Acquisition of Land Act 1981 applied to the acquisition, would be entitled to a notice under s. 12 of that Act. This means any owner, lessee and occupier of land proposed to be compulsorily acquired.

'Owner', in paragraph (b) above means, in relation to any land, a person, other than a mortgagee not in possession, who is for the time being entitled to dispose of the fee simple of the land, whether in possession or in reversion, and includes a person holding or entitled to the rents and profits of the land under a lease or agreement with an unexpired term exceeding three years (see s. 7(1) of the Acquisition of Land Act 1981). The protection does not extend to tenants for a month or any period less than a month, an occupier who is a statutory tenant within the meaning of the Rent Act 1977 or the Rent (Agriculture) Act 1976, or a licensee under an assured agricultural occupancy within the meaning of Part I of the Housing Act 1988 (s. 12 of the 1981 Act). In the case of ecclesiastical land, notice must also be served on the Church Commissioners.

'Land' is defined in the Interpretation Act 1978 as including buildings and other structures, land covered with water, and any estate, interest, easement, servitude or right in or over land. So gas, water and electricity undertakers and telecommunication operators who have apparatus in or over the land in question are included under s. 11(4).

In contrast with s. 11(2), which refers to the making of 'an objection in accordance with rules under s. 10', s. 11(3) refers only to the case 'where an objection is made'.

Amenity groups such as English Heritage, parish councils, environmental groups and consumer bodies have not been given 'statutory objector status' under s. 11(4). If these groups object to proposals, they have no right to call for a public local inquiry or public hearing. Inevitably, however, their views will be influential in causing the Secretary of State to exercise his discretion to refer the proposals to a public local inquiry or to hold a public hearing. If a public local inquiry is held, it is likely that amenity groups will appear. In practice even if promoters, not required to do so under rules, will be wise to consult widely with such bodies at an early stage and to take consultees' views into account in formulating their proposals.

The provisions of s. 250(2) and (3) of the Local Government Act 1972 are, by virtue of s. 11(5), applied to public local inquiries held under s. 11. These empower inspectors to compel persons to attend inquiries, to give evidence and to produce documents. Non-compliance constitutes a summary offence carrying a maximum penalty of a fine of level 3 on the standard scale, or six months' imprisonment or both. Provisions of s. 250(4) and (5) of the 1972 Act which relate to costs are applied both to public local inquiries and to public hearings under s. 11(2). The effect is that the Secretary of State may direct the costs incurred by him in relation to the inquiry or hearing, as certified by him, to be paid by such party to the inquiry as he shall direct. The Secretary of State may make orders to recoup his costs not only where the inquiry or hearing takes place but also where arrangements are made for it but it does not take place (s. 11(5)(b)). This follows a similar provision in s. 322(2) of the Town and Country Planning Act 1990. The Secretary of State is also empowered to order the costs incurred by one party at the inquiry or hearing to be paid by another party.

The Government proposes to charge promoters for the costs of holding public inquiries or hearings under s. 11. This contrasts with the policy not to charge for planning appeal inquiries. The justification given is that it is reasonable for promoters, rather than the taxpayer, to meet these costs because the promoter has chosen to initiate the development in question. It is also thought that the policy will encourage promoters to make greater efforts to settle with objectors in order to save costs at the inquiry or hearing. As against these arguments, it may be said that effective transport infrastructure is a prerequisite of economic recovery. To inhibit the carrying out of transport improvements would not be in the public interest.

Non-statutory guidelines are to be published regarding awards of costs as between parties. It is expected that the policy will be similar to that applicable to inquiries into planning appeals and proposals for compulsory acquisition. If so, one party will be able to recover from another any costs unnecessarily occasioned by the other's unreasonable conduct in relation to the inquiry or hearing.

3.5.4 Written representations

Where no statutory objector under s. 11(4) has called for a public local inquiry or hearing and the Secretary of State has not exercised his discretion to hold one, objections will be dealt with on the basis of written representations.

Rules about the making of written representations are to be prescribed. Draft rules, somewhat similar to those set out in the Town and Country Planning (Appeals) (Written Representations Procedure) Regulations 1987 (SI 1987/701), indicate that a copy of the objection will be served on the applicant. The applicant and other interested parties will be given an opportunity to comment on the objection, and the objector will in turn have a chance to reply.

In a case where there is no public local inquiry or public hearing, the Secretary of State will be required to consider all written representations in order to comply with his duty under s. 10(2). Although the duty applies only to objections which have been properly made, there is nothing to prevent the Secretary of State taking into account other objections if he thinks fit. Under s. 10(3) an objection is not required to be considered if it is withdrawn or appears to the Secretary of State to be frivolous or trivial, or to relate to matters which fall to be determined by a tribunal concerned with the assessment of compensation. The last-mentioned restriction, similar to one contained in s. 13(4) of the Acquisition of Land Act 1981, ensures that the determination of applications is not delayed by disputes which relate to matters which should properly be resolved by the Lands Tribunal.

3.6   DECISIONS ON APPLICATIONS

3.6.1   General power

The Secretary of State has a duty to determine an application made under s. 6 for a s. 1 or s. 3 order provided that the application has been duly made (see s. 6(1) discussed in 3.3 above) and the requirements of ss. 10 and 11 have been satisfied in relation to objections (see 3.5 above). Section 13(1) provides that the Secretary of State must determine:

(a)   to make an order . . . which gives effect to the proposals concerned without modifications; or

(b)   to make an order which gives effect to those proposals with modifications; or

(c)   not to make an order.

Similarly, those are his three options in relation to the making of orders by virtue of s. 7 (see 2.2 above).

It is clear from s. 13(2) that it is permissible for the Secretary of State to determine not to make an order if he considers that any of the objects of the order applied for could be achieved by other means. The Secretary of State can in this way ensure that the new procedures are not utilised where other authorisation procedures are available and would be more appropriate. For instance, it would not be permissible for a promoter to short-circuit the jurisdiction of a local authority by applying for a s. 1 or s. 3 order for works which could and should be authorised by planning permission.

Despite pressure in Parliament for it to be mandatory for the Secretary of State to reject an application under Part I of TAWA where alternative authorisation procedures are available, s. 13(2) is discretionary. This allows the Secretary of State the necessary flexibility to make an order authorising a full package of powers for a project, even if one of the matters (such as the closing of a railway station) could be authorised separately under other legislation. It should not be forgotten that the making of an order under Part I will not remove the need to obtain consent under other enactments, though the various procedures for obtaining such consents are to be assimilated as far as possible under regulations to be made under s. 15. (See further chapter 5.)

Section 13(3) empowers the Secretary of State to deal separately with several proposals contained in the same application and to make two or more orders on the same application. The Secretary of State may, for example, decide to make a final determination in respect of some of the proposals applied for but to defer consideration of the rest. This power will be useful in the case of multi-purpose orders which are allowed under s. 5(2). The Secretary of State will be able to deal with any proposals which are straightforward and unopposed without having to wait for the more controversial proposals to be considered at a public local inquiry or s. 11(2) hearing.

3.6.2 Modification of proposals

A special procedure is provided by s. 13(4), where the Secretary of State proposes to give effect to the proposals applied for subject to modifications which would, in his opinion, change them substantially. Before making any order, he must notify any person who appears to him to be likely to be affected by the modifications and give that person an opportunity of making representations within a period specified in the notice. Any representations duly made must be considered by him before the order is made.

It seems implicit in s. 13(4) that the same procedure should be gone through again if, having heard the representations, the Secretary of State is minded to vary the proposed modifications substantially so as to affect the proposals in a significant and different way.

Depending on the nature of the modifications and the representations received, it would be open to the Secretary of State to refer the modifications to a fresh public local inquiry or hearing under s. 11(2). The draft rules made under the Tribunals and Inquiries Act 1992 make provision for this contingency.

3.6.3 Publicity for the making or refusal of orders

Section 14 lays down the steps to be taken to publicise any determination to make or refuse an order under s. 1 or s. 3. Some steps are to be taken by the Secretary of State and others by the applicant.

Under s. 14(1)(a), the Secretary of State must, as soon as practicable after making a determination under s. 13(1) (whether making or declining to make an order), give notice of the determination stating the reasons for it to the person who applied for the order and to every local authority or property owner or occupier within s. 11(4) who made an objection which, not being withdrawn, was referred to a public local inquiry or hearing in accordance with s. 11(3). (For an explanation of the persons who fall within s. 11(4), see 3.5.3 above.) Notice of the determination must be published in the *London Gazette* as soon as practicable (s. 14(1)(b)).

Where the Secretary of State has determined to make an order, the *London Gazette* notice and the notice served under s. 14(1)(a) must state the name and address of the applicant and give such particulars of the terms of the order as the Secretary of State considers appropriate.

Where the Secretary of State has determined to make an order, the successful applicant must publish a copy of the notice given to him by the Secretary of State under s. 14(1)(a) in a local newspaper circulating in the area (or each of the areas) in which any works authorised by the order are to be carried out (s. 14(4)). The successful applicant is required as soon as practicable after the making of the order, to deposit in the office of the Clerk of the Parliaments a copy of the order and of the latest version of any plan or book of reference prepared in connection with the application (s. 14(5)(a) and (6)). The House of Lords Record Office keep a collection of plans and books of reference deposited in connection with schemes authorised by private Acts. The purpose of the requirement in s. 14(5)(a) is to enable that office to maintain a comprehensive record of documents relating to major transport schemes.

The successful applicant must also deposit a copy of those documents (or a copy of the relevant part of them) with every relevant local authority (namely each district council, London borough council and the Common Council of the City of London) in whose area works authorised by the order are to be carried out (s. 14(5)(b) and (7)). The local authority (or each of them) with whom documents are deposited in accordance with s. 14(5)(b) must make them available for inspection free of charge at all reasonable hours (s. 14(8)). This requirement has no time limit, the intention being to enable the public to have permanent access to orders and related documents which may have continuing local interest, not least in the event of questions arising as to the extent of the land subject to compulsory acquisition under the order. The local authorities given this duty are those responsible for maintaining the Land Charges Register.

With some minor modifications, these requirements apply also where an order is made on the initiative of the Secretary of State under s. 7 (see 2.2 above).

3.6.4 Commencement of orders

Where the Secretary of State determines to make an order, it may come into operation on the day on which notice of the determination is first published in the *London Gazette* under s. 14(1)(b). Alternatively, the Secretary of State may specify a later (but not an earlier) date for the commencement of the order in the order itself (see s. 13(5)).

This does not apply to an order which, by virtue of s. 12, is subject to special parliamentary procedure (s. 12(3)(a)). Such an order comes into operation in accordance with the Statutory Orders (Special Procedure) Act 1945 (see 3.8 below).

3.7 CHALLENGING THE VALIDITY OF ORDERS

An aggrieved party may challenge the validity of an order under s. 1 or s. 3, or of any provision in the order, by making an application to the High Court. However, the challenge may only be made on the grounds, and within the time limit, set out in s. 22(1). This limitation on the application of administrative law (discussed further below) is achieved by s. 22(3) which provides that, except as provided in s. 22(1) and (2), 'an order under section 1 or 3 above shall not, either before or after it has been made, be questioned in any legal proceedings whatever'.

The grounds on which a challenge can be made are that the order (or the provision in question) is not within the powers of the Act, or that any requirement imposed by or under the Act or the Tribunal and Inquiries Act 1992 has not been complied with. Although taken literally this provision appears to limit challenges to cases of *ultra vires* or non-compliance with procedural requirements, it is well settled that such a provision will be interpreted by the courts also to cover cases where the grounds of challenge are bad faith or that the Secretary of State has taken into account considerations which he ought not to have done, has failed to take into account considerations which he ought to have done, has come to his decision without any evidence to support it or has otherwise made a decision that no reasonable person would make (see *R* v *Secretary of State for the Environment ex parte Ostler* [1976] 3 All ER 90, per Lord Denning MR at pp. 93–4).

Any application questioning the validity of an order must be made within the period of 42 days beginning with the day on which notice of the Secretary of State's determination to make the order has been published in the *London Gazette* in accordance with s. 14(1)(b).

On an application under s. 22 the court may quash the order or any provision in it either generally or so far as it affects any property of the applicant, if satisfied either:

(a)   that the order or any provision in it is not within the powers of the Act; or
(b)   that there has been a failure to comply with any requirement imposed by or under the Act or the Tribunals and Inquiries Act 1992 *and* that the interests of the applicants have been substantially prejudiced by that failure.

Pending a final determination of the proceedings, the court may make an interim order suspending the operation of the order or any provision in it, either generally or so far as it affects any property of the applicant.

The provisions of s. 22 are based on similar provisions which apply in relation to highway orders and are contained in the Highways Act 1980, sch. 2, paras 2 to 4.

The inherent jurisdiction of the courts to determine whether statutory powers have been exceeded is not readily ousted. Any provision which purports to exclude the jurisdiction of the courts is interpreted restrictively (see *Halsbury's Laws*, 4th edn, London: Butterworths, 1989, vol. 1(1) para. 21 and the cases there cited). The high-water mark of the failure of the judiciary to give literal effect to an ouster clause was reached by the House of Lords in the case of *Anisminic Limited* v *The Foreign Compensation Commission* [1969] 1 All ER 208, where a determination was quashed notwithstanding a provision that the determination 'was not to be called into question in any court of law'. Nevertheless, para. 4 of sch. 2 to the Highways Act 1959 (now re-enacted as the Highways Act 1980, sch. 2, para. 4), which is in the same terms as s. 22(3) of TAWA, was held by the Court of Appeal in *R* v *Secretary of State for the Environment ex parte Ostler* [1976] 3 All ER 90 (reaffirming *Smith* v *East Elloe Rural District Council* [1956] 1 All ER 855) to bar an aggrieved party from making an application to the court after the expiry of the specified period of six weeks to challenge the validity of a decision of the Secretary of State confirming a highway order. *Anisminic* was distinguished on the basis that the decision of the Minister to confirm the highway order was in the nature of an administrative or executive decision rather than a judicial decision. However, all three judges in the *Ostler* case considered that a distinction could be drawn between a decision (such as the one in *Anisminic*) which is void *ab initio* because, being based on a mistaken view of the law, it is made outside the jurisdiction of the tribunal making it, and an actual decision made within jurisdiction though sought to be challenged (such as the one in *Ostler*). It could therefore be argued by an objector that, notwithstanding s. 22(3), an order might be capable of being challenged in the courts outside the six-week limit if (say) it included a provision which manifestly did not fall within s. 5.

From a promoter's point of view, however, the practical difficulty about the right of challenge conferred by s. 22 lies not in the theoretical possibility of a challenge after the six-week period on the grounds of *ultra vires* but in the fact that it enables an objector to challenge an order after it has been made on the grounds of some procedural defect in the application for the order. Thus it would be possible for an aggrieved person to claim months, perhaps years, after the application was made that (say) a notice required under the rules had not been properly served. Although an order cannot be quashed for a procedural defect unless the court is satisfied that the applicant has been substantially prejudiced, a pending action would engender uncertainty and delay.

The position as regards private or hybrid Bills is different. Standing Orders of each House provide for examiners to consider whether or not the promoters of a Bill have complied with the requirements of Standing Orders. Third parties are entitled to appear before the examiners to complain of any such non-compliance. However a Committee on a private or hybrid Bill may not inquire into compliance with the requirements of Standing Orders laying down the initial procedural steps relating to the Bill and, once the Bill has been enacted, the validity of the Act cannot be called into question.

During the passage of the Transport and Works Bill, promoters drew attention to the precedent in s. 10 of the Light Railways Act 1896, which provides that confirmation of an order by the Secretary of State shall be conclusive evidence that the requirements of the Act in respect of proceedings required to be taken before the making of the order have been complied with. They argued that since s. 10 of the 1896 Act is to remain in force in Scotland, a similar provision should apply to the new procedure in England and Wales. They suggested that rules under what is now s. 6 should make provision for the Secretary of State to determine, before the consideration of any application, that the requirements of the rules had been complied with; and that such a determination should raise a conclusive presumption that the requirements imposed under the rules had been complied with. These arguments did not find favour with the Government during the Bill's passage through the House of Commons; and the fact that all the stages of the Bill in the House of Lords had to be taken on one day because of the forthcoming election precluded the issue being considered by that House.

3.8 SPECIAL PARLIAMENTARY PROCEDURE

An order under s. 1 or s. 3 which would authorise compulsory acquisition of certain protected categories of land is, by virtue of s. 12, subject to additional parliamentary scrutiny under what is known as special parliamentary procedure ('SPP'). Section 12 applies to orders made under s. 1 or s. 3 the provisions of ss.

18 and 19 of, and paras 5 and 6 of sch. 3 to, the Acquisition of Land Act 1981 by providing that an order under s. 1 or s. 3 which authorises compulsory purchase is to be subject to SPP to the same extent as it would be by virtue of those provisions, if authorised under s. 2(1) of the 1981 Act.

The effect is to render subject to SPP an order under s. 1 or s. 3 which authorises the compulsory acquisition of:

(a) land held by the National Trust inalienably under s. 21 of the National Trust Act 1907 or s. 8 of the National Trust Act 1939 (see s. 18 of the 1981 Act);

(b) rights over land belonging to the National Trust and held by the Trust inalienably as above, unless the National Trust do not object to the making of the order (see sch. 3, para. 5 to the 1981 Act);

(c) land forming part of a common, which by s. 19(4) of the 1981 Act includes any land subject to be enclosed under the Inclosure Acts 1845 to 1882 and any town or village green, unless the Secretary of State has given a certificate under s. 19(1) of the 1981 Act;

(d) land forming part of an open space, defined in s. 19(4) as meaning any land laid out as a public garden, or used for the purposes of public recreation, or land being a disused burial ground, unless the Secretary of State has given a certificate under s. 19(1);

(e) land forming part of a fuel or field garden allotment, defined under s. 19(4) as meaning any allotment set out as a fuel allotment, or a field garden allotment, under an Inclosure Act, unless the Secretary of State has given a certificate under s. 19(1);

(f) rights over land forming part of a common, open space or fuel or field garden allotment (as defined above), unless the Secretary of State gives a certificate under sch. 3, para. 6(1) to the 1981 Act (see sch. 3, para. 6).

The certificate under s. 19(1) of the 1981 Act is a certificate that the Secretary of State is satisfied:

(i) that there has been or will be given in exchange for such land, other land, not being less in area and being equally advantageous to the persons, if any, entitled to rights of common or other rights, and to the public, and that the land given in exchange has been or will be vested in the persons in whom the land purchased was vested, and subject to the like rights, trusts and incidents as attach to the land purchased; or

(ii) that the land does not exceed 250 square yards in extent or is required for the widening or drainage of an existing highway or partly for the widening and partly for the drainage of such a highway and that the giving in exchange of other land is unnecessary, whether in the interests of the persons, if any, entitled to rights of common or other rights or in the interests of the public.

A certificate under sch. 3, para. 6(1) to the 1981 Act is a certificate that the Secretary of State is satisfied:

(i) that the land, when burdened with the right to be compulsorily acquired, will be no less advantageous to those persons in whom it is vested and other persons, if any, entitled to rights of common or other rights, and to the public, than it was before; or

(ii)   that there has been or will be given, in exchange for the right, additional land which will as respects the persons in whom there is vested the land over which the right is to be acquired, the persons, if any, entitled to rights of common or other rights over that land, and the public, be adequate to compensate them for the disadvantages which result from the acquisition of the right, and that the additional land has been or will be vested in the persons in whom there is vested the land over which the right is to be acquired, and subject to the like rights, trusts and incidents as attach to that land apart from the compulsory purchase order; or

(iii)   that the land affected by the right to be acquired does not exceed 250 square yards in extent, and that the giving of other land in exchange for the right is unnecessary, whether in the interest of the persons, if any, entitled to rights of common or other rights or in the interests of the public.

Before the Secretary of State gives a certificate under either provision he must give public notice of his intention to do so, give all interested persons an opportunity to make representations and objections and, if he thinks it expedient having regard to any representations and objections, hold a public inquiry.

Section 12 of TAWA does not, however, extend to s. 1 or s. 3 orders the provisions of s. 17 of the 1981 Act which apply SPP to orders under the 1981 Act authorising the compulsory acquisition of land belonging to a local authority or of land which has been acquired by statutory undertakers for the purposes of their undertaking. Instead, such bodies must rely on their rights under s. 11(3) of TAWA to require the Secretary of State to hold a local inquiry or hearing (see 3.5.3 above).

SPP is laid down in the Statutory Orders (Special Procedure) Act 1945 and the Standing Orders of both Houses of Parliament. A detailed description of SPP would be beyond the scope of this work but for a brief summary see 1.7. In outline, the effect of the procedure is that persons having a special interest are given the right to petition against the order. Petitioners may either object generally to the making of the order or may seek amendments. Whether or not any petitions are received, either House of Parliament may resolve that the order be annulled within a specified period. Petitions are referred to a Joint Committee of both Houses of Parliament. If the order is reported by the Joint Committee without amendment and has not been annulled, it will come into effect. If it is reported with amendments, has not been annulled and the responsible Minister agrees, it takes effect as so amended. If the Joint Committee reports that the order should not be approved, the order will not come into effect unless confirmed by Act of Parliament. (See s. 6 of the 1945 Act and 1.7.)

Section 12(2) provides an interface between SPP and the procedures under s. 9 of TAWA which relate to proposals of national significance (see further chapter 4). Where an order relates to proposals designated under s. 9 of TAWA to be of national significance, the principle of which has been approved by each House of Parliament in accordance with s. 9, the Chairman of Committees and the Chairman of Ways and Means may not certify that a petition against the order is proper to be heard by the Joint Committee if:

(a)   the petition is a petition of general objection; or

(b)   the petition is a petition for amendment and any of the amendments asked for would in the opinion of the Chairmen be inconsistent with such proposals.

The underlying principle is that a petition should not be entertained if it would require the Joint Committee to consider issues which have already been approved by Parliament under s. 9 of TAWA.

The provisions of Part I of TAWA are modified by s. 12(3) to make them consistent with SPP in cases where SPP is required. Section 12(3)(a) disapplies s. 13(5), under which a s. 1 or s. 3 order comes into operation on the publication of the determination by advertising in the *London Gazette* (see further 3.6 above). Instead the order will come into effect as provided in s. 6 of the Statutory Orders (Special Procedure) Act 1945. Section 12(3)(b), by making it clear that s. 22 will not apply in a case where an order is confirmed by Act of Parliament under s. 6(3) of the 1945 Act, ensures that the validity of an order which has been confirmed by Act of Parliament is not open to challenge in the courts. Section 12(3)(c) provides that, where an order is subject to SPP but is not confirmed by Act of Parliament, the time-limit within which its validity may be challenged under s. 22 is 42 days beginning with the day on which the order comes into operation under the 1945 Act instead of the usual period of 42 days beginning with the day on which the Secretary of State's determination to make the order is advertised in the *London Gazette*. (Section 22 is discussed further in 3.7 above.)

3.9   MODEL CLAUSES

Under s. 8 the Secretary of State is empowered to prescribe model clauses by order for incorporation in draft s. 1 or s. 3 orders. The power in s. 8 includes a power to revoke or amend any such order by virtue of s. 14 of the Interpretation Act 1978.

The model clauses will not remove from promoters the onus of ensuring that the draft order submitted with their application contains all the powers they require for the particular scheme proposed and makes the necessary provision for the protection of third parties. Their purpose is rather to promote consistency in the drafting of provisions of orders where that is possible. Promoters will need to satisfy themselves and the Department of Transport that any model provisions incorporated in draft orders are appropriate to the particular proposals in question and that no further provisions are needed. The intention is that promoters should have access to common form provisions in modern style which take account of relevant legislative changes. It follows that the model clauses will cover parts of orders which are fairly standard. However, the provisions will generally require some modification to make them fit the circumstances of individual cases, and draft orders will require to be completed by the addition of provisions tailored to the needs of the particular case in question. Section 8(3) therefore makes it clear that it will not be mandatory for a draft order to be based on the model clauses, or indeed to contain any provisions in the terms of the models in the order. On the other hand, it is likely that promoters will be encouraged to adhere to the terms of the model clauses where provisions in the order are intended to produce the same legal effect as equivalent provisions in the clauses.

Although not essential to the coming into operation of Part I of TAWA, it is proposed that an order (or orders) prescribing model clauses for railway orders (both overground and underground) and tramway orders will be made at the same time as the other subordinate legislation under Part I so as to assist promoters with their first applications under the new regime. The principal transport operators have been consulted on draft model clauses.

The attempt to standardise legislation, so far as appropriate, by providing model provisions for adoption by promoters (with or without modifications) is by no means new. The last century saw a series of 'clauses' Acts which were intended to save promoters expense and Parliament the task of scrutinising common form provisions (see further 1.3). With the passage of time the usefulness of some of these Acts has declined as their provisions have become increasingly outdated. The Tramways Act 1870 has now been repealed by TAWA and will be replaced by provisions in new model clauses. Of the others, only the Lands Clauses Acts have a modern equivalent – the Compulsory Purchase Act 1965. It is to be hoped that once the model clauses are published, they will be regularly updated so that they remain useful and relevant to promoters.

3.10   POWER TO APPLY FOR, OR OBJECT TO, ORDERS

Section 20 confers on any body which has power to promote or power to oppose Bills in Parliament, the power to apply for or to object to orders under ss. 1 and 3. If the power to promote or oppose Bills is subject to any condition, the exercise of the power to apply for or to object to orders under ss. 1 and 3 will be subject to a corresponding condition.

There is an exception to this in the case of the British Railways Board, the British Waterways Board, and London Regional Transport. Under s. 17 of the Transport Act 1962, which relates to the British Railways Board and the British Waterways Board, and sch. 2, para.18 to the London Regional Transport Act 1984 (the corresponding provision applying to London Regional Transport), these three bodies are only permitted to promote Bills with the consent of the Secretary of State. Section 20(3) of TAWA enables each of them to apply for orders under ss. 1 and 3 without the consent of the Secretary of State. Their powers to promote and oppose Bills are unaffected.

One of the reasons for dispensing with the need for the consent of the Secretary of State is to distance the Secretary of State from the decision whether any of those bodies should apply for a particular order under s. 1 or s. 3. It might otherwise be argued that the Secretary of State would be unfairly predisposed to approve the application by having given his initial consent to the making of the application. However, before a large programme of construction becomes the subject of an application for an order the financial aspects require to be approved by the Secretary of State as sponsor of the British Railways Board and London Regional Transport. So the Secretary of State retains some control over the initial decision to apply for an order under s. 1 or s. 3, even though his formal consent is no longer required.

Section 20 is principally required for bodies whose powers are governed by statutory constitutions. Natural persons and bodies constituted by Royal Charter do not require any express power to apply for or to object to the new orders. In the case of companies registered under the Companies Act 1985, it is likely that their powers will be in sufficiently wide terms to enable them to apply for or object to orders even if there is no express power to promote or oppose Bills. If any company does not have the necessary power, its memorandum of association may be changed by special resolution under s. 4 of the Companies Act 1985.

Under s. 239 of the Local Government Act 1972, county councils, district councils and London borough councils have powers both to promote and to oppose Bills, while parish councils and community councils may oppose (but not promote) Bills. These powers are, in both cases, subject to the restrictions set out in that section. The effect of s. 20(1) and (2) is that county councils, district councils and London borough councils may apply for or object to orders under ss. 1 and 3, and parish and community councils may object to such orders, subject to the restrictions contained in s. 239 of the 1972 Act. The effect of s. 20 of TAWA on s. 239(5) of the 1972 Act is uncertain. Section 239(5) prohibits an authority from making a payment to a member of the authority for acting as counsel or agent in promoting or opposing a Bill under that section. If that provision is viewed as imposing a condition on the power to oppose or promote Bills, it will also prohibit the making of a payment to a member of the authority for acting as counsel or agent in making or objecting to an application under s. 1 or s. 3. Those advising local authorities may well take the view that it is safest to refrain from making such payments.

An organisation which does not have power to petition against a Bill does not by virtue of s. 20 have power to oppose an order under s. 1 or s. 3. The *locus standi* of English Heritage to petition against the King's Cross Railways Bill was successfully challenged by the promoters before the court of referees. Insofar as that decision was based on lack of *vires* it would follow that they have no power to oppose applications for orders under s. 1 or s. 3.

3.11 TRANSPORT CONSULTATIVE COMMITTEES

Transport Consultative Committees are constituted under s. 56 of the Transport Act 1962. There are two types of committees – the Central Transport Consultative Committee for Great Britain, and various Area Transport Users' Consultative Committees for different areas of Great Britain designated by the Secretary of State. The London Regional Passengers' Committee was established by s. 40 of the London Regional Transport Act 1984 and is, by virtue of s. 41 of that Act, treated as an Area Transport Users Consultative Committee.

Under s. 56(4) of the Transport Act 1962, the functions of Area Transport Users' Consultative Committees are generally to consider and to make recommendations with respect to any matter affecting the services and facilities provided by the British Railways Board (or, in the case of the London Regional Passengers' Committee, by London Regional Transport):

(a)   which has been the subject of representations (other than representations appearing to the committee to be frivolous) made to the committee by or on behalf of users of those services or facilities; or

(b)   which has been referred to the committee by the Secretary of State for Transport, or by the British Railways Board or London Regional Transport; or

(c)   which appears to the committee to be a matter to which consideration ought to be given.

On receiving a recommendation by a Consultative Committee, the Minister may give directions to the British Railways Board or London Regional Transport with respect to the matters dealt with in the recommendation.

Before TAWA the remit of the committees did not extend to considering generally any question relating to the discontinuance or reduction of railway services. But notice of any proposed closure of passenger services from any station or on any line was required to be sent by the British Railways Board or London Regional Transport to the Area Committee for the area in which the station or line (or any part of the line) affected by the closure is situated. Under s. 56(8) of the Transport Act 1962, where an objection is received the Minister's consent to the closure is required. The Area Committee was required to consider the objection and any response by the British Railways Board or London Regional Transport and to report to the Minister on any hardship which they considered would be caused by the proposed closure. The report could contain proposals for alleviating the hardship but it was the duty of the committee to make a report which balanced the case for and the case against the proposal.

The effect of s. 21 of TAWA is to give a rather different role to the Area Transport Users' Consultative Committees where applications are made for orders under s. 1 or s. 7 of TAWA which would entail closures. The committees may consider and, if they think fit, make their own objections to any such proposals. They are not to be limited to fulfilling a purely representational role and are not to be required to present a balanced report about the proposals.

Several recent private Acts authorising light rail rapid transit systems have applied the provisions of s. 56 of the 1962 Act to closures of the new system. An example is s. 9(3) of the Greater Manchester (Light Rapid Transit System) (No.2) Act 1988. By virtue of s. 20(2) of the Interpretation Act 1978, the amendments made by s. 21 of TAWA to s. 56 of the 1962 Act will automatically be carried through to those systems.

The general procedures relating to closures of stations or services on railway lines of the British Railways Board or London Regional Transport are laid down in ss. 54 and 56 of the Transport Act 1962 and s. 54 of the Transport Act 1968. To summarise, the procedures provide for the publication of the proposals by advertising in local newspapers and for a six-week objection period. Where there are objections, the closure cannot proceed without the consent of the Secretary of State. It is expected that regulations made under s. 15 of TAWA will modify these closure procedures so as to ensure that the procedures can take place concurrently with procedures under Part I of TAWA. If consent to an order under s. 1 of TAWA is given, the Secretary of State will be enabled at the same time to give any necessary consent under s. 56 of the 1962 Act or s. 54 of the 1968 Act. See further chapter 5.

3.12   DELEGATION OF SECRETARY OF STATE'S FUNCTIONS
TO APPOINTED PERSONS

Section 23 enables the Secretary of State to delegate his powers to deal with applications for s. 1 or s. 3 orders to persons appointed by him. The delegation can be effected either generally for classes of applications specified in regulations, or on an *ad hoc* basis for a particular application. Where an application has been allocated to an appointed person, he will have the same powers and duties as the Secretary of State has under ss. 1 and 3 (see s. 23(3)(a)) and, if regulations so provide, any other specified powers and duties conferred on the Secretary of State under Part I of TAWA and under subordinate legislation made under Part I (see s. 23(3)(b)). Orders made by appointed persons are treated as if made by the Secretary of State (s. 23(5)) and the provisions of the Tribunals and Inquiries Act 1992 are applied (s. 23(9)). The provisions of s. 23 are similar to those in sch. 6 to the Town and Country Planning Act 1990 under which planning appeal functions of the Secretary of State may be delegated.

These powers will probably be used only if the Secretary of State is brought under pressure by large volumes of cases, or if it turns out that a significant number of applications relate to proposals thought to be too minor or uncontroversial to warrant consideration by the Secretary of State. As has been explained (see 1.9), the consultative paper published by the Government proposed a three-tier system, with local authorities dealing with the first-tier schemes (schemes of purely local significance). This proposal was not implemented in the Act, but has been replaced by the power in s. 23 which would enable schemes of purely local significance to be dealt with by persons appointed by the Secretary of State.

A significant limitation on the power to delegate is provided by s. 23(4), under which orders made by appointed persons may not authorise the compulsory acquisition of land or the compulsory creation or extinguishment of rights over land (including rights of navigation over water). In the main, therefore, an appointed person will only be able to make orders authorising the construction of works on land already owned by the transport operator.

Under s. 23(10) (as amended by the Transfer of Functions (Energy) Order 1992 (SI 1992/1314)) where the appointed person is an officer of the Department of Transport, the Department of the Environment, the Department of Trade and Industry or the Welsh Office, his functions are to be treated for the purposes of the Parliamentary Commissioner Act 1967 as functions of the department or office by whose Secretary of State he was appointed. Under the 1967 Act, the Parliamentary Commissioner for Administration (colloquially known as 'the ombudsman') is appointed to conduct investigations into actions taken by or on behalf of Government departments in the exercise of their administrative functions where complaints have been referred to him in accordance with the Act. The Departments of Transport, the Environment and Trade and Industry, and the Welsh Office are listed in sch. 2 to the 1967 Act as subject to investigation. The effect of s. 23(10) is to make actions of civil servants appointed under s. 23 subject to scrutiny by the Parliamentary Commissioner for Administration.

3.13   CROWN LAND

In the absence of express statutory provision, Crown interests cannot be compulsorily acquired. Section 25 (which is similar to s. 296 of the Town and Country Planning Act 1990, read with s. 293) reinforces this rule. No interest in land in which there is an interest belonging to Her Majesty in right of the Crown or of the Duchy of Lancaster or belonging to the Duchy of Cornwall, or belonging to a Government department, or held in trust for Her Majesty for the purposes of a Government department may be compulsorily acquired unless the necessary consent is obtained from the appropriate authority. The requirement to obtain a consent is not confined to the acquisition of the Crown or Duchy interest itself, but extends also to the acquisition of any non-Crown or non-Duchy interest in the land. Consent is therefore required to purchase, for example, a leasehold interest held in land the freehold of which belongs to the Crown.

Section 25(3) lays down who the appropriate authority is in each case. For example, the Crown Estate Commissioners are the appropriate authority in the case of land belonging to Her Majesty in right of the Crown and forming part of the Crown Estate. Any question as to who is the appropriate authority in any case may be referred to the Treasury, whose decision is final (s. 25(4)).

Where the appropriate consent has been obtained, the land in question may be included in orders made under s. 1 or s. 3. There is no power, however, to include land belonging to Her Majesty in her private capacity.

FOUR
SCHEMES OF NATIONAL SIGNIFICANCE

4.1 THE BACKGROUND

The Transport and Works Act 1992 recognises that some schemes have such far-reaching effects that it is appropriate for Parliament to retain a role in deciding whether or not they should go ahead. These schemes, described in the Act as being 'schemes of national significance', are dealt with in s. 9. The general effect of s. 9 is that schemes considered by the Secretary of State to be of national significance are required to be approved in principle by Parliament before proceeding to a public local inquiry. The approval of Parliament is an *additional* requirement; in other respects, the scheme is subject to exactly the same procedures as apply to applications for, and approval of, other s. 1 or s. 3 schemes.

The Joint Committee on Private Bill Procedure gave some consideration to whether Parliament should continue to be involved where schemes raise issues of high significance. They noted (para. 23 of the Report) that 'in exceptional cases of projects involving, for example, novel forms of technology or widespread environmental effects, it is right that Parliament should be able to express an opinion even when the final decision is one for the Minister'. Reference was made in the Report to the general means whereby Parliament may concern itself with major or controversial proposals. The means referred to were parliamentary debates on a Government motion (e.g., the debates in 1987 on the Inspector's Report on the Public Inquiry on Sizewell) and the granting of planning permission by means of special development orders under the Town and Country Planning Act 1971, which require parliamentary endorsement.

The Joint Committee, in recommending that all works proposals where planning considerations are dominant should be authorised by non-parliamentary procedures, did not expressly reserve for Parliament any special role in the case of particularly important schemes. This was based on the assumption that private Bill proposals rarely involve issues of high significance (para. 24 of the Report) and that, in the opinion of the Committee, private Bills 'are not . . . an appropriate system for authorising works of purely local significance'. The Committee were concerned mainly with the authorisation procedures for what they saw as run of the mill schemes, that is to say purely local schemes. They referred only briefly to schemes which are exceptional because, for example, they raise issues of high environmental significance. The Committee went on to conclude that they would not recommend any restriction on the right of the Government to bring works schemes to Parliament by way of hybrid Bills or special development orders (para. 32 of the Report).

The Government's response to the Report was that proposals of national significance should receive special treatment, and that there should be built into the new procedure provision for proposals of national significance to be referred to Parliament for decision. It was initially proposed (*Private Bills and New Procedures – A Consultation Document*, Cm 1110, London: HMSO, 1990, para. 29) that, in the case of projects considered by the Secretary of State to be of national importance, the statutory instrument containing the order authorising the scheme should be subject to affirmative resolution by each House of Parliament with a single debate on the floor of each House. The order would not come into effect until the statutory instrument had been approved by Parliament in this way. The Government considered parliamentary intervention would not be sufficiently safeguarded by relying only on the existing possibilities referred to in the Joint Committee's Report. They concluded (para. 26) that those who believe that Parliament should decide on projects of national significance would not be satisfied by the holding of a parliamentary debate if the debate gave no express decisive role to Parliament. Special development orders would be inappropriate since they would not confer on transport schemes protection from nuisance actions. In any event, parliamentary endorsement of special development orders, which often involve detailed scrutiny of proposals in committee, would be likely to lengthen substantially the authorisation procedures. Hybrid Bills would not solve the problem either, since these would not be appropriate in the case of schemes which the Government did not wish to sponsor.

The Government's stated objective was to ensure that Parliament retained a decisive role in considering proposals of national significance while at the same time avoiding lengthy duplication in Parliament of the detailed examination which would already have taken place as part of the new order-making procedure.

The Government's initial proposals were modified to take account of comments made to the Department of Transport in response to the consultative paper. The promoters of large projects made the point that public local inquiries are ill-suited to investigate the overall merits of schemes of national significance. By their very nature they are concerned with examining matters of local, rather than national, importance. Local inquiries, already cumbersome, might well be over-burdened if charged with hearing arguments on the policy and principle of a large scale scheme as well as with considering more detailed local issues. It was also considered that if Parliament was going to veto an important scheme, it should do so early in the decision-making process rather than after a full local inquiry had been held, putting both promoters and objectors to unnecessary trouble and expense. The Council on Tribunals was concerned that the inquiry system could be brought into disrepute if, after a long and thorough inquiry, the whole process were overturned in Parliament – perhaps by a single vote.

The Government concluded (Commons Second Reading H.C. *Hansard*, 2 December 1991, cols 43 and 44) that it would assist the conduct of local inquiries into large projects if the project had been given the initial approval of Parliament. The proceedings would be held in the knowledge that the strategic framework of the scheme had been sanctioned by Parliament. While it could be argued that no decision affecting the scheme should be made until all its details had been thoroughly investigated, it was simply not practical to defer making a decision in principle until the scheme and all other options had been worked out in fine detail. No decision in principle might mean no decision at all; and it was essential for the prosperity of the country to arrive at difficult decisions. The Government was therefore persuaded that Parliament should be called upon at an early stage to decide whether a scheme should proceed to be considered by a public local inquiry. However, the matter would not be brought before Parliament until the draft order had been submitted (accompanied by an environmental statement) and the objection period had expired. Parliament would therefore consider the matter with some knowledge of the environmental background and the nature of any objections.

This procedure does not, of course, preclude the possibility of the issues raised by a scheme being brought to the attention of Parliament in other ways. One device, canvassed by the Joint Committee, that the scheme could be debated by Parliament on a Government motion, remains an additional option. Another method might be the setting up by the Government of a commission to advise the Secretary of State on the issues of principle raised by a proposed scheme. Most importantly, the hybrid Bill procedure (discussed in 4.6 below) is available for major schemes supported by the Government.

4.2   WHAT SCHEMES ARE 'SCHEMES OF NATIONAL SIGNIFICANCE'?

Section 9 provides that where an application for an order authorising a s. 1 or s. 3 scheme is made, the special s. 9 procedure applies to 'proposals which in the opinion of the Secretary of State are of national significance'. Whether a scheme is or is not of national significance falls wholly to be decided by the Secretary of State. The determination has to be made within the period of eight weeks beginning with the day on which the application is received by him.

No indication is given in the Act as to the criteria which may or should be taken into account by the Secretary of State in reaching his decision – the matter is simply left to his discretion. However, as a matter of common sense, one would expect the Secretary of State to have regard to any information about the scheme submitted with the application and, in particular, the contents of the environmental statement (see 3.3 above).

The period within which objections to any applications for a scheme must be made is to be prescribed in rules made under s. 10 and is expected to be six weeks from the date of the application. The period of eight weeks was deliberately chosen to be two weeks longer than the objection period so as to enable the Secretary of State to take into account any relevant issues raised by objectors.

The main criticism that may be made is that the jurisdiction of Parliament should not depend on the discretion of the Secretary of State, particularly where no statutory indication is given as to how the discretion should be exercised. Not surprisingly, this comment was made repeatedly, not merely by bodies responding to the consultative document, but throughout the Bill's progress through Parliament (see Commons Second Reading H.C., *Hansard*, 2 December 1991, col. 49; Parliamentary Debates, H.C., *Hansard*, Standing Committee A, Transport and Works Bill, Sixth Sitting, 14 January 1992, cols. 187-195; House of Lords (when all stages of the Bill were considered together to enable it to pass before the pre-election dissolution of Parliament) Parliamentary Debate H.L. *Hansard*, 13 March 1992, col. 1524). It was suggested in Standing Committee that Parliament should reserve to itself the right to require a scheme to be brought before it if, for instance, no fewer than 100 MPs signed an Early Day Motion to that effect.

These arguments were resisted by the Government, as were all attempts to specify in the Bill criteria to which the Secretary of State should have regard in making his decision. The Government argued against any limitation on the Secretary of State's discretion. Each case should be decided on its individual merits, different factors being relevant to different types of schemes, and it was essential that maximum flexibility should be retained. However, the Minister indicated that guidance notes would be published.

It is not therefore possible to predict with any certainty what types of projects will be treated as schemes of national significance. But it seems likely that, for a scheme to require the approval of Parliament, it would have to affect a significant part of the country rather than just a small part of it. This might be thought to be the case where the proposals affect a substantial area as in the case of a new railway such as Crossrail (which includes a proposed underground railway in London from Paddington Station to Liverpool Street Station) extending over the areas of several local authorities; or as in the case of a major tidal energy barrage, where the effect of the scheme would be to benefit a significant part of the country. Schemes may also qualify if their environmental effects are thought to raise issues of national importance. The decision is essentially political. To take a specific example, the London Underground Act 1992 authorises an extension of the Jubilee underground line, including substantial underground works at Westminster. The construction of the Westminster works would affect the area immediately adjoining the Palace of Westminster and would necessitate the demolition of 1–3 Bridge Street opposite the Palace. During the Bill's passage through Parliament, its impact on the locality near the Palace attracted particular scrutiny, with the result that the original proposals in the Bill as deposited were considerably modified. Had the Jubilee extension scheme been promoted using the new order-making procedures, it seems probable that the Secretary of State would have considered it appropriate for the scheme to come before Parliament.

The Secretary of State's decision whether or not a scheme is to be treated as one of national significance would be open to challenge in the courts by judicial review on the grounds that the Secretary of State acted unreasonably by considering irrelevant matters or by failing to consider relevant ones.

In practice, since the Secretary of State's decision is essentially political, the views of Parliament will play an important part. It would be difficult to claim that an issue which has attracted the widespread attention of peers and Members of Parliament is one of merely local significance. It therefore seems likely, and appropriate, that if a particular project excites considerable parliamentary interest, the Secretary of State will decide that it is a scheme of national significance. If in doubt, it will be safer for the Secretary of State to determine that a scheme is of national significance, since this is less likely to be challenged than a decision that a scheme does not require parliamentary sanction.

4.3 THE PROCEDURE FOR DEALING WITH SCHEMES OF NATIONAL SIGNIFICANCE

Where the Secretary of State receives an application under s. 6 for a s. 1 or s. 3 order, he may, within eight weeks beginning with the date on which the application is received, decide that in his opinion the application relates to proposals of national significance. Before the end of the period he must then publicise that decision by publishing a notice in the *London Gazette* identifying the application and the proposals which he has determined are of national significance.

The period of eight weeks is two weeks longer than the period which is to be prescribed by rules for the making of objections, so the Secretary of State will be able to consider any pertinent matters raised by objectors. This tight timetable should not, in practice, present any difficulties. Promoters of any scheme that might conceivably qualify to be treated as being of national significance will almost certainly have engaged in detailed dialogue with the relevant Government departments well before the formal application is made, not least because a scheme of this sort is likely to involve at least an element of public expenditure, such as a grant under s. 56 of the Transport Act 1968.

A notice similar to that in the *London Gazette* must also be published in a local newspaper circulating in the area (or each of the areas) in which any proposed works are to be carried out. A copy of the notice must be sent to:

(a)   the applicant;

(b)   any objecting local authority (which term includes a county council, a district council, a London borough council, the Common Council of the City of London, the Council of the Isles of Scilly and a Passenger Transport Executive) for an area in which any works authorised by the proposed order are to be carried out; and

(c)   any objecting owner, lessee or occupier of any land which is, or in which interests are, to be compulsorily acquired. (These last expressions are explained further in 3.5.3.)

The local newspaper notice must be published, and the notices sent out to the objectors, as soon as practicable after the publication of the *London Gazette* notice.

The Secretary of State's decision need not relate to the entire scheme covered by the application. Section 9(1) enables the Secretary of State to determine that some only of the proposals to which the application relates are of national significance. If that is the case, care will be needed to ensure that the notices required to be served and published in newspapers make it clear which of the proposals are to be treated as being of national significance.

Once the Secretary of State has determined that proposals are of national significance, they must be approved by each House of Parliament before any order on the application can be made. The restriction extends to all proposals in the application and is not confined to those of national significance. Parliamentary approval is signified by the passing of a resolution in each House of Parliament on a motion moved by a Minister of the Crown which identifies the proposals in question.

The motion cannot be considered by either House of Parliament until at least eight weeks after the publication of the notice in the *London Gazette* under s. 9(2). The eight-week period is intended to give peers and Members of Parliament an opportunity to study the proposals. The Government has indicated that copies of the order submitted by the promoters and all the accompanying documents, including the environmental statements, will be deposited in Parliament. Copies of any objections made will also be available. A summary of the case for and against the proposals and the alternatives that have been examined will be prepared for the assistance of Parliament. The eight week period will also enable the promoters and any other interested parties to express their views to peers and Members of Parliament.

There is no statutory deadline for debating the motion. The timetable will depend on the pressures on parliamentary business and on whether Parliament is in recess. In the case of any application made after April in any year, a motion to approve proposals of national significance is unlikely to come before either House of Parliament before the following November.

4.4   THE EFFECT OF PARLIAMENTARY APPROVAL

If Parliament does not approve the proposals in principle, no order on the application may be made by the Secretary of State. If, on the other hand, a resolution approving the scheme has been passed by Parliament, the Secretary of State may not make an order on the application which includes any provision that is inconsistent with the proposals approved by the resolution. There is, however, nothing to prevent the Secretary of State from declining to make an order at all.

Provision is made by s. 9(5) for Parliament to sanction modifications of proposals originally approved under s. 9. Again, sanction is given by a resolution passed on a motion moved by a Minister of the Crown. It is interesting that there is, in this case, no equivalent of the eight-week waiting period which applies in relation to the original motion. It would theoretically be possible for very little notice to be given to Parliament of any modifications required to be authorised.

The philosophy behind this system of parliamentary approval is easy to express. It is for Parliament to sanction the proposals in principle. Once approved, the proposals can be worked up to produce a number of variants, any of which fit within the approved framework. The role of the inspector at the public local inquiry is, on the whole, to be confined to the consideration of the detail of the scheme rather than its broad outline. In this task, he will be assisted by the knowledge that the principle of the scheme has received parliamentary backing. The Secretary of State retains a discretion to refuse to make an order but, if he does make one, its provisions must not conflict with proposals which have been approved by Parliament, whether by the original resolution or by a subsequent supplementary resolution.

Although the underlying rationale of s. 9 is clear, it is likely to prove very difficult to apply. The conceptual difficulty lies in differentiating between the essential ingredients of a scheme and its details. The issues in any particular case will be, first, what precisely should Parliament be asked to approve and, secondly, what exactly Parliament has approved. The answer to the first question is political; the answer to the second will turn on the exact wording of the motion put before Parliament. It is clear that the drafting of the motion will be of the utmost importance. If it is drafted generally, the Secretary of State will have considerable latitude. If it is drafted so as to cover a number of very specific matters, there may be insufficient room for manoeuvre. Since the motion is to be moved by a Minister of the Crown, its drafting will lie neither with the promoters nor with Parliament but with the Executive.

An obvious example (and one which was raised during the Bill's passage through Parliament) is the construction of an important new railway connection. Is the essential feature of the scheme to be sanctioned the construction of a fast railway line between two specified points, or should Parliament be asked to approve the route of the new railway? The answer to this question will depend on the circumstances of each individual case. When the matter was raised by a Member of Parliament in Standing Committee with reference to the Channel Tunnel Link, the Minister revealed the inherent difficulties:

> I cannot today give him the wording of that resolution. However he is right to say that a decision has been taken that the Link would be desirable. It is a question of where that Link should go. I cannot say exactly where it will be, but we see the resolution as a line of route expressing a general corridor into the area. That general corridor would not be definitive – there may be variations as a result of local representations and the public inquiry. (H.C. Deb., *Hansard*, Standing Committee A, Transport and Works Bill, Sixth Sitting, 14 January 1992, col. 199.)

Even if the terms of the motion approved by Parliament are clear, it is not certain to what extent an inspector will consider himself precluded from re-examining issues which have been approved by Parliament. The sanctioning of the principle of a scheme by an initial resolution has a well-established equivalent in hybrid Bill procedure. In the case of hybrid Bills (which are further discussed in 4.6 below), each House of Parliament is given the opportunity of discussing the issues raised by the Bill at the second reading debate. Subject to any indication or instruction to the contrary, the second reading of the Bill is taken to remove from the promoters the onus of proving the expediency of the Bill. It is no part of the functions of the Select Committee inquiry into a hybrid Bill to conduct roving investigations into its general merits. The Committee's role is limited to hearing those affected parties who petition and to reducing as far as possible the hardship and inconvenience which would be inflicted on them if the Bill were passed into law. It follows that no amendment destructive of the principle of the Bill may be made by the Committee in the absence of any special instruction by the House.

That the application of these rules relating to hybrid Bills does not give rise to problems is to a great extent attributable to the centralised nature of parliamentary proceedings. Chairmen of Select Committees of either House are advised by House officials: in particular, in the Commons, the Counsel to the Speaker and, in the Lords, by the Counsel to the Chairman of Committees. The resolution of questions of procedure is rarely influenced by political pressures. Because all proceedings take place in the Palace of Westminster, interested parties are able to consult quickly and easily. A settled, if arcane, body of practice has therefore been built up and is well understood both by House officials and by parliamentary practitioners.

In contrast, it seems unlikely that the analogous division of responsibilities between Parliament, public local inquiries and the Secretary of State contemplated by s. 9 will be consistently and predictably applied. The Government will be under great political pressure when settling the terms of the parliamentary motion of approval. Inspectors will have varying views as to their exact functions. Unlike chairmen of Select Committees, they will not have the benefit of guidance on specific problems from an adviser who is seen to be authoritative and non-political.

Where Parliament has approved the national policy of the scheme, an attempt will be made to restrict the remit of the public local inquiry by rules under s. 9 of the Tribunals and Inquiries Act 1992. It seems unlikely that this will resolve the difficulties mentioned above. The draft rules do not prohibit the giving of oral evidence at inquiries which challenges the overall expediency of proposals already approved under s. 9, but leave the matter to the inspector's discretion. It has been indicated that inspectors are to be free to hear evidence on matters of policy where the evidence is both important and was not available to Parliament when the issues were debated. Whether such evidence is or is not new and weighty is a matter of judgment and would presumably fall to be decided by the inspector. With no rules of *locus standi* to curb debate, only the toughest of inspectors will refuse to hear arguments from objectors which go to the heart rather than to the detail of the scheme. Uncertainty over the inspector's role is exacerbated by the fact that a parliamentary resolution is not intended to be conclusive sanction for a scheme. It remains open to the Secretary of State to refuse to make the order altogether or to go back to Parliament with a modifying resolution. The effect is to invite continuing debate on the general merits of the scheme despite parliamentary approval.

4.5 SCHEMES OF NATIONAL SIGNIFICANCE INITIATED BY THE SECRETARY OF STATE

Reference already has been made to the power of the Secretary of State to initiate schemes for defence or safety purposes (see 2.2). Where such a scheme is deemed by the Secretary of State to be of national significance, the procedures of s. 9 apply but in a modified form.

Notices of the schemes required to be published in the *London Gazette* and national newspapers under s. 7(3) must identify any proposals which have been identified as being of national significance. There is no need for additional notices to be published under s. 9(2) or (3). It follows that there is no requirement for the Secretary of State to notify any objector to the proposed scheme. A motion of approval must be put before Parliament. As in the ordinary case, a minimum period of eight weeks must elapse between the publication of the s. 7 notice in the *London Gazette* and the motion of approval being considered by Parliament. No order may be made by the Secretary of State unless and until the motion of approval has been passed by each House of Parliament.

4.6 HYBRID BILLS

The new procedures for schemes of national significance are likely to prove less than satisfactory in general. In the case of schemes supported by the Government, they appear entirely inappropriate.

Schemes of national significance will generally need Government backing if they are to get off the ground. Often they are large scale projects involving considerable public expenditure. Important overground or underground railway schemes are at present, almost without exception, promoted by London Regional Transport (or its subsidiary London Underground Limited) or by the British Railways Board. Up to now, it has been necessary for those bodies to seek the Secretary of State's approval to such schemes because they are empowered to promote Bills only with his consent (see s. 17 of the Transport Act 1962 and the London Regional Transport Act 1984 sch. 2, para. 18). The formal requirement to obtain the Secretary of State's approval to schemes is now removed by s. 20 of TAWA, which gives to London Regional Transport and the British Railways Board the right to apply for orders under s. 1 without the consent of the Secretary of State (see 3.10). In reality, however, it will continue to be necessary for either body to obtain ministerial approval before embarking on a scheme of any magnitude because of the public funding involved. Most schemes for the provision of public transport facilities are financed at least partly by grants under s. 56 of the Transport Act 1968.

A criticism frequently levied against the promotion by British Rail or London Regional Transport of private Bills to authorise large scale railway schemes (such as the King's Cross Railways Bill) is that the Government, though not itself promoting the Bill, is alleged to be actively assisting the promoters. The promoters have successfully sought ministerial consent to promote the Bill. Governmental support is demonstrated by Ministers speaking in favour of the Bill on the floor of the House. Yet the Government has to distance itself from the promotion of the Bill. The ambiguous stance of the Government, even if sometimes embarrassing, does not give rise to any real difficulty in this context, however, since the passing of a private Bill is a matter for Parliament and not the Government.

Of more concern is the conflict which would arise if the new order-making procedure were used to authorise schemes which have, in effect, been considered and approved by the Secretary of State even before a formal application is made under TAWA.

It is likely that these difficulties will be resolved by continued use being made by the Government of the hybrid Bill procedure. This approach is consistent with the Joint Committee's recommendation that the right of the Government to promote hybrid Bills should not be restricted.

The nature of a hybrid Bill has already been touched on in chapter 1. A hybrid Bill is a public Bill, that is to say a Bill relating to matters of public policy and introduced directly by a Member of Parliament – generally by a Minister – which also has the character of a private Bill in that it affects the interests of specific individuals or bodies as distinct from all individuals or bodies of a similar category. In order to protect these private rights, some of the procedures laid down in the Standing Orders of each House of Parliament for private Bills are also applicable to hybrid Bills. So, for example, persons directly affected by the Bill are given the opportunity to petition against the Bill in each House and to be heard on their petition by a Select Committee of the House.

The problems (discussed in 1.4) which have arisen in private Bill procedures and which led to the passing of TAWA do not apply to hybrid Bills. This is because hybrid Bills enjoy a number of procedural advantages over private Bills:

(a)   Subject to receiving authorisation from the Standing Orders Committee of the House of Commons, a hybrid Bill can be introduced at any time in any given Session of Parliament.

(b)   Once a hybrid Bill has received a second reading in either House, the principle of the Bill is deemed to have been accepted in that House and, accordingly, the promoters (the Government) are not required to make out the case for the Bill before the Select Committee. They are only required to answer the arguments put forward by any petitioners who, similarly, are only entitled to argue a case against some – but not all – of the provisions of the Bill. Amendments destructive of the purposes of the Bill cannot be made.

(c)   Throughout the passage of a hybrid Bill, the Government are entitled, and expected, to whip their supporters at each stage on the floor of each House.

(d)   The Government can counter filibustering by tabling and passing a 'guillotine' motion to curtail debate on the Bill. Proceedings are not therefore subject to being 'talked out'. If any stage becomes too prolonged, it is open to the Government to curtail debate on the remainder of that stage. So, for example, amendments made to a hybrid Bill at the Committee stage in the House of Commons, which may be fatal to a private Bill's progress at the subsequent Consideration stage in that House, do not pose any threat to progress on the hybrid Bill.

(e)   The Select Committee is likely to consist of nine members of whom any three constitute a quorum. In the case of a private Bill, the Select Committee usually consists of four members (three being a quorum) in the Commons and five members (four being a quorum) in the Lords. Individual members of the Select Committee for a hybrid Bill therefore have many more opportunities to absent themselves from the Committee proceedings to deal with their other parliamentary duties without leaving the Committee inquorate. The Felixstowe Bill (a private Bill) demonstrated how difficulties arise when two members of the Committee are absent at any time. The same situation occurred in relation to the King's Cross Railways Bill.

The advantages of hybrid Bill procedure over the new order-making power largely lie in the speed of Select Committee proceedings when compared to the proceedings of public local inquiries. The Severn Bridges Bill (a hybrid Bill) was introduced into Parliament in November 1990 and received Royal Assent in February 1992. In the case of another hybrid Bill, the Channel Tunnel Bill, which was more controversial, the Bill was introduced in April 1986 and passed in July 1987. The speed with which these schemes were authorised does not indicate that opposition to them was disregarded but rather that the Government achieved satisfactory settlement with many of the petitioners – a process always stimulated by the approach of the date set for the commencement of the Select Committee proceedings.

When compared to highways schemes which are conducted by public local inquiries, hybrid Bill procedures are singularly efficient. On average it takes 11 years for a highways scheme to be approved, and only two years for a new highway to be constructed.

There are many who would argue that major transport infrastructure schemes, such as the proposed high-speed Channel Link, should not become bogged down in political and local controversy. As the Minister said at the Second Reading of the Transport and Works Act, 'If the country is to prosper, it must be able to make difficult decisions of this kind' (House of Commons, H.C. Deb., *Hansard*, 2 December 1991, col. 44).

FIVE
PLANNING PERMISSION, OTHER STATUTORY CONSENTS AND BLIGHT NOTICES

5.1 INTRODUCTION

This chapter concerns ss. 15 to 19 of TAWA which deal with the relationship between the new s. 1 and s. 3 orders and the consents, permissions and licences which may be required under other enactments. Undoubtedly the most important of these is the requirement to obtain planning permission under the Town and Country Planning Act 1990, s. 16, and this will be considered first. The approach of TAWA towards this requirement is to subsume the procedure for obtaining planning permission in the procedure for the new s. 1 and s. 3 orders. However, in the case of two other requirements of a planning nature – namely those for listed building consent and conservation area consent under the Planning (Listed Buildings and Conservation Areas) Act 1990 – the Act provides for the basic features of the consents to be retained (s. 17), with the result that they must be given separately from the decision on the s. 1 or s. 3 order.

Hazardous substances consent under the Planning (Hazardous Substances) Act 1990 is dealt with by s. 18, while Coast Protection Act consent under s. 34 of the Coast Protection Act 1949 is dealt with by s. 19. In both cases, as with planning permission, the Act subsumes the procedures in the new s. 1 and s. 3 procedure.

Section 15 deals with cases, such as s. 17, where the procedures for obtaining statutory consents, etc. are not to be subsumed. In such cases, the Secretary of State is given a power by regulations to assimilate the procedures with that of an application under s. 6 for a s. 1 or s. 3 order.

Section 16(2) – which deals with blight notices – raises different issues and is dealt with at the end of the chapter.

Section 70 provides that the other provisions of TAWA shall come into force on such day as the Secretary of State may by order appoint; and different days may be appointed for different purposes. The Department of Transport has indicated that Part I of TAWA (which includes ss. 15 to 19) will be brought into force by 1 January 1993 (see chapter 2.5).

5.2   PLANNING PERMISSION

5.2.1   The Joint Committee's recommendations

In chapter 1 we saw how criticism of private Bills for works schemes tended to involve not only unfavourable comparisons with the town and country planning system and its provision for public local inquiries, but also expressions of unease as to the actual relationship between the planning system and statutory authorisation by means of private Act. The Joint Committee on Private Bill Procedure considered that private Bills were not an appropriate system for authorising works of purely local significance, and that a public local inquiry was the best way of considering proposals for any such works. Having rejected the feasibility of introducing a public local inquiry stage into the private Bill system, or the introduction of the Scottish private legislation procedure, the Joint Committee concluded that, where planning considerations are dominant, all works proposals for which private Bill approval would be required should be authorised through non-parliamentary procedures, involving, where necessary, the holding of public local inquiries (Joint Committee on Private Bill Procedure, *Report*, HL Paper 97/HC 625, London: HMSO 1988).

Part I of TAWA provides for the establishment of such new procedures in the case of railways, tramways, other guided transport systems, waterways and matters specified by the Secretary of State under s. 3 (see chapters 2 and 3). The removal from Parliament to the Executive of the means of authorisation for such schemes does not, however, make it unnecessary to consider the relationship between the new procedures created by the Act and the town and country planning system. On the contrary, the policy of the Act in this regard is novel, complex and controversial.

The Joint Committee considered that the new order-making procedures should be capable of delivering to a promoter every authorisation which could have been obtained if the promoter were still able to proceed by way of private Bill. One such authorisation which follows automatically from the conferring of works powers by private Act is that of planning permission. The Town and Country Planning General Development Order 1988 (SI 1988/1813), sch. 1, Part II, class A, provides that development authorised by a local or private Act of Parliament, which designates specifically the nature of the development authorised and the land upon which it may be carried out, is permitted development, for which planning permission is automatically granted by art. 3. Development is, however, not permitted if it consists of or includes:

(a)   the erection, construction, alteration or extension of any building, bridge, aqueduct, pier or dam; or
(b)   the formation, laying out or alteration of a means of access to any highway used by vehicular traffic,

unless the prior approval of the relevant planning authority is obtained. That authority's power to refuse permission, or impose conditions, is constrained in that such refusal or conditions may be imposed only where the authority is satisfied that:

(i)   the development (other than the provision of or works carried out to a dam) ought to be and could reasonably be carried out elsewhere on the land; or

(ii)   the design or external appearance of any building, bridge, aqueduct, pier or dam would injure the amenity of the neighbourhood and is reasonably capable of modification to avoid such injury.

In practice, all major works for which approval is sought by way of private Bill were able to satisfy the requirements referred to above, in that they were specifically described in the Bill (usually by reference to numbered works) and shown on the plans and sections deposited with the Bill in Parliament.

The Joint Committee envisaged that 'the making of the railway order would have effect to grant a permission of the same form as that presently granted to works authorised by private Bill' (*Report*, para. 48). The Government's Consultation Document did not specifically endorse the Joint Committee's recommendation, but merely stated that 'in the interests of flexibility the new procedure should allow promoters the option of seeking planning permission separately (direct from the local planning authority) *as an alternative to seeking planning permission by means of the order*' (*Private Bills and New Procedures – A Consultation Document*, Cm 1110, London: HMSO, 1990, emphasis supplied). The Joint Committee had itself suggested that promoters might on occasion find it expedient to obtain planning permission in the ordinary way before applying for an order, but the Government's reference to seeking planning permission by means of the order was generally interpreted as indicating either an intention to extend the categories of permitted development in the General Development Order so as to cover the new orders (as recommended by the Joint Committee), or else an intention to provide in the order, as made, for the automatic grant of planning permission for the specific works mentioned in that order, subject to the same or similar exceptions as those set out in class A of Part II.

5.2.2 TAWA's approach

To the surprise of many, TAWA rejects both of these approaches. Instead, s. 16 amends the Town and Country Planning Act 1990, s. 90 (which gives power to deem planning permission to be granted in certain cases where development is authorised by a Government department), by inserting as s. 90(2A) a provision that, on making an order under s. 1 or s. 3 of TAWA which includes a provision for development, the Secretary of State may direct that planning permission for that development shall be deemed to be granted, subject to such conditions (if any) as may be specified in the direction.

The Government's decision to depart from the existing practice in the case of private Bills, and not to grant automatic planning permission for works authorised by s. 1 or s. 3 orders, caused considerable concern, especially to promoters, such as the British Railways Board, who feared that the wholly permissive nature of the new s. 90(2A) would result in uncertainty and delay. These fears were forcefully expressed by the Solicitor to the British Railways Board (Simon Osborne, Esq.) at a conference on the Bill in January 1992, attended by the Minister responsible for handling the Bill in its Commons Committee stages and his senior officials. In Mr Osborne's view, the General

Development Order approach was to be preferred, because of the certainty it offered. He was not persuaded that purely permissive powers were required in order to give effect to the Joint Committee's recommendation that promoters of the new orders should be able, if they so wish, to seek planning approval from the local planning authority for some or all aspects of the proposed scheme, and he pointed out that, under the private Bill system, there was nothing to prevent the promoter of a private Bill from seeking planning permission in the normal way for development which would be authorised under a private Bill, instead of relying on planning consent granted under the General Development Order. In his view the permissive nature of the provision could be used to delay implementation of a scheme which the Government did not wish to see go ahead, thereby avoiding the necessity of rejecting the scheme outright.

5.2.3 Debates in Parliament

The Government's proposals on planning consent came under detailed scrutiny during the Bill's passage through the House of Commons, and the arguments advanced on either side are worthy of consideration, both for the light that they shed upon how the new system may actually work in practice and as a graphic example of the basic policy dilemma which lies behind the whole of Part I of the Act, namely, how best to reconcile the need for speedy and effective authorisations of infrastructure projects with the system of development control which has evolved in England and Wales since 1947 (and in particular the importance placed by that system upon local decision-making).

In Standing Committee and on Report, amendments were moved to cl. 16(1) (as it then was) which would have given effect to the Joint Committee's proposal that works authorised by s. 1 or s. 3 orders should be treated as permitted development. One of the MPs who put forward such amendments was Roger Moate, who had been a member of the Joint Committee; the other was Peter Snape, an Opposition transport spokesman. Both were concerned that important railway projects could be delayed or frustrated unless the new order-making system followed that of private Bills. Mr Moate considered that 'an element of doubt, flexibility and discretion is now being introduced which could delay matters or require further planning processes. That would not help many desirable developments' (House of Commons, H.C. Deb., *Hansard*, Standing Committee A, Transport and Works Bill, Seventh Sitting, 16 January 1992, col. 230), whilst in Mr Snape's words, 'people are concerned about the long, built-in delays in Britain's planning procedures, especially on transport infrastructure. We do not want to create a further barrier in legislation that would cause even greater delay to some much-needed projects' (ibid., col. 231). Of major concern to both was the dilemma which might confront a promoter in deciding whether to work-up the proposed scheme to the stage where it would be possible for the Secretary of State to grant full (as opposed to merely outline) planning permission if he decided to make the order. If the promoter did so, but the order were rejected, considerable expenditure would have been wasted. On the other hand, if all reserved matters had to go to the local planning authority (following a grant of outline permission) there would be the probability of further delays before the project could begin.

Both MPs drew a comparison between the proposed treatment for planning purposes of, on the one hand, the new orders for railways, tramways, coastal construction, etc. and, on the other, the existing treatment of harbour works authorised by orders under ss. 14 or 16 of the Harbours Act 1964. The Town and Country Planning General Development Order 1988, sch. 1, Part II, class A, referred to above, covers not only a local or private Act of Parliament, but also 'any order made under section 14 or 16 of the Harbours Act 1964', with the result that works authorised by such orders enjoy the status of permitted development, subject to the same exceptions as apply in the case of works authorised by private Act (see above). To the critics of cl. 16, it appeared anomalous that the Government was proposing a radically different approach for s. 1 and s. 3 orders, particularly since the Government was not taking the opportunity presented by the Transport and Works Bill to change the relationship between planning control and harbour orders under the 1964 Act.

In essence, the Government's view was that it would be in the best interests of everyone, including promoters, if the planning merits of a particular project were considered on a case-by-case basis, rather than by a blanket permission, subject to standard exceptions, as under the General Development Order. In its view, the latter approach, involving automatic planning permission deemed to be granted with the order, would encourage objectors to raise planning issues at the local inquiry, even where planning permission had been granted prior to the inquiry into the order, or where the local planning authority had advised that planning permission was not needed. Under the approach contained in s. 90 of the Town and Country Planning Act 1990, on the other hand, the inspector would be able to disallow the raising of planning issues in such circumstances. It is difficult to see, however, why it should be any more difficult in practice for an inspector to disallow evidence relating exclusively to planning issues in this case than in the case where the General Development Order would, strictly speaking, supply a planning permission which has already been granted. In neither case is the inspector being asked to decide (or report) upon planning issues, and the discretion afforded to an inspector in the running of the inquiry should be sufficient to avoid any unnecessary evidence having to be heard.

A more powerful argument advanced by the Government in favour of the s. 16 approach is that the promoter will have more control over the planning matters to be decided under the order-making process than would be the case with the General Development Order approach. As has been seen, Part II, class A contains certain substantial exceptions, as a result of which the relevant planning authority can, for example, require the proposed location of a bridge or a particular building to be moved to another location on the designated land (which, given the linear nature of that land, could be a significant distance away), or require the design or external appearance of the bridge or building to be modified in the interests of neighbourhood amenity. Under the approach adopted by the General Development Order there would be no power for the Secretary of State, when making the s. 1 or s. 3 order, to override any of these exceptions and grant planning permission for the bridge or building to be in a particular location, or of a particular design or external appearance, even where the promoter has been able to supply sufficient detail on such matters at the inquiry stage.

5.2.4   Effect of s. 16

The approach taken in s. 16 gives the promoter the ability to decide, in effect, how much planning consent to seek through the s. 1 or s. 3 order-making process. The other side of the coin is that the promoter who does not wish to seek full permission for every aspect of the project will not be able to assume that only the reserved matters set out in Part II, class A will be referred to the relevant planning authority for approval. Instead the Secretary of State will have the power to decide the grounds on which the authority might object to the detailed designs, to take one example.

The Government's insistence on flexibility means that new s. 90(2A) of the Town and Country Planning Act 1990 is expressed in permissive terms – 'the Secretary of State *may* direct that planning permission for that development shall be deemed to be granted . . .'. As has already been mentioned, the permissive nature of the provision in the Bill led to fears that an applicant for an order who also wishes the Secretary of State to grant planning permission for the scheme may find that, although successful in the application for an order, the Secretary of State might decline to grant planning permission. When this possibility was raised at the Report stage of the Bill in the House of Commons, the Parliamentary Under-Secretary of State for Transport (Patrick McLoughlin) responded as follows:

Although . . . the Secretary of State could, in theory, withhold or delay deemed planning consent, one has to ask why he would want to do so. The planning merits are likely to be such an important and integral aspect of the approval process where development is involved that it is scarcely conceivable that the Secretary of State would approve an order without at the same time granting planning permission. The promoter would be bound to question the decision of the Secretary of State, and the Secretary of State would have to provide reasons. Such a decision would probably be unlawful, because it would be unreasonable, and no reasonable Secretary of State would have made it. . . . For those who remain sceptical, I can give an unqualified assurance that on all applications in which planning permission is sought as part of the order, the Secretary of State would always make a determination on the works order and deemed planning permission at the same time. (House of Commons, H.C. Debs., *Hansard*, 20 February 1992, cols. 558–9.)

The assurance just quoted proved to be as far as the Government was prepared to go to appease critics of s. 16(1), during the passage of the Transport and Works Bill. However, in July 1992 it was announced that the Applications Rules to be made under s. 6 of TAWA will require the promoter to state specifically whether he wishes the Secretary of State to grant deemed (sic.) planning permission and to identify those matters which the promoter is content to reserve for subsequent approval by the local planning authority.

This decision represents a further attempt to reduce the risk (albeit, in the Government's view, theoretical) that the Secretary of State might fail to take a decision on the planning question, when making a s. 1 or s. 3 order. Faced with a specific planning application, the Secretary of State would in practice be legally bound to decide the matter.

Nevertheless, the s. 16 approach means that promoters of (in particular) railway projects, having become used to the exceptions set out in Part II, class A, will now be required to take what may often be difficult decisions concerning the scope and nature of the planning application. The down-side of flexibility is uncertainty, and much will depend initially upon the attitude taken by inspectors at individual inquiries (not to mention the Secretary of State himself). Only once the results of the first few inquiries into both minor and major projects have been analysed will it be possible too see whether fine tuning – or a more radical change – is necessary.

5.3   LISTED BUILDINGS AND CONSERVATION AREAS

The Planning (Listed Buildings and Conservation Areas) Act 1990 imposes special restrictions upon the demolition, alteration or extension of any building of special architectural or historic interest, contained in a list kept by the Secretary of State under s. 1 (a 'listed building'), and of any building located within an area designated by the local planning authority under s. 69 as being of special architectural or historic interest the character or appearance of which it is desirable to preserve or enhance (a 'conservation area'). A person wishing either to demolish a listed building or a building in a conservation area, or to alter or extend such a building in any manner which would affect its character, must apply to the local planning authority for listed building consent or, as the case may be, conservation area consent.

By s. 10, the application shall be made in such form as the local planning authority may require and shall contain:

(a)   sufficient particulars to identify the building to which it relates, including a plan;

(b)   such other plans or drawings as are necessary to describe the works which are the subject of the application; and

(c)   such other particulars as may be required by the authority.

In London, English Heritage is given power to direct the local planning authority as to the granting of the application, to authorise the authority to determine it as they think fit, or to direct them to refuse the application.

By s. 12 of the 1990 Act, the Secretary of State may give directions requiring applications (for listed building consent) to be referred to him instead of being dealt with by the local planning authority.

5.3.1   Private Bills and listed buildings

In the late-1980s, promoters of private Bills relating to railways in London began to insert in those Bills a provision designed to ensure that the authorisation of the works by Parliament would override the restrictions contained in what was then the Town and Country Planning Act 1971 relating to listed buildings and conservation areas. The first such provision was contained in the King's Cross Railways Bill (1988) and concerned, in particular, the demolition of the Great Northern Hotel as part of a comprehensive redevelopment of King's Cross Station. The provision was subjected to much criticism, both inside and outside Parliament, based upon claims – by now familiar to readers of this Guide – that the promoters were attempting to use the private Bill route to override important parts of the town and country planning system, and that legislators were inherently less qualified to pronounce upon such matters as the architectural or historic importance of a particular building than were the local planning authority and English Heritage. The House of Commons Opposed Committee was persuaded by these arguments, and in 1990 removed the provision from the Bill, urging other Committees faced with similar provisions to do likewise. However, only a few months later, a House of Lords Opposed Committee allowed a similar provision to remain in the Bill for what eventually became the London Underground (Safety Measures) Act 1992, although that provision had been modified so as to specify both the buildings concerned and the nature of the works proposed to them.

The Committee on the Safety Measures Bill issued a Special Report detailing the reasons why they had decided to allow the 'listed buildings' provision to remain in the Bill (House of Lords, *Special Report from the Select Committee on The London Underground (Safety Measures) Bill* (H.L.), HL Paper 14, London: HMSO, 1990). The Committee found that there was an urgent need for the works proposed by the Bill and that the promoters' plans for meeting that need were viable and appropriate. If the promoters were to be required to seek listed building consent or conservation area consent, they would have to submit detailed plans of any building which was to replace the demolished building before the demolition took place. In the case of certain buildings which required to be demolished at Tottenham Court Road, in order to facilitate the construction of a new London Underground ticket hall, the Committee was informed that it would be at least five years before a new building could be constructed over the site of the new ticket hall. Given these circumstances, the Committee accepted that it was not practicable for detailed plans for the new building to be drawn up at the stage when the Bill was before the Committee for its consideration, and that the process of securing agreement to the plans would unnecessarily delay the construction of the new ticket hall beneath the site. Given that the works were needed as soon as possible, that their feasibility had been accepted and that the usual planning procedures (i.e., the necessity for planning permission) would apply to the development of the site above ground level (over the new ticket hall), the Committee considered that the inclusion of the listed building provision in the Bill was justified.

When the Bill was debated on the floor of the House of Lords on 21 March 1991, the Minister of State, Lord Brabazon of Tara, gave the Government's view of such provisions. While acknowledging the importance of upholding the normal statutory arrangements for protecting listed buildings, the Government considered that there is a restricted class of strategically important developments being promoted in pursuance of Government policy that could be at risk if promoters were not able to secure all the necessary consents for their projects from one procedure. Lord Brabazon acknowledged that there was some force in the argument that if Parliament sees fit to authorise such schemes it would be unreasonable for the promoters to be required additionally to apply for listed building consent to demolish or alter the buildings concerned. 'Blanket' clauses, which failed to specify the affected buildings and the measures proposed, would, however, not be acceptable to the Government. The Safety Measures Bill fell within the restricted class just referred to, and the Government supported the retention of the amended provision, as the Opposed Committee had decided. (House of Lords, H.L. Debs.,*Hansard*, 21 March 1991, cols. 786–8).

The Government's support for provisions in private Bills disapplying listed building and conservation area controls was therefore limited to strategically important developments being promoted in pursuance of Government policy objectives. Had the Safety Measures Bill not fallen within that category the Government would undoubtedly have reported against the provision, and it is likely that it would have been rejected before the Bill reached the statute book. In such circumstances, the promoters could well have found the powers given them by Parliament being effectively overridden by the local planning authority, or English Heritage, if the application for listed building consent were refused. An appeal to the Secretary of State is possible under the 1990 Act, but the delay, cost and uncertainty in such a course – involving a further hearing by way of public local inquiry – would have been considerable.

5.3.2   TAWA's approach

The Government's solution to the problem posed by the appearance of listed building, etc. provisions in private Bills, whilst pragmatic, would, however, never have been completely satisfactory. The ideal solution would have been to have let all the relevant consents, including planning permission and listed building or conservation area consent, be determined by a single authority following a comprehensive hearing into the matter. The difficulty with that solution was that by the late-1980s a large and influential body of opinion had concluded that an Opposed Private Bill Committee was not a suitable forum for determining such questions. The approach taken by TAWA – namely, to remove the authorisation of various infrastructure projects from Parliament to the Secretary of State – frees the Government from this difficulty, and it is therefore not surprising that the Act's treatment of listed building and conservation area consents in no way depends upon the type or importance of the scheme in question. Instead, s. 17 amends the Planning (Listed Buildings and Conservation Areas) Act 1990, s. 12 (see above) by the insertion of a new subsection (3A), which provides that an application for listed building consent shall, without the need for any direction by the Secretary of State, be referred to the Secretary of State, rather than being dealt with by the local planning authority, in any case where such consent is required in consequence of proposals included in an application for an order under s. 1 or s. 3 of TAWA.

Although s. 17 itself does not specifically mention conservation area consent, the effect of s. 74(3) of the 1990 Act is to make new s. 12(3A) cover both applications for listed building consent and applications for conservation area consent.

The purpose of new s. 12(3A) is to enable the Secretary of State to determine the application for listed building or conservation area consent concurrently with the determination of the application for a s. 1 or s. 3 order under TAWA. It is important, however, to note that this approach is not the same as removing the requirement for listed building consent from proposals in s. 1 or s. 3 orders. Such an approach could have been taken on the basis that the Secretary of State, advised if necessary by an inspector having experience in matters of listed building and conservation areas, not to mention his officials, is a more expert and appropriate authority for determining such planning matters than is a committee of MPs or peers. However, TAWA rejects this approach in favour of one involving separate (albeit concurrent) decision-making by a single authority.

5.3.3 Consequences of s. 17

Certain important consequences follow from this decision. On a procedural level, the promoter of a s. 1 or s. 3 order will be required to make an application for listed building consent or conservation area consent to the local planning authority, even though the effect of new s. 12(3A) will be to refer that application automatically to the Secretary of State. It should be noted that this differs from the case of planning permission, where the promoter will be required to state in his application for the order whether he wishes the Secretary of State to grant deemed planning permission under new s. 90(2A) of the Town and Country Planning Act 1990 (see 5.2.4 above).

Where a listed building or conservation area is to be materially affected by a s. 1 or s. 3 order, the promoter will thus be required to comply with the provisions of s. 10 of the Planning (Listed Buildings and Conservation Areas) Act 1990, referred to above. Section 10(2)(c) requires the applicant to provide such other particulars as may be required by the local planning authority. The degree of detail that is required in respect of the application is therefore a matter primarily for the local planning authority, even though, once made, the application will be determined not by them but by the Secretary of State. A promoter of, for example, a railway scheme which is opposed by a local authority through whose area the line is to run may be apprehensive lest that body, as local planning authority, requires the application for listed building consent to contain details which the promoter is unable to supply at that stage, i.e., when he is making his application to the Secretary of State for a s. 1 order. In the case of the London Underground (Safety Measures) Bill referred to earlier, the House of Lords Committee was in no doubt that 'to obtain consent under the normal planning procedures, the promoters would have to submit detailed plans of any building which was to replace the demolished building before the demolition took place'. It would therefore appear that, if the facts in the Safety Measures case – which should not be regarded as exceptional – were to arise in relation to an application for a s. 1 order, the promoters might find themselves unable to make an application for listed building consent which complies with s. 10, with the result that the Secretary of State could be unable to determine that issue concurrently with the s. 1 application.

It should be mentioned that s. 15 of TAWA contains a power for the Secretary of State to make regulations for the purpose of assimilating the procedure for obtaining other statutory consents (which would include listed building and conservation area consents) with the procedure for obtaining a s. 1 or s. 3 order. Section 15 is dealt with in detail in 5.6 below. Regulations made under that section may exclude or modify the application of any enactment. However, while s. 15 could, on the face of it, be used to amend the Planning (Listed Buildings and Conservation Areas) Act 1990 so as to enable the Secretary of State to ensure that applications are made directly to him, rather than to the local planning authority, the terms of s. 17 make it clear that this is not the intention. Furthermore, it may be doubted whether it would be appropriate to vary the requirements of the Planning (Listed Buildings and Conservation Areas) Act 1990, s. 10, by means of s. 15 regulations, so as to fetter the local planning authority's ability to require the promoter to provide in his application certain particulars such as, for example, the details of any structure which it is intended should eventually replace a listed building which is proposed to be demolished.

While, therefore, it is impossible at this stage to predict precisely how the new system will work, it would seem that the policy behind s. 17 – namely, to retain listed building and conservation area consents as separate statutory requirements – could make it difficult for a promoter faced with circumstances similar to those in the Safety Measures case to run an application for listed building consent concurrently with that for a s. 1 order, and so obtain all necessary authorisations by means of a single process. In such a case, it is necessary to consider how the listed building application would be determined, once the promoter is able to supply the requisite details. The wording of new s. 12(3A) of the Planning (Listed Buildings and Conservation Areas) Act 1990 is, it would seem, wide enough to ensure that the application will be referred to the Secretary of State, even if it is submitted by the promoter to the local planning authority after the s. 1 order has been made by the Secretary of State. Were this not to be so, the promoter could find that the implementation of the scheme is further delayed, whilst the local planning authority considers the application and (perhaps) refuses it, necessitating an appeal to the Secretary of State.

New s. 12(3A) requires an application to be referred to the Secretary of State instead of being dealt with by the local planning authority 'in any case where the consent is required in consequence of proposals included in an application for' a s. 1 or s. 3 order. In the case of major schemes it will often be possible for objectors to argue that the proposals can be satisfactorily implemented (even within the limits of deviation set out in the application) without demolishing or altering a particular listed building. Given the objective nature of the wording in s. 12(3A), it is possible that determined objectors might attempt to challenge by means of judicial review the Secretary of State's decision to grant consent following a purported referral under that subsection – or the actual referral itself before any decision is taken – on the ground that the consent is not required in consequence of the proposals. It may be doubted, however, whether a court would be inclined to get involved in such questions, and promoters will be able to reduce any risk by ensuring that the application is sufficiently detailed as regards their proposals relating to a listed building or conservation area so that any criticism of their plans would have to relate to those proposals rather than to whether the proposals require listed building, etc. consent.

Before leaving s. 17 of TAWA it is necessary to say something of the way in which the Secretary of State must determine applications referred to him under new s. 12(3A). The decision on the listed building or conservation area consent must be made separately from (although it may be concurrent with) the decision on the application for a s. 1 or s. 3 order. Where an inquiry is to be held following objections to the latter application it is the Government's intention that the Secretary of State will presumably give both the promoter and the local planning authority an opportunity of appearing before the inspector in connection with the listed building or conservation area application, since the inquiry in respect of the latter will be held concurrently. In this way the Secretary of State will comply with s. 12(4) of the Planning (Listed Buildings and Conservation Areas) Act 1990, which requires the Secretary of State to afford the applicant and the local planning authority an opportunity of appearing before, and being heard by, a person appointed by the Secretary of State, should either of them so require (see 5.6 below). It would seem to follow, therefore, that where there is no hearing in respect of the application for a s. 1 or s. 3 order, the Secretary of State would be required to afford the parties an opportunity of being heard solely in respect of the application for listed building or conservation area consent.

5.4 HAZARDOUS SUBSTANCES

Section 18 deals with hazardous substances consent under the Planning (Hazardous Substances) Act 1990. Its approach is similar to that taken by s. 16 in the case of planning permission, namely, to subsume the decision-making process in respect of such consent with the process in respect of s. 1 or s. 3 orders, thereby making it unnecessary for applicants for such orders to apply separately for hazardous substances consent.

Section 18 inserts a new s. 12(2A) into that Act, which gives power to deem hazardous substances consent to be granted in certain cases. New s. 12(2A) provides that, on making an order under s. 1 or s. 3 of TAWA which includes any provision that would involve the presence of a hazardous substance in circumstances requiring hazardous substances consent, the Secretary of State may direct that such consent shall be deemed to be granted, subject to such conditions (if any) as may be specified in the direction.

The Planning (Hazardous Substances) Act 1990 provides that, in most cases, the district council is the hazardous substances authority for its area. Where a hazardous substance (as specified in regulations) is present on, over or under land in a controlled quantity (as so specified), hazardous substances consent must be obtained from the authority.

In contrast with the approach taken in the case of listed building consent, s. 18 is based on the assumption that it would be inappropriate to require an applicant for a s. 1 or s. 3 order to make separate application to the local authority for hazardous substances consent, which could then be called in by the Secretary of State. If the hazardous substances authority objected to the proposed storage of such a substance in controlled quantities in connection with a scheme to be authorised by a s. 1 or s. 3 order, that authority could presumably object under s. 11 to the application for the order and demand an inquiry or hearing in accordance with s. 11(3).

5.5 COAST PROTECTION CONSENT

Although the procedures described in ss. 16 and 18 have been said to be subsumed in the s. 1 and s. 3 order-making process, it is nevertheless the case that the Secretary of State must make a separate decision on planning permission and hazardous substances consent, if he chooses to deal with them on making a s. 1 or s. 3 order. In the case of consent under s. 34 of the Coast Protection Act 1949, however, the degree of subsumption can be said to be total. Section 19 provides that any operations authorised by an order under s. 1 or s. 3 of TAWA are to be exempt from the requirement to obtain the Secretary of State's consent under s. 34 of the CPA.

Section 34 of the CPA provides that no person shall without the consent of the Secretary of State carry out the following operations, namely:

(a)   construct, alter or improve any works on, under or over any part of the seashore lying below the level of mean high-water springs;

(b)   deposit any object or any materials on any such part of the seashore as aforesaid; or

(c)   remove any object or any materials from any such part of the seashore lying below the level of mean low-water springs,

if the operation (whether while being carried out or subsequently) causes or is likely to result in obstruction or danger to navigation. The Secretary of State has power to impose conditions upon giving his consent (s. 34(3)).

The scope of s. 34 is restricted by s. 35, which contains a number of exceptions, now increased by s. 19 of TAWA which adds as s. 35(1)(h) the exemption relating to activities under s. 1 and s. 3 orders, just described.

The approach adopted by s. 19 is at variance with the former practice in respect of works below high-water mark authorised by private Acts, or which are authorised by harbour orders under ss. 14 or 16 of the Harbours Act 1964. In all cases it was common to find provisions expressly preserving the separate requirement to obtain the consent of the Secretary of State under s. 34 of the CPA. (A rare example of an exception is to be found in s. 56(3)(c) of the Thames Barrier and Flood Prevention Act 1972.) During the passage of the Transport and Works Bill, the Government accepted that (in view of what is now s. 19) it would be anomalous if applicants for harbour revision orders and harbour empowerment orders were still to be required to obtain separate consent under the CPA. Section 63(3) of TAWA accordingly exempts operations authorised by such orders from the requirement to obtain consent under s. 34 of that Act.

5.6   ASSIMILATION OF PROCEDURES

We have seen in 5.2 to 5.5 above that TAWA has two ways of handling the relationship between s. 1 and s. 3 orders and other statutory consents. Section 16 (town and country planning), s. 18 (hazardous substances) and s. 19 (coast protection) provide for the procedures for obtaining those other consents to be subsumed by the new order-making procedures in Part I of the Act. No separate applications are therefore necessary (any planning application, for example, being contained in the s. 1 or s. 3 application); and either the Secretary of State is empowered to give consent on making the s. 1 or s. 3 order or else, in the case of s. 19, the consent requirement is overridden.

The approach adopted by s. 17 (listed buildings and conservation areas) and s. 21 (transport consultative committees) is different, in that both the basic procedure leading to the decision whether to grant consent and the decision itself are retained.

5.6.1   Need for a regulation-making power

The Government's initial view was, in effect, that all necessary statutory consents should be obtainable through the s. 1 or s. 3 application procedure and that the order itself would be able to grant such consents. As a consequence, orders which granted consents that were the responsibility of more than one Secretary of State would have been made jointly.

By the time the Transport and Works Bill was introduced, however, the Government had had second thoughts. In order to implement the approach proposed in the Consultation Document, TAWA would have had to have identified and amended all the enactments dealing with every relevant consent, licence, etc., and the procedures related thereto. Such a course was accordingly rejected as impractical as a general measure, although, as we have seen, it is used to varying degrees in the case of the specific consents mentioned in ss. 16, 18 and 19.

The Government's realisation of the impracticability (on a general level) of the solution it had originally proposed to the problem of other statutory consents led it inevitably to the conclusion that separate decision-making for such consents would have to be retained. In the case of listed building consent (s. 17), it appears that the Government considered there to be policy reasons why such a course should be adopted, quite apart from the practical difficulties of subsuming procedures with those of the s. 1 or s. 3 orders. On the other hand, it would clearly have been undesirable – and contrary to both the recommendations of the Joint Committee on Private Bill Procedure and the Government's own Consultation Document – merely to have left the promoter of a s. 1 or s. 3 order to obtain any other statutory consents in the normal manner, without any regard for the fact that the promoter was seeking a s. 1 or s. 3 order in respect of matters consisting of or comprising activities directly related to those other consents.

5.6.2   The s. 15 power

Accordingly, s. 15(1) and (2) confer a power upon the Secretary of State to make regulations adapting or modifying the procedures in respect of any such other statutory consent, permission or licence with a view to assimilating them (wholly or partly) with the procedure for obtaining a s. 1 or s. 3 order. Section 15 in particular contemplates that proceedings relating to these may be held concurrently with proceedings relating to the order. For example, in the case of a scheme which involved the promoter seeking listed building consent (see 5.3 above), it would be possible for regulations to ensure that the holding of an inquiry into objections to an application for a s. 1 order could be held concurrently with the inquiry into the application for listed building consent, thereby satisfying s. 12(4) of the Planning (Listed Buildings and Conservation

Areas) Act 1990. The same is true of scheduled monument consent under the Ancient Monuments and Archaeological Areas Act 1979.

Section 15(3) provides that regulations made under s. 15 may include provision:

(a)   excluding or modifying the application of any enactment; or

(b)   authorising the Secretary of State to give directions or take such other steps as may be appropriate for the purpose of securing the assimilation of procedures.

Under s. 15(4), the power to make regulations under s. 15 is subject to negative-resolution procedure.

It was mentioned earlier that, although s. 15 is largely a pragmatic solution to a practical problem, the decision to retain separate applications and decision-making for certain forms of consents is one of policy, based upon the perceived importance of the consents. One interesting example concerns the licences for the deposit of substances and articles in the sea, required under Part II of the Food and Environment Protection Act 1985. In the Transport and Works Bill as originally introduced, this requirement was not to apply 'to anything done for the purpose of carrying out works authorised by an order under' s. 1 or s. 3 (cl. 19). As can be seen, this provision bore a striking resemblance to s. 19 (relating to coast protection consent) which is the most extreme form of 'subsumption' found in TAWA. In Standing Committee in the House of Commons, however, cl. 19 was removed, with the result that an application for such a licence must be made by the applicant for a s. 1 or s. 3 order, although the procedure for obtaining the licence can be assimilated by regulations under s. 15, should the Secretary of State choose to do so.

The conclusion which can be drawn from the deletion of cl. 19 is that the Government considered, on reflection, that a licence to carry out dumping at sea should not, in effect, be automatically granted in respect of any activity which could be said to relate to the execution of works authorised by a s. 1 or s. 3 order.

5.7   BLIGHT NOTICES

Section 16(2) enhances the rights of an individual or business to obtain compensation for planning blight in the case of projects which would formerly have proceeded by way of private Bill but which are now to be authorised by s. 1 or s. 3 orders.

Planning blight arises where certain formal proposals exist which would result in land being used for public purposes, for example, for the creation of a new highway. In certain circumstances, the owner of land may find that its value is adversely affected by the proposals. In such circumstances the owner may find it impossible to sell the land at all, or to sell it for anything like its value prior to the publication of the proposals.

The Town and Country Planning Act 1990 provides a mechanism whereby such an owner may require the appropriate authority (i.e., the body having designs on the land) to purchase it on payment of its 'unblighted' value. The classes of blighted land are set out in sch. 13 to that Act, and the categories of person entitled to serve blight notices upon the appropriate authority are dealt with in ss. 149 to 171. Broadly speaking, these are resident owner-occupiers of dwelling-houses and owner-occupiers of certain forms of small businesses.

Land affected by a private Bill does not fall within the classes set out in sch. 13. Accordingly, although land could be severely blighted while a Bill to build, for example, a new railway line was progressing through Parliament, its owner would be unable to require the promoter to purchase the land by the service of a blight notice. Only once the Bill had been enacted would the blight provisions in the 1990 Act bite. Conversely, in the case of a highway project, the owner would be entitled to serve a notice as soon as the land was shown on a plan approved by the local highway authority or (in the case of a trunk road or motorway) published by the Secretary of State and notified to the highway authority.

In certain cases, land within the limits of deviation set out in a private Bill might in practice be covered by the blight notice provisions, before enactment of the Bill, for example if the local planning authority or the Secretary of State had 'safeguarded' the land for the purpose of the proposed works, or if those works were contemplated in a development plan. From the owner's viewpoint, however, it seemed illogical that highway proposals automatically fell within sch. 13 whereas works proposals in a private Bill did not.

Section 16(2) inserts in sch. 13 a new para. 23, which covers land:

    (a)   the compulsory acquisition of which is authorised by an order under s. 1 or s. 3 of TAWA;

    (b)   which falls within the limits of deviation within which powers of compulsory acquisition conferred by such an order are exercisable; or

    (c)   which is the subject of a proposal, contained in an application made in accordance with rules under s. 6 of that Act or in a draft order prepared under s. 7(3) of that Act, that it should be such land.

It will be seen that (c) above represents a change from the position in the case of private Bills, and brings schemes subject to application for s. 1 or s. 3 orders basically into line with the position in the case of highways, etc. By including (c) TAWA has in effect provided an automatic mechanism for deterring rash applications for s. 1 or s. 3 orders. A promoter who runs into difficulties in funding purchases of properties subject to blight notices would be unlikely to convince the Secretary of State to make the order.

SIX
THE AUTHORISATION OF SCOTTISH TRANSPORT SYSTEMS

6.1 SCOTTISH PRIVATE LEGISLATION PROCEDURE

The Private Legislation Procedure (Scotland) Act 1936 is a consolidation of the Private Legislation Procedure (Scotland) Act 1899 and an amending Act passed in 1933. The 1936 Act provides the machinery by which persons must proceed if they wish to obtain parliamentary powers in regard to certain matters affecting public or private interests in Scotland. The procedure is different from that relating to a private Bill in the case of England and Wales, described in chapter 1. At first the proceedings relate to a draft provisional order, which if opposed gives rise to an inquiry before Commissioners in Scotland. If the order is made, it is not valid until it has been confirmed by Parliament by means of a Confirmation Act.

The scope of orders under the 1936 Act is far wider than is the case for other special procedure orders, described in chapter 1, where the subject matter is limited to the particular concerns of the enabling Act. The 1936 Act, by contrast, covers virtually every matter in respect of which persons are entitled to seek parliamentary powers by means of a private Bill.

Petitions for a provisional order must be deposited at the Scottish Office in London together with a draft of the order on or before 27 November, or on or before 27 March. Petitions against the order must be deposited not later than six weeks after 11 December or 11 April (these being the final dates for the publication of notices).

If the Chairman of Committees of the House of Lords and the Chairman of Ways and Means in the House of Commons consider that the contents of the draft order 'relate to matters outside Scotland to such an extent, or raise questions of public policy of such novelty and importance that they ought to be dealt with by private Bill and not by provisional order' (s. 2(2)), they report accordingly and proceedings on the order come to an end, although the promoters are then able to proceed with the same measures by way of a private Bill (known, in these circumstances, as a substituted Bill).

Assuming the Chairmen do not report as just described, the draft order is referred to Examiners to determine whether certain general orders (equivalent to

Standing Orders in the case of private Bills) have been complied with. If a provisional order is opposed (or if the Secretary of State so decides in the case of an unopposed order) an inquiry is held before Commissioners sitting in Scotland. The Commissioners are drawn from three panels, one panel each from the Lords and Commons and one consisting of suitably qualified non-parliamentarians (in 1988, this panel consisted of five academics, four solicitors, four businessmen, three trade unionists, a surveyor, an estate manager and a former MP). The procedure at the inquiry is similar to that of an Opposed Private Bill Committee, but the Commissioners report to the Secretary of State, who must refuse the order if that is the Commissioners' conclusion.

At this stage (assuming the order is not refused) the procedure for a confirmation Bill commences. This Bill, which gives validity to the provisional order, must be presented to Parliament (by a Minister having responsibility for Scotland) as soon as practicable after the order is made and issued. Bills to confirm orders where no inquiry has been held proceed under s. 7 of the 1936 Act, while those which have been to inquiry proceed under s. 9. A s. 7 Bill is deemed in each House to have passed all its stages up to and including committee; a s. 9 Bill is read a first time and is then subject to another opportunity for petitions, which may lead to a further inquiry being held before a Joint Committee of Lords and Commons (in Westminster) if a motion to refer the Bill to such a committee is passed by the House in which the confirmation Bill originates. If that Committee reports that the order ought to be confirmed the Bill is ordered for consideration or third reading, depending upon whether it has been amended, before going to the second House (where there is no opportunity to petition against the confirmation Bill).

6.2 THE JOINT COMMITTEE'S RECOMMENDATIONS AND THE GOVERNMENT'S RESPONSE

The 1936 Act system is an ingenious blend of parliamentary and executive powers, with the important feature of providing for an inquiry to be held locally. The Joint Committee on Private Bill Procedure found that between 1958 and 1985 only 21 orders required to be examined by Commissioners in Scotland, and between 1978 and 1985 only one. Confirmation Bills were committed to a Joint Committee only twice, in 1904 and 1985. The latter case, which concerned the Lothian Regional Council (Edinburgh Western Relief Road) Order, required the Joint Committee hearing the matter to sit for 17 days, over a period of six weeks. The inquiry before Commissioners on the same matter had in fact been the longest such hearing ever, lasting 52 days, over three and a half months.

The Joint Committee on Private Bill Procedure heard much evidence regarding the circumstances surrounding the Edinburgh case (which are interesting, although unfortunately beyond the scope of the present work), but concluded that it was an exceptional case and that there was no general trend towards more contentious orders or longer inquiries. The Joint Committee accordingly recommended to both Houses 'not to over-react in ways which might upset a procedure which is basically working well' (Joint Committee on Private Bill Procedure, *Report*, HL Paper 97/HC 625, London: HMSO, 1988, p. 44). The Committee went on, however, to state that legislation:

to set up new systems of ministerial Orders for rail and tramway works, and to extend the scope of the Harbours Act, should extend to Scotland. The Committee acknowledge that the burden of Scottish private legislation upon Parliament is slight. However, these recommendations are founded upon the principles that decisions should be taken in the forum ordained by Parliament, and that Parliament is not the right place to consider works proposals of purely local significance; and the Committee consider that these principles are equally true on either side of the Border. (ibid., p. 45)

The Government did not agree. In its Consultation Document, the Joint Committee's exhortation to Parliament not to over-react was quoted with approval, but the recommendation that the new order-making powers should nevertheless extend to Scotland was ignored. Accordingly, in TAWA, both s. 1 orders (relating to railways, tramways, etc.) and s. 3 orders (relating to inland waterways and works interfering with navigational rights) apply only in the case of England and Wales.

6.3   RAILWAY AUTHORISATIONS AFTER THE ACT

The Government's vote of confidence in the 1936 Act system means that promoters of railway works in Scotland may continue to seek authorisation by means of provisional orders under the procedure described in 6.1 above. In certain circumstances, however, it may be possible to obtain such authorisation by means of a light railway order under the Light Railways Acts 1896 to 1912. These Acts are repealed by TAWA in relation to England and Wales, in consequence of the introduction of s. 1 orders (s. 68 and sch. 4, Part I), but the Government's decision not to extend the new system to Scotland means that the procedure under the Light Railways Acts will continue to be available there for those wishing and able to make use of it.

As is stated in chapter 1, the Department of Transport does not consider most of British Rail's lines to be light railways, and, in practice, the light railways procedure tends to be used only in the case of such projects as sidings or small spurs of track, or for railways of an essentially 'leisure' nature such as those run on former British Rail routes.

Application for a light railway order is made now to the Secretary of State. The detailed procedure is covered by rules which, broadly speaking, follow the procedure for a private Bill under the Standing Orders of Parliament. Notice of the application must be advertised and copies of the draft order, together with any plans, sections and book of reference (in the case of compulsory acquisition) must be deposited with local authorities and various Government departments. Notices must be served on landowners whose land is intended to be taken (or shown within the limits of deviation on the plans).

Objections must be made in writing to the Secretary of State not later than the last day of the month after the month in which the application is made. Where objections are made and not withdrawn the Secretary of State causes an inquiry to be held, but s. 9(3) of the 1896 Act provides that he may not make an order if the magnitude of the project, or some other factor, is such that he forms the opinion that the proposals ought to be submitted to Parliament. In such a case the Secretary of State may make an order as a provisional order for submission to Parliament.

Compulsory purchase may be authorised by a light railway order, but only by means of the Lands Clauses Acts and not the Compulsory Purchase Act 1965. Present Government policy is to refuse applications for compulsory purchase powers if the land is required solely for a 'leisure' railway. Unlike a Scottish provisional order, a light railway order does not confer deemed planning permission under the General Development Order.

6.4   HARBOUR ORDERS

The amendments in TAWA of the Harbours Act 1964, which expand the order-making powers in that Act, extend to Scotland. The alternative of proceeding by means of a provisional order is abolished, as are the differences in procedure between Scottish harbour orders and those for England and Wales (see chapter 7, especially 7.3 and 7.11).

SEVEN
HARBOURS

7.1 INTRODUCTION

Although the majority of TAWA concerns railways and other guided transport systems, it also contains provisions which are of great importance both to those involved in the ports industry and to anyone else interested in the law relating to development in harbour areas. The significance of these provisions is, however, somewhat obscured by the fact that they consist entirely of amendments of other legislation, primarily the Harbours Act 1964.

This chapter will describe, in general terms, the order-making procedures under that Act before analysing the changes wrought by TAWA. These changes came into force on 15 July 1992 (Transport and Works Act 1992 (Commencement No. 1) Order 1992 (SI 1992/1347)).

7.2 HARBOUR REVISION ORDERS AND HARBOUR EMPOWERMENT ORDERS

The Harbours Act 1964 is a good example of the movement away from authorisation by private Act of Parliament and towards authorisation by ministerial or executive order, described in chapter 1 – another good example being Part I of TAWA itself.

7.2.1 Types of Harbour Authority

Virtually all significant ports and harbours in the United Kingdom are managed by bodies having statutory powers (and duties) to do so. These statutory harbour authorities (as they are known) can take different forms. Some are local authorities (e.g., Bristol), some are 'ordinary' registered companies (e.g., Fosdyke and Mostyn) and some statutory companies (e.g. Mersey and Felixstowe). Many harbour authorities are of the kind known – somewhat inaccurately – as port trusts. These bodies were established by Parliament but, unlike the statutory companies, are controlled not by shareholders but by a specially constituted body, sometimes known as commissioners. Examples of this type of authority are Port of Tyne, Ipswich, and Cromarty Firth. The Ports

Act 1991 contains provisions enabling this kind of harbour authority to be privatised, thereby enabling the greater powers of a registered company to be utilised in connection with the development of the harbour, its assets and facilities. Tees and Hartlepool, Clyde, Forth, Medway and Tilbury have changed their status from port trust to registered company in consequence of the Ports Act 1991.

Prior to the 1964 Act, the special legislation under which statutory harbour authorities carried out their functions was contained in various local Acts. A degree of standardisation had been achieved with the passing of the Harbours, Docks, and Piers Clauses Act 1847, but this Act was not automatically applicable – it had to be applied specifically to a particular harbour by means of a local Act.

The 1964 Act was passed in response to the recommendations of the Committee of Inquiry into the major ports of Great Britain, contained in a 1962 report known as the Rochdale Report (after the Committee's Chairman, Viscount Rochdale). The 1964 Act introduced new forms of order-making procedure which were intended to reduce the need for private Acts (i) where an existing statutory harbour authority required an addition or alteration to its statutory powers and duties, and (ii) where it was desirable to create a new harbour authority in order to manage a harbour. Orders of the first kind are known as 'harbour revision orders' and orders of the second kind, 'harbour empowerment orders'. Before describing them, however, some of the terminology used in the 1964 Act should be explained.

7.2.2 Harbours and harbour authorities

In the 1964 Act, 'harbour' means (subject to an exception which is irrelevant for present purposes) any harbour, whether natural or artificial, and any port, haven, estuary, tidal or other river or inland waterway navigated by sea-going ships. It specifically includes a dock (used by sea-going ships), a wharf and, in Scotland, a boatslip being a marine work (itself a defined expression of some complexity).

As can be seen, the definition of 'harbour' is very wide, being based to a large extent on geographical features, and is capable of covering areas wholly lacking in any 'built' features such as quays, wharves or jetties.

'Harbour authority' in the 1964 Act means any person (which includes, by virtue of the Interpretation Act 1978, a body corporate such as a company or 'port trust') in whom are vested – under the 1964 Act itself, another Act, an order or other instrument or provisional order – powers or duties of improving, maintaining, or managing a harbour.

7.2.3 Harbour revision orders

Of the two kinds of order described above, the more common is the harbour revision order. Section 14 of the 1964 Act provides that there may, in relation to a harbour which is being improved, maintained or managed by a harbour authority in the exercise of and performance of statutory powers and duties, be made by the appropriate Minister an order known as a harbour revision order for achieving all or any of the objects specified in sch. 2 to the Act. Several of these objects are extended by TAWA and are discussed below.

Harbour revision orders are normally applied for by the harbour authority for the harbour concerned, but a person appearing to the appropriate Minister to have a substantial interest, or a body representative of persons appearing to him to have such an interest, may also make an application. In certain circumstances the appropriate Minister may himself promote a harbour revision order (Harbours Act 1964, s. 15).

Section 14(2)(b) of the 1964 Act contains an important qualification upon the appropriate Minister's powers. It is discussed at 7.4 below.

7.2.4 Harbour empowerment orders

Harbour revision orders are used in cases where a statutory harbour authority already exists. Harbour empowerment orders, by contrast, deal with the situation where there is no such authority, but it can be shown that there ought to be. Section 16(1) to (3) of the 1964 Act sets out the criteria to be applied in the case of (respectively, and broadly speaking) a harbour, a fishery harbour (within the meaning of s. 21 of the Sea Fish Industry Act 1951) and (in Scotland) a marine work. Instead of being confined to the list of objects in sch. 2, the Secretary of State (or, in certain cases the Minister of Agriculture, Fisheries and Food) may, on an application made to him, make an order conferring on the applicant, some other designated person or a body to be constituted for the purpose of the order, all such powers as are requisite for bringing about the achievement of one or more of the objects set out in s. 16(1),(2) or (3) (as the case may be). Those objects are the improvement, maintenance or management of the harbour/fishery harbour/marine work and the construction of various dock or harbour facilities. Section 16(5) contains a qualification upon the Secretary of State's powers similar to s. 14(2)(b) of the 1964 Act and is discussed at 7.4 below.

The procedure in the case of both harbour revision orders and harbour empowerment orders contains provision for the making of formal objections, and for the holding of a public local inquiry into those objections. If the order is made following an inquiry, an objector may in certain circumstances be able to challenge it again, before it has come into force, by appearing before a Joint Committee of Lords and Commons under what is known as special parliamentary procedure (see chapter 1). TAWA drastically reduces the circumstances in which special parliamentary procedure will apply (see 7.11 below).

In Scotland, all harbour revision orders and harbour empowerment orders were formerly subject to special parliamentary procedure. TAWA removes this difference, thus putting Scottish orders on an equal footing with those relating to England and Wales.

7.3 HARBOUR ORDERS AND PRIVATE ACTS

Despite the order-making powers contained in the Harbours Act 1964, a large number of private Acts (and Scottish provisional orders) passed since 1964 were concerned with harbours, including two – the Felixstowe Dock and Railway Act 1987 and the Associated British Ports Act 1990 – whose controversial nature increased calls for a thorough re-examination of the private Bill system (see chapter 1).

There were two reasons for this continued use of private Bills. First, the scope of the powers conferred upon the Executive by ss. 14 and 16 of the 1964 Act was limited in nature and, in particular, meant that those powers could not be invoked adequately in order to facilitate the creation of significant leisure – as opposed to commercial – facilities, such as marinas. Secondly, s. 62 of the 1964 Act expressly preserved the ability to promote a private Bill (or provisional order) even though some or all of the objects of the Bill or provisional order could be achieved by a harbour revision order or harbour empowerment order. Without s. 62, promoters of private Bills or provisional orders would have been unable to prove that part of the Preamble which states that the objects of the Bill or order cannot be achieved without the authority of Parliament.

The Joint Committee on Private Bill Procedure recommended action on both fronts, by widening the scope of harbour orders 'so as to allow general powers to be included and a wider range of development to be authorised', and by repealing s. 62 (Joint Committee on Private Bill Procedure, *Report*, HL Paper 97/HC 625, London: HMSO 1988, para.60). The Government's Consultation Document concurred (*Private Bills and New Procedures – A Consultation Document – The Government's Response to the Report of the Joint Committee on Private Bill Procedure*, Cm. 1110, London: HMSO, 1990). The result is TAWA, s. 63, and sch. 3. Schedule 3, para. 8 repeals s. 62 of the 1964 Act, so that promoters seeking to achieve aims which are within the scope of a harbour order may no longer proceed by way of private Bill (or Scottish provisional order). The extensions of the harbour order powers are dealt with in the following paragraphs of this chapter.

7.4 MARINAS AND OTHER RECREATIONAL FACILITIES

Section 14(2)(b) of the Harbours Act 1964, as originally enacted, contained the restriction that the appropriate Minister could not make a harbour revision order unless he was:

> satisfied that the making of the order is desirable in the interests of securing the improvement, maintenance or management of the harbour in an efficient or economical manner or of facilitating the efficient and economic transport of goods or passengers by sea.

In most cases this restriction had the effect of precluding the use of a harbour revision order for the purposes of constructing such facilities as marinas. Section 16(5) of the Act contained an even tighter restriction on the power to make a harbour empowerment order, in that the person making the order had to be satisfied that it was 'desirable in the interests of facilitating the efficient and economic transport of goods or passengers by sea'.

Schedule 3, para. 1(2) amends s. 14(2)(b) of the 1964 Act by adding at the end the words 'or in the interests of the recreational use of sea-going ships'. Paragraph 2(2) adds the same words to the end of s. 16(5). It is therefore now clear that, whatever the nature of the harbour in question, a harbour revision order or harbour empowerment order can be used in the case of matters relating to the recreational use of the harbour by yachts, motor launches, etc.

7.5   REDUCTION OF HARBOUR FACILITIES

The Harbours Act 1964, s. 14(2)(b), at least on first reading, has a strongly positive ring, leading some to conclude that it cannot be used to sanction a negative act such as closing down part of the harbour. In fact, there could well be circumstances where the management of the harbour in an efficient and economical manner might require the retrenchment of a harbour authority's activities. The Government concluded, however, that the opportunity presented by TAWA should not be missed to put the matter beyond doubt. Paragraph 1(3) of sch. 3 accordingly inserts a new s. 14(2B) into the 1964 Act, which states that nothing in s. 14(2)(b) shall prevent the making of an order for facilitating:

(a)   the closing of part of the harbour;
(b)   a reduction in the facilities available in the harbour; or
(c)   the disposal of property not required for the purposes of the harbour,
if the appropriate Minister is satisfied that the making of the order is desirable on grounds other than those specified in that subsection.

Schedule 3, para. 9(4) inserts into the list of objects in sch. 2 to the 1964 Act a new para. 8A enabling the authority to close part of the harbour or to reduce the facilities available there. The disposal of property vested in the harbour authority for harbour purposes, which is no longer required for those purposes, is already specifically set out in sch. 2 as an object for the attainment of which a harbour revision order may be made. However, new s. 14(2B) (read with the amended s. 14(3)) makes it unnecessary to justify either this object, or the new objects of closure or reduction of harbour facilities set out in para. 8A, by reference to the requirements of s. 14(2)(b). In future, therefore, it will be possible for a harbour revision order to sanction the closure of commercial facilities irrespective of whether this is in the interests of the harbour business itself. One example might be where a harbour authority decides to close cargo-handling facilities adjacent to a residential area, in consequence of complaints about noise, and to sell the surplus land for additional housing, even though there is no shortage of potential customers wishing to use those facilities.

Schedule 3, para. 1(4) amends s. 14(3) of the 1964 Act so as to enable harbour revision orders to be made for achieving one or more of the objects mentioned in sch. 2, whether the order falls within s. 14(2)(b) or within the new s. 14(2B) discussed above.

Before leaving this topic it is important to mention that the extended power to close facilities at a harbour does not extend to the complete closure of the harbour. The Government decided that this step – which would usually require the dissolution of the harbour authority as a statutory authority – should not be taken by executive order, but should be left to Parliament. Any proposal to close a harbour will, therefore, have to be contained in a private Bill (or Scottish provisional order).

7.6   HARBOUR AUTHORITIES HAVING SEVERAL HARBOURS

Some harbour authorities have statutory responsibility for more than one harbour, or are members of the same group of companies as those having such responsibility for other harbours. One example is Sea Containers, several of whose subsidiaries are harbour authorities. Another is Associated British Ports, who, in the past, found it necessary from time to time to promote a private Bill containing provisions which were intended to apply to various of their harbours.

Harbour revision orders now require to have the same flexibility and, accordingly, sch. 3, para. 1(5) inserts a new s. 14(4A) into the 1964 Act. This provides that where two or more harbours are being improved, maintained or managed by the same harbour authority, or by harbour authorities which are members of the same group of companies, a harbour revision order may relate to more than one of the harbours.

What if proposals relating to one harbour attract opposition (in the form of objections) but proposals relating to the other (or others) do not? It appears that in such circumstances the Department or Ministry would consider splitting the application (and consequently the procedure) so as to enable an inquiry to be held into the contested provisions, while the uncontested provisions are dealt with as a separate unopposed order.

7.7   FOOTPATHS AND MAPS

In 1989, the harbour revision order procedure was invoked at Blyth, Northumberland, in order to divert a right of way which would otherwise have run through a newly created cargo-handling area, raising problems of safety as well as customs security (Blyth Harbour Revision Order 1989 (SI 1989/874)). TAWA contains amendments to the 1964 Act which are intended to define the circumstances in which a harbour revision order can be used for the stopping up or diversion of footpaths and bridleways.

Schedule 3, para. 9(3) inserts new sch. 2, para. 7A into the 1964 Act, thereby adding, as an express object, the extinguishing or diverting of public rights of way over footpaths or bridleways for the purpose of works described in the order or ancillary to those works. This makes it unnecessary to rely upon the 'sweeping-up' provision in sch. 2, para. 17. It should be noted that sch. 2, para. 7A refers to 'works described in the order', not works authorised by the order. As in the Blyth case, the works requiring the diversion or stopping up of a footpath will usually be entirely above high-water mark, and thus will not require authorisation by harbour revision order.

Schedule 3, para. 10(3) inserts in sch. 3, para. 3 to the 1964 Act an important procedural requirement where a draft harbour revision order or harbour empowerment order proposes the extinguishment or diversion of a public right of way over a footpath or bridleway. In such cases the applicant must serve on every local authority in the area a notice stating where details of the draft order and relevant map may be inspected and stating that if the local authority desires to make an objection to the inclusion in the order of the provision in question it should do so in writing before the end of 42 days from the date on which the notice was served.

Schedule 3, para. 3 places a restriction upon the powers of the Secretary of State or Minister in the case of harbour revision orders or harbour empowerment orders which propose to stop up or divert rights of way over a footpath or bridleway, by the insertion of new s. 17(2A) into the 1964 Act, prohibiting the making of the order unless the Secretary of State or Minister is satisfied that an alternative right of way has been or will be provided or that the provision of an alternative right of way is not required. This restriction is in line with the analogous provisions of s. 251 of the Town and Country Planning Act 1990, which deal with stoppings-up and diversions in connection with development. New s. 17(2B) (also added by sch. 3, para. 3) further provides that the Secretary of State or Minister shall not make a harbour revision order or harbour empowerment order which provides for diverting a public right of way over a footpath or bridleway unless he is satisfied that the path or way will not be substantially less convenient to the public in consequence of the diversion. This provision follows s. 119 of the Highways Act 1980.

Schedule 3, paras 1(7) and 2(5) insert, respectively, new ss. 14(5A) and 16(7A) into the 1964 Act. These new subsections provide that where a harbour revision order or harbour empowerment order includes provision for extinguishing or diverting a public right of way over a footpath or bridleway there must be annexed to the order a map of a scale not less than 1:2500 on which the path or way concerned and, in the case of a diversion, the new path or way, are plainly delineated. This is the scale currently prescribed in the Public Path Orders and Extinguishment of Public Rights of Way Orders Regulations 1983 (SI 1983/23).

Having inserted references to specific-scale maps in the case of rights of way, it was logical to make similar changes to the existing requirements in the 1964 Act regarding maps in connection with harbour revision orders and harbour empowerment orders authorising the compulsory purchase of land. Accordingly, sch. 3, paras 1(6), 2(4) and 4 amend the references to 'large-scale' maps in ss. 14(5), 16(7) and 18(3) of the 1964 Act, by substituting references to maps of a scale of not less than 1:2500. The definition of 'large-scale' in s. 57(1) is repealed by sch.4, Part II.

7.8   WORKS IN THE HARBOUR

A large number of the harbour revision orders made since 1964 have been for the authorisation of works below high-water mark. The reasons why such works require statutory authorisation are described in chapter 1 (1.3). It is curious that the draftsman of sch. 2 to the 1964 Act did not include the construction of works in the harbour amongst the list of objects, but works orders have in practice been held to fall within para. 4 of that schedule, which, *inter alia*, allows for the conferring on the harbour authority of powers in addition to those already conferred by local statutory provision.

7.8.1   Licensing powers

Harbour authorities have in certain cases obtained powers by private Act to control activities (including works) by third parties within the harbour. This control takes the form of a licensing power, which until about 20 years ago was usually framed in such a way as to constitute merely a further restriction upon the licensee's ability to construct below high-water mark. In particular, the grant of the licence did not empower the licensee to carry out the works notwithstanding the inevitable interference which the works would cause to public rights of navigation which subsist over tidal waters.

In a number of more modern private Acts (such as the Medway Port Authority Act 1973 and the Port of Tyne Act 1991) the licence is expressly stated to give authority for construction, etc. notwithstanding any interference with public rights of navigation or other public rights (such as rights of fishing). The licensee is thereby freed from the need to obtain separate statutory authorisation by means of a private Act or harbour revision order (if appropriate).

The Cowes Harbour Revision Order 1989 (SI 1989/1941) included a licensing power in terms similar to those just described, and this was followed in harbour revision orders for Newhaven and Heysham. The use of harbour revision orders to create licensing powers of this kind appeared to some to be at the margins of what was permitted by s. 14 of the 1964 Act. TAWA, again, gave the Government the opportunity to put the question beyond doubt, and the result is sch. 3, para. 9(3), which inserts into the 1964 Act new sch. 2, para. 7B. This object consists of extinguishing public rights of navigation for the purposes of works described in the order or works ancillary to such works, or permitting interference with the enjoyment of such rights for the purposes of such works or for the purposes of works carried out by a person authorised by the authority to carry them out.

7.8.2 Effects of works on rights of navigation

New sch. 2, para.7B is a close and rather interesting provision. The reference to extinguishing public rights of navigation contrasts with the later reference to interference with such rights. Extinguishment of rights suggests their complete elimination over an area of water not limited to the space taken up by the physical structure of the actual works. Extinguishment might be appropriate in the case of the construction of an enclosed dock whose water area had formerly been washed by the tide. The absence of any reference to extinguishment in the part of para. 7B dealing with works carried out by authorised persons (i.e., licensees) can be explained on the basis that works such as enclosed docks are unlikely to be built under licensing powers, and perhaps even ought not to be so built. It would be theoretically possible for enclosed docks to be built under licensing powers, and a harbour revision order sought merely for the extinguishment of public rights of navigation in the docks, since para. 7B refers to extinguishing such rights for the purposes of works described in the order, and thus appears not to be limited to works authorised by the order itself. This would still ensure that there was a separate right to object to, and an examination of, a proposal to extinguish public rights of navigation.

The reference to permitting interference with the enjoyment of public rights of navigation for the purposes of works described in the order is strictly unnecessary in the case of works authorised by the order, since it is the statutory authority of the order which itself gives immunity against claims based upon public nuisance. Railway works authorised by s. 1 orders similarly enjoy immunity against nuisance, and it does not appear to be envisaged that s. 1 orders will expressly confer such an immunity.

The main reason for new sch. 2, para. 7B of the 1964 Act is contained in the opening and closing words and has already been touched upon, namely to state expressly that harbour revision orders and harbour empowerment orders may contain licensing powers which allow the licensee to interfere with public rights of navigation for the purposes of the licensed works.

7.8.3 What works may be licensed?

New sch. 2, para. 7B clarifies the position of licensees' powers, as regards public rights of navigation. But what kind of works may be licensed by the harbour authority under powers conferred by harbour revision order? Provided that the overall requirement of s. 14(2)(b) of the 1964 Act is satisfied, it has been considered that sch. 2, para. 4 to that Act confers upon the harbour authority the power to control any works or activity by third parties which concern or might affect the functioning of the harbour. Schedule 2, para. 3(c), as originally enacted, referred expressly to the regulation of activities by others in connection with the harbour or harbour operations but, given the narrowness of the expression 'harbour operations' (e.g., cargo handling, passenger embarking and disembarking, warehousing, etc.), this provision did little more than cover the activities of those, such as terminal operators, using the harbour for harbour purposes.

Schedule 3, para. 9(2) amends sch. 2, para. 3(c) of the 1964 Act by omitting the words 'in connection with the harbour' and replacing 'harbour operations' with the phrase 'activities relating to the harbour'. This is certainly far wider than the previous formulation in para. 3(c) and will reduce the need to rely upon para. 4 in order to justify powers to licence activities which are not of the kind which the harbour authority itself would want to carry out, but which have an impact upon the harbour such as to justify the authority having power (in the first instance at least) to ensure that the proposals are not unduly harmful to its own activities or to those of other harbour users.

7.8.4 Coast protection consent

Before leaving the subject of harbour works, it is necessary to mention s. 63(3) of TAWA, which inserts new s. 35(1)(i) into the Coast Protection Act 1949. The effect of this amendment is to exempt operations authorised by a harbour revision order or harbour empowerment order from the requirement to obtain the consent of the Secretary of State under s. 34 of that Act. The circumstances in which such consent is necessary are set out in chapter 5 (5.5).

7.9   HARBOUR BUSINESSES, DEVELOPMENT OF LAND AND DELEGATION OF FUNCTIONS

Those harbour authorities which are solely the creation of statute (namely, statutory companies and port trusts) may do only what their statutory provisions expressly or impliedly authorise. In this respect they differ from a harbour authority company, which has a memorandum and articles which may permit a wider range of activities than those concerned solely with the carrying out of the company's functions as statutory harbour authority.

In recent years, as competition between ports has grown, those harbour authorities which are statutory companies or port trusts have sought from Parliament wider powers to enable them to take full advantage of their facilities and expertise and compete on more equal terms with those authorities which do not derive the totality of their powers from statute. The abolition of the dock labour scheme in 1990 and the passing of the Ports Act 1991 have further intensified competition. The Mersey Docks and Harbour Act 1992 is a recent instance of a statutory company obtaining from Parliament further powers (modelled upon those already enjoyed by Associated British Ports under the Transport Act 1981) so as to be able to compete fairly with other harbour authorities, including the newly privatised port trusts such as Medway and Tees and Hartlepool. Port trusts which choose not to become privatised, however, face the difficulty that the Government may be reluctant to agree to a widening of their powers, in certain cases, on the basis that, unlike companies, they lack what is perceived by some as the discipline which comes from having shareholders.

7.9.1 Harbour businesses

TAWA attempts to reduce the need for further private Acts for the extension of a harbour authority's 'business' powers, while continuing to signal that harbour authorities *per se* cannot expect to be put wholly in the position of a registered company.

Section 63(2) of TAWA deals with the ability of harbour authorities to run businesses. It amends the Docks and Harbours Act 1966, s. 37, which empowers such authorities to acquire harbour businesses and set up companies engaged in harbour businesses. Under s. 37 as enacted, the only businesses which could be acquired or set up were those wholly or mainly engaged in 'harbour operations', as defined in the 1964 Act, and inland clearance depots. The range of permitted activities was, therefore, somewhat limited, and excluded even such things as the provision of transport services to and from the harbour. Section 63(2) amends s. 37 of the 1966 Act by replacing references to harbour operations with references to activities relating to harbours (cf. 7.8 above). Section 63(2)(c), however, inserts new s. 37(2A), which provides that nothing in s. 37(2) as amended shall be construed as authorising a harbour authority to delegate to another body any function that it could not otherwise delegate, for example, its statutory functions. If a harbour authority wishes to delegate any such functions to a subsidiary, it will need to apply for a harbour revision order (see below).

Section 63(2)(d) removes the need for Ministerial consent before a harbour authority engages in any of the activities covered in s. 37 of the 1966 Act.

7.9.2 Development of land

As the nature of cargo-handling operations changed in the years since the Second World War, especially with the growth of containerisation, a number of the larger harbour authorities found themselves with considerable amounts of land which were not needed – or likely to be needed – for cargo-handling purposes. Many authorities were reluctant merely to dispose of the surplus land to a developer, but wished to be active participants in the redevelopment process, thereby ensuring harmonisation with the continuing port activities as well as having the chance to reap greater rewards which could be ploughed back into the harbour business. Several port trusts therefore sought and obtained statutory powers to develop (either alone or with others) land no longer required for harbour purposes, with a view to its disposal after development, and to acquire by agreement other land for development with the surplus land. Examples are to be found in the Tees and Hartlepools Port Authority Act 1966 and sch. 3 to the Transport Act 1981 (in the case of Associated British Ports). A somewhat wider power – which encompasses harbour businesses – is contained in the Port of Tyne Act 1990.

Schedule 3, para. 9(5) inserts a new sch. 2, para. 9A into the 1964 Act – a provision which follows the Tees and ABP example, just described.

7.9.3 Delegation of functions

Schedule 3, para. 9(5) also inserts a new sch. 2, para. 9B into the 1964 Act, the result of which is to enable a harbour revision order to authorise the authority to delegate the performance of any of its functions except those relating to its regulatory or conservancy functions, that is to say:

(a)   a duty imposed on the authority by or under any enactment;
(b)   the making of byelaws;
(c)   the levying of ship, passenger and goods dues;
(d)   the appointment of harbour, dock and pier masters;
(e)   the nomination of persons to act as constables; and
(f)   functions relating to the laying down of buoys, the erection of light-houses and the exhibition of lights, beacons and sea-marks, so far as those functions are exercisable for the purposes of the safety of navigation.

7.10 CONSERVATION AND THE ENVIRONMENT

As introduced, the harbours provisions of the Transport and Works Bill contained no matters of a specifically environmental nature. As enacted, TAWA contains two such provisions which, together, take the ports industry into uncharted waters. Schedule 3, para. 9(6) inserts new para. 16A into sch. 2 to the 1964 Act (the list of objects for the achievement of which harbour revision orders may be made). The object in new para. 16A is imposing or conferring on the authority duties or powers (including powers to make byelaws) for the conservation of the natural beauty of all or any part of the harbour or of any of the fauna, flora or geological or physiographical features in the harbour and all other natural features.

This provision was introduced as a back-bench amendment to the Transport and Works Bill during its Report Stage on 4 March 1992, and was accepted by the Government, apparently in response to the representations of various amenity bodies who had been supported by Opposition Members during the Committee Stage of the Bill.

A harbour authority is unlikely to promote a harbour revision order to impose on itself environmental duties which it regards as inimical to its general interests, but others might seek to do so, if they can show a substantial interest (Harbours Act 1964, s. 14(2)(a)). Even assuming, however, that a third party applicant satisfied this requirement it would still be necessary to overcome the restriction in s. 14(2)(b) of the 1964 Act, the relevant provisions of which, as we have seen, have a strongly commercial flavour, speaking as they do of 'the improvement, maintenance or management of the harbour in an efficient and economical manner'. A harbour revision order whose environmental provisions significantly impaired the harbour authority's ability to provide for the loading and unloading of goods and the embarking and disembarking of passengers would be unlikely to satisfy the s. 14(2)(b) requirement.

Schedule 3, para. 6 goes considerably further than new para. 16A. It inserts new s. 48A into the 1964 Act, entitled 'Environmental duties of harbour authorities'. The section provides as follows:

It shall be the duty of a harbour authority in formulating or considering any proposals relating to its functions under any enactment to have regard to—
 (a)   the conservation of the natural beauty of the countryside and of flora, fauna and geological or physiographical features of special interest;
 (b)   the desirability of preserving for the public any freedom of access to places of natural beauty; and
 (c)   the desirability of maintaining the availability to the public of any facility for visiting or inspecting any building, site or object of archaeological, architectural or historic interest;
and to take into account any effect which the proposals may have on the natural beauty of the countryside, flora, fauna or any such feature or facility.

When, on 21 January 1992, Joan Walley MP moved an amendment to the Bill, in identical terms to new s. 48A, the Minister for Shipping (Patrick McLoughlin MP) said that it was:

a recipe for confusion about what the harbour authority is supposed to do beyond complying with its established statutory requirements. It also seems to be a recipe for litigation and judicial reviews. Moreover it is not the purpose of the Bill to impose general duties on the harbour authorities . . . It is not as if the ports industry is particularly free of controls over the way environmental issues are safeguarded and the interests of conservation protected . . . I have to question why the ports industry should be specially singled out by having such a general duty imposed on it, when no similar duty is placed on industrial and commercial concerns generally'. (House of Commons, H.C. Debs., *Hansard*, Standing Committee A, Transport and Works Bill, Tenth Sitting, 21 January 1992, cols. 337–8.)

On 11 March 1992, the Prime Minister announced that he was calling a general election for 9 April, and, following a rearrangement of business, the

Transport and Works Bill came before the House of Lords on 13 March for its Second Reading and remaining stages. If the Bill had failed to get through all its Lords stages that day, it is highly likely that it would have been lost.

During the Committee Stage, Lord Clinton-Davis moved an amendment to insert new s. 48A to the 1964 Act. This time the Government's response was different. Lord Brabazon of Tara said:

> we accept that the duty which this amendment imposes could be seen as supplementary to the raft of existing legislation dealing with these matters. In particular, the general duty (which, indeed, some harbours already have in their local Acts) would pull together these various requirements and plug any possible gaps in the existing framework, so as to ensure that these important matters are given proper attention in the way the harbour authorities carry out their functions. I am most grateful to the noble Lord, Lord Clinton-Davis, for having moved the amendment. I recommend that the Committee accept it. (House of Lords, H.L. Debs., *Hansard*, 13 March 1992, col. 1517.)

As Lord Brabazon remarked, it is the case that some harbour authorities already have general environmental duties, along the lines of s. 48A, in their local legislation (e.g., Milford Haven Conservancy Act 1983; Hayle Harbour Act 1989). In fact, it is likely that one of the original purposes of new sch. 2, para. 16A to the 1964 Act was to enable individual harbour revision orders to impose general environmental duties of the kind found in those Acts where the Secretary of State or Minister of Agriculture was satisfied that the special circumstances of the harbour required it, and those duties would not conflict with the purposes for which the harbour authority was established. The introduction of s. 48A, however, makes this irrelevant, and the references to duties in new para. 16A must therefore now be read as going beyond s. 48A.

It is possible that new s. 48A will be reconsidered as part of a general review of coastal planning and environmental policy, as suggested by the House of Commons Select Committee on the Environment in March 1992. Meanwhile, it remains to be seen how that section, and new sch. 2, para. 16A, will work in practice.

7.11 SPECIAL PARLIAMENTARY PROCEDURE

Special parliamentary procedure was created by the Statutory Orders (Special Procedure) Act 1945. It is described in detail in chapter 1 (1.7). Prior to TAWA, under the 1964 Act (as amended in 1981) an objector to a harbour revision order or harbour empowerment order affecting a harbour in England or Wales could not only require his objection to be considered at a public local inquiry but, if the order was nevertheless made following that inquiry, the objector could invoke special parliamentary procedure by giving notice that he maintained his objection. In such circumstances, assuming the objection met certain requirements under the Standing Orders, the objector could challenge the order, or seek its amendment, before a Joint Committee of Lords and Commons. Although made, the order would be in abeyance pending the Joint Committee's decision.

In the case of Scotland, all harbour revision orders and harbour empowerment orders were automatically subject to special parliamentary procedure irrespective of objections, with the result that they had to be laid before Parliament and were subject to negative resolution procedure. There were technical reasons for this distinction, which stems from 1981 when automatic special parliamentary procedure was abolished in the case of orders relating to England or Wales.

As mentioned in chapter 1, special parliamentary procedure has fallen from favour in recent years, largely for the same reasons as private Bills. TAWA represents a significant victory for the critics of special parliamentary procedure, in that the procedure's scope in connection with harbour orders is severely curtailed.

Schedule 3, para. 10(4) amends sch. 3 to the 1964 Act, with the result that special parliamentary procedure can now apply only in relation to proposals in an order to acquire compulsorily land which is held inalienably by the National Trust or land forming part of a common, open space, etc. This parallels the application of special parliamentary procedure in the case of the new order-making powers for railways, etc. contained in Part 1 of TAWA (see 3.8).

Schedule 3, paras 5(4) and 10(5) make further amendments to sch. 3 to the 1964 Act so as to abolish automatic special parliamentary procedure in the case of Scottish harbour revision orders and harbour empowerment orders, which henceforth are treated in exactly the same way as orders relating to harbours in England or Wales. The technical difficulties referred to earlier are no longer relevant, given the virtually total removal of special parliamentary procedure in the case of harbour orders.

One important consequence of the change in procedure for Scottish harbour orders is that it becomes necessary for the Government to implement in respect of such orders Council Directive 85/337/EEC of 27 June 1985 (OJ No. L175, 5.7.85, p.40) on the assessment of the effects of certain public and private projects on the environment. Previously such orders were treated as Acts of the United Kingdom legislature by reason of their being laid before Parliament and subject to negative resolution procedure, and thus did not fall within the scope of the Directive, which requires certain proposed projects to be subject to environmental assessment. Now, however, Scottish orders have lost that immunity, and the Government is required to implement the Directive for Scotland as it did for England and Wales by means of the Harbour Works (Assessment of Environmental Effects) Regulations 1988 (SI 1988/1336). This requirement has been met by the making of the Harbour Works (Assessment of Environmental Effects) Regulations 1992 (SI 1992/1421) which came into force on 15 July 1992.

Schedule 3, para. 10(7) omits paras 8A and 8B of sch. 3 to the 1964 Act. These provided for special parliamentary procedure to apply where an objection or representation about proposed modifications to a draft order were maintained in the case of a harbour revision order promoted by the Secretary of State under s. 15. Since such an order cannot concern the compulsory purchase of land, special parliamentary procedure can be totally withdrawn.

7.12 FEES, COSTS AND TECHNICAL CHANGES

Schedule 3, para. 10(2) amends sch. 3 to the 1964 Act by inserting new para. 1B. This provides that such fees as may be determined by the Secretary of State shall be payable on the making of an application for a harbour revision order. By virtue of s. 17 and Part VII of sch. 3, this also applies to harbour empowerment orders.

Fees are payable in the case of private Bills, and s. 6 of TAWA contains a power to charge fees in the case of the new orders under Part I. It is therefore not surprising that the Government took the opportunity to introduce a similar power in the case of harbour revision orders and harbour empowerment orders. The Government has, however, stated that fees will be set at a level to ensure the recovery of costs in processing the order, and that there is no intention to make a profit.

Section 47 of the 1964 Act applies the Local Government Act 1972, s. 250, which provides for the holding of inquiries. That section contains provisions relating to the payment of costs in connection with such inquiries which, in the case of the 1964 Act, will be public local inquiries held to consider opposed applications for harbour orders. The power to award costs in s. 250 does not, however, extend to the case where an inquiry is arranged but does not take place. Schedule 3, para. 5(2) accordingly amends s. 47 of the 1964 Act by inserting a new subsection (1A). This provides that the power to make orders as to costs under s. 250(5) of the 1972 Act should be exercisable in the circumstances just described, thus allowing costs to be awarded where, for example, an inquiry is cancelled at the last minute because of the unreasonably late withdrawal of a prospective party to the inquiry. Similar provision is made in the case of the new orders under Part I of TAWA.

Schedule 3, para. 5(3) inserts new s. 47(2A) into the 1964 Act, which extends the Scottish equivalent of the s. 250 power (namely, s. 210(8) of the Local Government (Scotland) Act 1973) in the case of Scottish harbour orders.

Schedule 3, para. 1(4)(b) and (c) makes two changes to s. 14(3) of the 1964 Act, which deals with the contents of a harbour revision order. The first adds the words 'or in connection with' after the words 'for the purposes of' so that a harbour revision order may contain any supplemental, consequential or incidental provisions appearing to the appropriate Minister to be requisite or expedient for the purposes of *or in connection with* the order. The words 'in connection with' already occur in the corresponding provision (s. 16(6)) dealing with harbour empowerment orders, and no satisfactory explanation has ever been given for their absence from s. 14(3) which, it was argued, could have prevented harbour revision orders from including, for example, environmental safeguards, in the case of harbour works authorised by the order.

The second change to s. 14(3) inserts words which enable a harbour revision order to exclude or modify general Acts and statutory instruments, as well as those of a local nature. One possible use of this power would be the disapplication of the provisions in the Town and Country Planning General Development Order which confer deemed planning permission in the case of works authorised by a harbour revision order. Similar disapplication provisions appeared from time to time in private Bills of the late-1980s, but this tended to be in response to complaints that the promoters were attempting to avoid facing a public local inquiry. Such a criticism cannot be levelled at the harbour revision order procedure, which contains a requirement that an inquiry be held if an opposed order is to proceed.

Finally, two repeals of harbour legislation should be mentioned. Section 65 of TAWA repeals the remaining provisions of the General Pier and Harbour Act 1861, which provided for provisional orders to be made in respect of the formation, management and maintenance of piers and harbours and for works costing up to £100,000. Such orders had to be confirmed by Act of Parliament. The 1861 Act was, for most purposes, superseded by the creation of the harbour order powers in the 1964 Act, and the expansion of those powers by TAWA means that the 1861 Act can now be repealed. The second repeal is that of the Fishery Harbours Act 1915. This enabled the Minister of Agriculture, Fisheries and Food to make provisional orders similar to those under the 1961 Act, in the case of fishery harbours.

EIGHT
INLAND WATERWAYS AND WORKS
AFFECTING RIGHTS OF NAVIGATION

8.1 INTRODUCTION

In the previous chapter the scope and nature of harbour revision orders and harbour empowerment orders were described. Notwithstanding the changes made by TAWA to the Harbours Act 1964, there will continue to be cases where works affecting rights of navigation cannot be authorised by an order under that Act. For instance, the definition of 'harbour' in the 1964 Act, although capable of covering non-tidal rivers and inland waterways, requires the waters in question to be capable of navigation by sea-going ships, while, on the other hand, an area of the territorial sea may be so distant from the land as to be incapable of forming part of a natural harbour, haven, estuary, etc. Furthermore, a harbour may lack a statutory harbour authority, and the works proposed in it may not justify the creation of such a body, thereby ruling out the use of a harbour empowerment order. Even if a harbour authority does exist, the proposed works may not be covered by sch. 2 to the 1964 Act, nor satisfy the requirements of s. 14(2)(b) (see chapter 7).

Before TAWA, the statutory authorisation required to secure immunity for the works from claims in nuisance had, in such cases, to be obtained by private Act (or Scottish provisional order).

The Joint Committee on Private Bill Procedure accepted the point, made by Lord Caithness (Minister of State, Department of the Environment) in a House of Lords debate in April 1988, that once one goes beyond low-water mark the normal considerations which planning authorities take into account in dealing with planning applications become of less importance. As the Minister said:

the normal limit of local authority jurisdiction, and hence of the scope of the planning system, is the mean low-water mark. There are a number of exceptions to this rule, for example in enclosed bays or in harbours for which the local authority is the harbour authority. But the low-water mark is a sensible boundary line. Once one goes beyond it, the normal considerations which local planning authorities take into account when considering planning applications, which relate mainly to the appropriateness of the proposed land use to the uses of neighbouring land, become of less importance. Once out at sea, issues of navigation and fishery have to be considered on which even coastal local authorities do not have, and generally do not need to have, any expertise. Local authorities have a legitimate interest in what goes on just off their shores, but this does not mean that they should be given control. In practice, very few developments are undertaken offshore; each one raises different issues, and, in the absence of any appropriate authority, such projects can be decided only by Parliament. (House of Lords, H.L. Debs, *Hansard*, 27 April 1988, col. 287.)

By accepting this analysis, the Joint Committee in effect rejected the suggestion that developments affecting rights of navigation could properly be dealt with by means of the planning system without the need for separate statutory authorisation. They considered that such authorisation could in many cases be provided by an expansion of the order-making powers under the Harbours Act 1964 (see chapter 7) but, in cases where development could not be authorised even by these expanded powers, the Joint Committee appeared to conclude that a private Bill would still be required, although it would be limited solely to those aspects of the scheme which required statutory authorisation.

By the time the Government issued its Consultation Document in 1990, the views expressed by Lord Caithness had been modified. Although continuing to accept the necessity of a form of authorisation separate from the planning process in the case of works which interfere with rights of navigation, the Government decided that, if a new order-making power was to be introduced for railways, trams, etc., it would be anomalous to leave those coastal and other developments falling outside the scope of harbour orders to continue to be dealt with by private Bill:

> The Government considers that a flexible and enduring system should provide a means of dealing with essentially works proposals other than by private Bill ... the Government considers it preferable to draft the legislation establishing the order-making procedure covering rail and light rapid transit proposals in such a way that it can be extended by subordinate legislation for use to authorise other works projects (such as barrages and canal works) which would otherwise require approval by means of a private Act of Parliament. (*Private Bills and New Procedures – A Consultation Document*, Cm 1110, London: HMSO, 1990.)

8.2   THE NEW S.3 ORDERS

The result of the Government's deliberation is ss. 3 and 4 of TAWA. Section 3 empowers the Secretary of State to make orders:

(a)   which would authorise the construction or operation in England and Wales of inland waterways (defined as including both natural and artificial waterways, and waterways within parts of the sea within Great Britain, but not managed or maintained by a harbour authority); or

(b)   which would authorise the carrying out of works which interfere with rights of navigation in waters within or adjacent to England and Wales, up to the seaward limits of the territorial sea.

The power in (b) above is subject to the qualification that the works must be of a description prescribed by order under s. 4. Any such orders will be subject to affirmative resolution procedure, which is appropriate given that the Secretary of State would be in effect removing a category of matters from Parliamentary scrutiny (by private Bill) each time an order is made.

The types of works that are likely to be prescribed under s. 4 will include such things as tidal barrages, artificial islands (e.g., such as that proposed in the Hook Island (Poole Bay) Bill), coastal reclamation (e.g., for residential development) and outfall pipes from generating stations.

Section 3(2) provides that the Secretary of State shall not make an order under s. 3 if in his opinion the primary object of the order could be achieved by means of an order under the Harbours Act 1964. The effect of this provision will be to ensure that a harbour revision order or harbour empowerment order is used for the purpose of authorising works below high-water mark, rather than a s. 3 order, where the primary object of the scheme complies with the requirements of s. 14(2)(b) of, and sch. 2 to, the 1964 Act (in the case of a harbour revision order) or s. 16(5) (in the case of a harbour empowerment order). If only a subsidiary aspect of the scheme falls within the scope of harbour order powers, it will be possible to use a s. 3 order to obtain all the necessary authorisations.

Schedule 1 to TAWA sets out the matters within ss. 1 and 3, and the description of these matters at 3.2 therefore applies equally to s. 3 orders. The method of application and the other procedural and related matters dealt with in 3.3 to 3.13 also apply to s. 3 orders.

As to the commencement of the s. 3 procedure, see chapter 2.5.

NINE
TRAMWAYS (LIGHT RAIL RAPID TRANSIT SYSTEMS)

9.1 INTRODUCTION

The development of the new sophisticated rapid transit systems has made them an increasingly popular way of easing traffic congestion in urban areas. A rapid transit system may be described as a public transport system which uses a special infrastructure to give a greater capacity and/or more rapid movement of people than can be achieved by using buses and ordinary roads. By convention, the term 'rapid transit system' is used for a system that is employed exclusively (or nearly so) for passengers and is not operated as part of a national railway network. One of the systems encompassed by the term is a light rail rapid transit system which continues the tramway tradition of steel wheel on steel rail technology and has the ability to fit into existing street patterns, either by sharing roads with other traffic or by running on its own reserve tracks. Such systems come within the definition of 'tramway' under s. 67(1) of TAWA (see 3.1.2). The advantage of light rail systems over other forms of rapid transit systems is the ability of the vehicles to travel both on and off the road. While there are still two traditional tramways in operation in the British Isles – in Blackpool and in the Isle of Man – there are currently several proposals to introduce new light rail rapid transit systems. At the time of writing, the system in Manchester has just been opened.

The Joint Committee on Private Bill Procedure found that the provisions of the Tramways Act 1870, the only legislation specifically regulating tramways, were outdated and inadequate to meet modern requirements (Joint Committee on Private Bill Procedure, *Report*, HL Paper 97/HC 625, London: HMSO, 1988, paras. 57 and 58). Their recommendations were implemented by TAWA. The 1870 Act is repealed. Henceforth the construction and modification of tramways will be authorised by orders made under s. 1 of TAWA instead of by private Acts or the procedures in the 1870 Act (see chapters 2 and 3). Part II of TAWA makes provision for the safety of tramways (see chapters 10, 11 and 12). This chapter is concerned with the miscellaneous administrative matters dealt with in Part III of TAWA.

9.2   LEASING OF TRAMWAYS IN OPERATION AT ROYAL ASSENT

Section 60 of TAWA enables a person authorised by or under statute to operate a tramway in operation at the passing of the Act (16 March 1992) to enter into agreements which grant another person the right to operate the whole or part of the tramway for an agreed period. The agreement may also grant to the lessee related statutory rights. An agreement under s. 60 may only be made with the consent of the Secretary of State.

The need for this power arises because statutory powers can be exercised only by the person on whom they are conferred and in accordance with the statutory provisions under which they were granted. Recent private Acts authorising light rail rapid transit systems have commonly contained provisions authorising the 'leasing' of the undertaking. See, for instance, s. 54 of the Midland Metro Act 1989. But in the absence of express statutory authority, an undertaking such as a tramway which is constructed and operated under statutory powers cannot be carried on by another person. The grant of the right to operate the tramway system should not, of course, be confused with the power of tramway operators under general property law to grant ordinary leases or agreements relating to the physical assets forming part of the tramway undertaking, such as the track, apparatus or rolling stock.

Old established tramway operations do not usually have the statutory power to permit another person to operate the tramway. The absence of such authority has caused problems to at least two undertakings – at Blackpool and Llandudno – where the Blackpool Borough Council and the Aberconwy Borough Council respectively have in the past wished to enter into full leasing arrangements but were unable to do so. Section 60 confers the requisite power.

The power is confined to existing tramways because it is envisaged that orders under s. 1 of TAWA authorising tramways in the future will, where appropriate, confer authority on the operator to enter into leasing and agency arrangements. These powers will probably be exercisable only with the Secretary of State's consent. Model clauses under s. 8 may well include such a provision which is expressly authorised by TAWA, sch. 1, para. 15 (see further 3.2.4).

9.3   APPLICATION OF PUBLIC SERVICE VEHICLES LEGISLATION

The Public Passenger Vehicles Act 1981 regulates the safety and operation of 'public service vehicles', a term defined in s. 1 of that Act to mean:

a motor vehicle (other than a tramcar) which —
    (a)   being a vehicle adapted to carry more than eight passengers, is used for carrying passengers for hire or reward; or
    (b)   being a vehicle not so adapted, is used for carrying passengers for hire or reward at separate fares in the course of a business carrying passengers.

It follows that tramcars are not covered by the regulatory regime of the 1981 Act. Section 61 of TAWA makes amendments to the 1981 Act so as to apply some of the provisions in that Act to tramcars. The remaining provisions continue not to apply to tramcars since the definition of 'public service vehicle' has not been generally extended to include tramcars. The following provisions have been applied:

(a)   Regulations under ss. 24 and 25 of the 1981 Act make provision for regulating the conduct, when acting as such, of drivers, inspectors and conductors of public service vehicles and of passengers on such vehicles. The power to make the regulations has now been extended to enable them to apply to drivers, inspectors and conductors of, and passengers on, tramcars (see s. 61(2) and (3) of TAWA). The regulations currently in force made under ss. 24 and 25 of the 1981 Act are the Public Service Vehicles (Conduct of Drivers, Inspectors, Conductors and Passengers) Regulations 1990 (SI 1990/1020).

(b)   A person carrying on the business of operating tramcars is to be under the same duty as that imposed by s. 27 of the 1981 Act on operators of public service vehicles to keep such accounts and records in relation to the business and to make to the Secretary of State such financial and statistical returns, and in such manner and at such times, as the Secretary of State may from time to time require (see s. 61(4) of TAWA). The duty under s. 27 of the 1981 Act does not apply to the British Railways Board, London Regional Transport or any subsidiary of London Regional Transport (see s. 27(3) of the 1981 Act).

(c)   Regulations made under s. 60 of the 1981 Act with respect to the carriage of luggage and goods on public service vehicles, and the safe custody and redelivery or disposal of any property accidentally left in such a vehicle and fixing charges for lost property may now be made to apply to luggage and goods on, and property accidentally left in, tramcars (see s. 61(5) of TAWA).

(d)   Regulations under ss. 24, 25 and 60 of the 1981 Act, as amended by s. 61 of TAWA, which apply to tramcars may amend or exclude any provision of an Act or instrument of local application whose subject matter is the same as that of the regulations (see s. 60(1B) of the 1981 Act inserted by s. 61(6) of TAWA). This power enables the regulations to ensure uniformity by amending or replacing specific provisions dealing with (say) lost property on tramcars which had been included on an *ad hoc* basis in private Acts authorising the operation of tramway systems.

9.4   EXCLUSION OF HACKNEY CARRIAGE LEGISLATION

Prior to TAWA, the safety of tramcars and the conduct of drivers of, and passengers on, tramcars fell under the regulatory regime laid down in the hackney carriage legislation. This legislation was originally designed to regulate horse-drawn carriages which plied for hire and, after the introduction of motor vehicles, was retained and adapted to apply instead to taxi cabs or London cabs. The term 'hackney carriage' is still used to describe the motor cabs which replaced horse-drawn carriages. As one would expect, the hackney carriage legislation was never very appropriate to regulate tramcars, still less modern light rail rapid transit systems.

The effect of s. 62 of TAWA is to disapply the hackney carriage legislation from tramcars. Instead, the conduct of drivers and passengers is to be regulated by regulations made under ss. 24 and 25 of the Public Passenger Vehicles Act 1981 (see s. 61 of TAWA and 9.3 above) and the safety of all tramways (whether authorised by statute or not) comes under the jurisdiction of HM Railway Inspectorate (see s. 42 of TAWA and 11.3 below).

In London, the legislation regulating hackney carriages is to be found in a series of statutes, from the London Hackney Carriage Act 1831 to the London Cab Acts 1968 and 1973. In the rest of England and Wales, the relevant legislation is contained in the Town Police Clauses Acts 1847 and 1889 and the Local Government (Miscellaneous Provisions) Act 1976. Immediately before the coming into force of s. 62 of TAWA, this legislation applied to tramcars partly by virtue of s. 48 of the Tramways Act 1870 and partly because tramcars fell within the definition of 'hackney carriage' contained in the Metropolitan Public Carriage Act 1869. Section 62 makes the amendment to the hackney carriage legislation necessary to exclude tramcars from its ambit.

TEN
RAIL CROSSINGS

10.1 STOPPING UP AND DIVERSION OF FOOTPATHS AND BRIDLEWAYS CROSSING RAILWAYS

10.1.1 Outline

Sections 118 to 123 of the Highways Act 1980 provide for the stopping up or diversion of footpaths and bridleways. However, these powers are only exercisable in limited circumstances – in the case of a stopping up, where the path or way is no longer needed for public use (see s. 118(1)) or, in the case of a diversion, if the diverted path or way will not be substantially less convenient to the public (see s. 119(6)). Sections 118 to 123 do not permit the stopping up or diversion of paths or ways solely on safety grounds, so, before the passing of TAWA, specific statutory authority was generally needed to close a level crossing for that reason.

The Joint Committee recommended that the Highways Act 1980 should be extended so as to permit stopping-up orders to be made on safety grounds using the Highways Act procedures, including confirmation by the Secretary of State following, if necessary, a public local inquiry (Joint Committee on Private Bill Procedure, *Report*, HL Paper 97/HC 625, London: HMSO, 1988, para. 49). This recommendation was accepted by the Government subject to the proviso that public safety should be weighed against other relevant considerations in deciding whether a footpath or bridleway crossing a railway is to be stopped up or diverted (see *Private Bills and New Procedures – A Consultation Document*, Cm 1110, London: HMSO, 1990, para. 40).

The amendments to the Highways Act implementing these proposals are contained in s. 47 of, and sch. 2 to, TAWA. Power is provided for two new types of order to be made under Part VIII of the Highways Act 1980 – rail crossing extinguishment orders and rail crossing diversion orders. These orders are made under procedures similar to those which apply to the making of public path extinguishment or diversion orders under ss. 118 and 119 of the Highways Act 1980. The orders will generally be made by the council in whose area the crossing is situated, on the application of the railway operator. Opposed applications require to be confirmed by the Secretary of State for the Environment after consultation with the Secretary of State for Transport. In an opposed case, the Secretary of State for the Environment will arrange for a public inquiry or hearing to take place, or for there to be written representations.

These new procedures do not apply to footpaths and bridleways crossing railways in Scotland, which the Government proposes to consider in a wider context when undertaking a general review of countryside access issues in Scotland.

10.1.2   Rail crossing extinguishment orders

The new s. 118A of the Highways Act 1980 (set out in TAWA, sch. 2, para. 3) empowers a council to make a rail crossing extinguishment order, that is to say an order extinguishing a footpath or bridleway in their area which crosses a railway otherwise than by tunnel or bridge. The council may make the order if it appears to them to be expedient in the interests of the safety of members of the public using or likely to use the path or way.

'Council' here means a county council, a district council, a London borough council or the Common Council of the City of London (Highways Act 1980, s. 329(1)). The procedure applies to tramways as well as railways but not to tramways which are laid along a carriageway (s. 118A(8), definition of 'railway').

So as to avoid a path or way coming to a dead end, the public right of way over the path or way may be extinguished not only over the crossing itself but also up to the intersection of the path or way with another highway over which the public have a similar right of way.

An order may not be confirmed by the Secretary of State or, if unopposed, by the council unless the Secretary of State or council are satisfied that it is expedient to confirm the order having regard to *all* the circumstances (not just the interests of safety). Under s. 118A(4) of the 1980 Act, they must, in particular, consider whether it is reasonably practicable to make the crossing safe for use by the public and, if the extinguishment order is to be made, that appropriate arrangements have been made to ensure that barriers and signs are erected and maintained. The Department of the Environment proposes to issue guidelines as to the matters which should be taken into account by the Secretary of State or councils in confirming rail crossing extinguishment orders. In all cases the Secretary of State will have to strike a balance between safety, expense and the convenience of the public. It is therefore likely that guidelines will make it clear that matters to be considered should include the existing use made by the public of the crossing, the availability of an alternative crossing, whether it would be possible to make the crossing safe by adopting measures such as the construction of a footbridge or tunnel or the putting up of signs, and the expense of taking those measures. If the Secretary of State or council come to the conclusion that instead of the right of way being extinguished the crossing should be made safe, s. 48 of TAWA enables the Secretary of State by order to require the railway operator to provide a tunnel or bridge. Orders under s. 48 are considered further at 10.2 below.

It is envisaged that, in general, rail crossing extinguishment orders will be made on the application of the railway operator, defined in new s. 118A(8) as being 'any person carrying on a railway undertaking which includes maintaining the permanent way'. In such a case, the council may require the railway operator to enter into an agreement with them to pay the whole or part of the expense of erecting or maintaining barriers and signs at the point where the path or way leading to the crossing is to be stopped up (see s. 118(5)).

Orders are to be in a prescribed form containing a map defining the land over which the public right of way is extinguished (see s. 118A(6)).

10.1.3 Rail crossing diversion orders

The new s. 119A of the Highways Act 1980 (set out in TAWA, sch. 2, para. 4) enables a council in the interests of the safety of members of the public to divert a footpath or bridleway crossing a railway rather than totally extinguishing it under s. 118A. Such an order, known as a rail crossing diversion order, has the effect of altering the route of a path or way by creating a new path or way to effect the diversion and then extinguishing the former right of way over the crossing and up to the intersection of the path or way with the newly created route. If facilities need to be provided for the convenient exercise of the new right of way (such as the provision of stiles or gates), the order is to be timed so that the new route is available with the necessary facilities before the old route is closed (see s. 119A(7)).

As in the case of a rail crossing extinguishment order, an order may not be confirmed (by the Secretary of State or, if unopposed, by the council) unless the Secretary of State or council are satisfied that it is expedient to do so having regard to all the circumstances, and in particular to whether it is reasonably practicable to make the crossing safe for use by the public and what arrangements have been made for ensuring that, if the order is confirmed, any appropriate barriers and signs are erected and maintained (see s. 119A(4)). Administrative guidelines are to be issued setting out the criteria in the same way as for rail crossing extinguishment orders. Under the powers conferred by s. 119 of the Highways Act 1980, a footpath or bridleway cannot be diverted if the path or way will become substantially less convenient to the public in consequence of the diversion. The criteria under s. 119A are different. The guidelines will probably include the convenience of the diverted route as a matter to be considered, but one to be balanced against the need for public safety and the inconvenience to the public if the path or way were extinguished altogether under s. 118A. As in the case of an extinguishment order, consideration of measures which could be adopted to make the crossing safe might prompt the making of an order under s. 48 for the provision of a bridge or tunnel (see further 10.2 below).

A diversion under s. 119A of the 1980 Act can only alter the termination of the path or way if the old point of termination is on a highway over which a right of way on foot or by horse (as the case may be) subsists and the new point of termination is on the same highway or on another connecting highway over which the same sort of right of way subsists (see s. 119A(5)). The intention is that the power should be used only to divert a right of way and not in effect to create a new path or way.

If the rail crossing diversion order is made by the highway authority, they will survey the new path or way and carry out any work which appears to them to be necessary to bring it into a fit condition for use by the public as a footpath or bridleway. If the order is made by a council other than the highway authority, the highway authority concerned may survey the new path or way and certify what work (if any) appears to them to be necessary to bring it into a fit condition and will serve a copy of the certificate on the authority who made the order. The work will either be carried out by the authority who made the order or by the highway authority, the costs being recouped in the first instance from the authority making the order (see s. 27 of the Highways Act 1980, as applied by s. 119A(11) of that Act). In either case, if the order is made on the application of the railway operator, the council making the order may recoup the whole or part of the costs concerned from the operator. Similarly, where the order is made on the application of the operator, the council may recover from the operator the whole or part of any compensation payable under s. 28 of the Highways Act 1980 (see 10.1.5 below) and the whole or part of the costs of erecting or maintaining barriers or signs (s. 119A(8)). These costs relate to the initial bringing of the new path or way into a fit condition and the stopping up of the old path. So far as the costs of maintenance are concerned, the order may require the operator to maintain all or part of the new footpath or bridleway (see s. 119A(6)).

A rail crossing diversion order must be in a prescribed form containing a map showing both the pre-order route and the post-order route of the path or way and, as respects the new route, any part already subject to a public right of way and the part to be subject to a new right of way (s. 119A(9)).

'Railway' and 'railway operator' have the same meaning here as for rail crossing extinguishment orders (see 10.1.2 above).

10.1.4 Procedure for making or confirming rail crossing extinguishment or diversion orders

The procedure for the making and confirmation of rail crossing extinguishment or diversion orders is the same as that laid down in sch. 6 to the Highways Act 1980 for the making and confirmation of public path creation, extinguishment or diversion orders (see ss. 118A(7) and 119A(10)).

A detailed explanation of sch. 6 would be outside the scope of this work. Broadly, the council making the order must advertise it, by placing newspaper advertisements, giving notice to interested persons, including the owners, occupiers and lessees of affected land, and displaying notices at the end of the ways and paths concerned. An opportunity is given for the making of representations or objections. If any are received, the Secretary of State may either arrange for a local inquiry to be held or, alternatively, may give the person the right to be heard. A local inquiry must be held where an objection is received from a local authority.

An unopposed order may be confirmed either by the Secretary of State or by the council making it. An opposed order may only be determined by the Secretary of State who may, after considering the report of the person appointed to hold the inquiry or to hear representations or objections, decline to confirm it or confirm it with or without modification. Provision is made for the publication of an order which has been confirmed.

The procedure for a rail crossing diversion order differs from that for a public path creation or diversion order in one important respect. A public path creation or diversion order to which objection is made by statutory undertakers on the ground that the order provides for the creation of a public right of way over land covered by works used for the purposes of their undertaking is, under sch. 6, para. 2 to the Highways Act 1980, subject to special parliamentary procedure. This requirement has not been applied to the new rail crossing diversion orders under s. 119A of the 1980 Act, consistently with the Government's policy to keep to a minimum matters relating to works which are required to be brought before Parliament.

Under s. 121(4) of the Highways Act 1980, as amended by TAWA, sch. 2, para. 6(4), the Secretary of State may not make or confirm a rail crossing extinguishment or diversion order if the order extinguishes a right of way over land under, in, upon, over, along or across which there is any apparatus belonging to or used by any statutory undertakers for the purpose of their undertaking, unless the undertakers have consented to the making or confirmation of the order. The consent may be conditional upon the inclusion in the order of protective provisions but may not be unreasonably withheld, any question whether the withholding of such a consent is unreasonable or whether any requirement is reasonable being determined by the Secretary of State. 'Statutory undertakers' here include gas suppliers, water and sewage undertakers, telecommunication system operators, public electricity suppliers, the Post Office and the Civil Aviation Authority.

10.1.5 Miscellaneous matters relating to rail crossing extinguishment or diversion orders

Where a path or way lies partly within and partly outside the area of a council, the council may make a rail crossing extinguishment or diversion order over the whole of the path or way. But, with respect to any part of the path or way which is inside their area, the council must consult with the other council, and with respect to any part of the path or way outside their area, they may only act with the consent of the other council. A council is required to consult with the Countryside Commission with respect to any part of a path or way in a National Park (s. 120(1) and (2) of the Highways Act 1980, as amended by TAWA, sch. 2, para. 5). Where a proposed diversion of a path or way would have the effect that a different authority would become the highway authority of the path, notice must be given to the existing highway authority (s. 120(4) of the Highways Act 1980, as amended by TAWA, sch. 2, para. 5).

The Secretary of State is given default powers to make rail crossing extinguishment or diversion orders if he is satisfied that this should be done in the interests of safety, that no council has submitted an order to him but if an order were submitted he would have power to confirm it (see s. 120(3) as amended by TAWA, sch. 2, para. 5). Although in general the Secretary of State may not exercise these powers without consultation with the council concerned, he need not consult if, after six months from receiving from the railway operator a request to make an order, the council have neither confirmed the order nor submitted it to the Secretary of State (see s. 120(3A) as inserted by TAWA, sch. 2, para. 5).

Under s. 28 of the Highways Act 1980 (applied in relation to rail crossing diversion and extinguishment orders by s. 121(2) of the Highways Act 1980, as amended by TAWA, sch. 2, para. 6(3)) compensation may be payable to a person who shows that the value of his interest in land is depreciated, or that he has suffered damage by being disturbed in his enjoyment of land, in consequence of the operation of a rail crossing extinguishment or diversion order. In the case of rail crossing diversion orders made on the application of a railway operator, the operator may be required to pay the whole or part of that compensation (see s. 119A(8)(a) of the Highways Act 1980, inserted by TAWA, sch. 2, para. 4).

Councils exercising their functions in relation to the making of rail crossing extinguishment and diversion orders are required to have due regard to the needs of agriculture and forestry (see s. 29 of the Highways Act 1980 applied to such orders by s. 121(3) of the 1980 Act as amended by TAWA, sch. 2, para. 6(4)).

Under s. 293 of the Highways Act 1980 as amended by TAWA, sch. 2, para. 7, an authorised person may enter land for the purpose of surveying it in connection with the making of a rail crossing extinguishment or diversion order.

To the extent that a new footpath or bridleway created under a rail crossing diversion order is not to be maintained at the expense of the transport operator under the terms of the order, it will be maintainable at public expense (see s. 36(2) of the Highways Act 1980, as amended by s. 64 of TAWA).

10.2   TUNNELS AND BRIDGES FOR FOOTPATHS AND BRIDLEWAYS CROSSING RAILWAYS

Section 48 of TAWA provides an alternative method by which the problem of an unsafe footpath or bridleway crossing a railway or tramway can be solved. If the Secretary of State considers that the crossing constitutes a danger to members of the public using it, he may make an order requiring a transport operator to provide a tunnel or bridge to carry the path or way under or over a rail or tramway. Alternatively, the operator may be ordered to improve an existing tunnel or bridge situated reasonably near the level-crossing in question. Presumably the latter alternative will be used if there is a conveniently placed bridge or tunnel to which the path or way may be diverted.

The power under s. 48 may be exercised only where the transport operator has sought an order extinguishing or diverting the public right of way over the footpath or bridleway in question, either by making an application under s. 6 of TAWA or by requesting the council to make a rail crossing extinguishment or diversion order under s. 118A or s. 119A of the Highways Act 1980 (see s. 48(1)(b), read with the definition of 'closure or diversion application' in s. 48(8)). 'Transport operator' is defined in the same way as for ss. 118A and 119A of the 1980 Act, i.e. not as the person operating the railway or tramway in question but as the person responsible for maintaining the permanent way (s. 48(8)). Section 51 of TAWA amends the Level Crossings Act 1983 so as to define 'operator' in the same way for the purposes of that Act, which deals with safety arrangements at level-crossings.

The order may include particulars as to the tunnel or bridge to be provided or improvements to be made (s. 48(3)). Planning permission will have to be obtained for its design unless the order is made under s. 1 of TAWA and the Secretary of State directs that planning permission shall be deemed to be granted under s. 90(2A) of the Town and Country Planning Act 1990, as inserted by s. 16(1) of TAWA (see further 5.2).

Not less than two months before making the order the Secretary of State must send a written notice with a draft of the proposed order to the transport operator and to each local authority in whose area the crossing (or any proposed new crossing) is situated (s. 48(4) and (5)). 'Local authority' here means any of the following – a county council, a district council, a London borough council, the Common Council of the City of London, a parish or community council and a parish meeting of a parish not having a separate parish council (s. 48(8)). While there is no express requirement that the Secretary of State must consider any representations made by the operator or local authority, it is implicit that he will not be acting reasonably unless he does so. Indeed s. 48(5) acknowledges that, no doubt in response to representations made, the final order may be a modified version of the one originally circulated.

A transport operator ordered to build a bridge or tunnel will be in a difficult position if he does not already have the necessary ancillary powers and rights. Clearly the operator will need the right permanently to acquire the land (if not already owned by him) on either side of the track on which each end of the tunnel or bridge will be constructed and to have temporary use of, and access to, working sites. For this reason s. 48(6) and (7) provides that the operator is only to be under a duty to use his best endeavours to comply with the order rather than under an absolute duty to do so. The duty imposed on him includes a duty to use his best endeavours to obtain any powers or rights required to provide or build the tunnel or bridge either by private treaty or compulsorily (probably by applying for a s. 1 order). There is no express sanction for failure to comply with this duty; as is the case with all statutory duties, the order of mandamus would lie to enforce it.

The power under s. 48 is an important ancillary to the Secretary of State's functions in relation to the determination of rail crossing extinguishment or diversion orders. The incidence of accidents at level-crossings is distressingly high. Indeed, it may be argued that it is intrinsically dangerous for persons to cross a railway track on the level on foot or by horse or bicycle, especially if the track is used by fast modern trains. From the point of view of the transport operator, the problem could frequently be solved by the stopping up or diversion of the path or way – a last resort often opposed by bodies such as the Ramblers Association. However, an operator who requests the Secretary of State or a council to make an order for that purpose runs the risk that he may instead be required to provide a tunnel or bridge at his expense. It should, however, be noted that no order requiring the provision of a bridge or tunnel may be made unless the original procedure was initiated by the transport operator himself.

An order requiring the provision of a bridge or tunnel must be made within the period of two years from the time when the application for the closure or diversion of the path or way in question is made by the transport operator.

Because s. 48 is ancillary to the Secretary of State's functions in relation to the closure or diversion of footpaths and bridleways under Part I of TAWA or the Highways Act 1980 which do not extend to Scotland, s. 48 does not extend there either.

10.3   SAFETY AT PRIVATE CROSSINGS IN ENGLAND, WALES AND SCOTLAND

10.3.1   Power to place signs and barriers at private crossings

Section 52 confers on the operator of a railway or tramway the power to provide signs or barriers at private level-crossings, i.e. places where the railway or tramway is crossed by a length of road or path to which the public does not have access. 'Barrier' here includes a gate and 'crossing sign' means any object or device (whether fixed or portable), or any line or mark on the road or path in question, for conveying to users of the road or path warnings, information, requirements, restrictions or prohibitions relating to the crossing in question (see s. 56(1)).

The signs or barriers to be provided must be of a character authorised by the Secretary of State either generally in regulations or by specific authorisation (s. 52(1)). The authorisation may relate to the size and colour of a crossing sign and whether or not it is illuminated (by lighting or the use of reflectors or reflecting material), and the nature of the warnings, information, requirements, restrictions or prohibitions conveyed by it (s. 52(3)).

It is implicit in s. 52 that the power to place signs on private land must include the power to enter the land for this purpose. However, the power is subject to the restrictions in s. 53. A transport operator may only enter land and place signs with the consent of the owner or in accordance with an authorisation given by the Secretary of State (s. 53(1)). In order to obtain such authorisation the operator must, after making reasonable efforts to obtain the consent of every owner of the land, serve notice on every owner whose consent he has not obtained. The notice must give details of the proposal and indicate that the Secretary of State will consider any representations made by the owner within a 42-day period from the date of the notice. The operator may then refer the proposals to the Secretary of State for authorisation who, after considering any representations duly made within the period of 42 days of the last notice served, may authorise the proposals with or without modifications or direct the operator not to carry them out (s. 53(4)). Authorisation may be given by the Secretary of State subject to conditions. In particular, he may direct the operator to pay compensation to the owner (s. 53(5)). The amount of the compensation, if not agreed, is determined by the Lands Tribunal (s. 53(6)).

Where a crossing sign or barrier has been placed at a private crossing in accordance with ss. 52 to 54, the operator may for the purpose of maintaining the sign or barrier enter land and do works without the consent of the owner (s. 53(7)(b)). In addition, he may enter land and do works without the owner's consent if it is necessary to do so in order to comply with a direction given by the Secretary of State to place a sign or barrier there (see s. 53(7)(a) and 10.3.2 below).

'Owner' in these provisions is given an extended meaning by s. 53(9) and includes not only the freeholder but also a leaseholder or tenant other than a tenant for a month or any period less than a month, or a mortgagee not in possession. There is a corresponding definition of 'owner' for Scotland.

10.3.2 Secretary of State's powers in relation to signs and barriers at private crossings

The Secretary of State may direct the operator of a railway or tramway to place crossing signs or barriers of a specified character at a private crossing (s. 52(2)). Such a direction is enforceable in relation to a private crossing in England and Wales by an order of mandamus on the application of the Secretary of State. If the crossing is in Scotland, the direction is enforceable by order of the Court of Session on an application by the Lord Advocate under s. 45 of the Court of Session Act 1988 (s. 54(3)). In addition, if the operator fails to comply with such a direction or fails to maintain a sign or barrier which has been placed at a private crossing in accordance with ss. 52 to 54, the Secretary of State may himself carry out the necessary work and recover the cost from the operator (s. 54(1) and (2)). The Secretary of State has the right for these purposes to enter land without the consent of the owner (s. 53(8)).

Section 124 of the Transport Act 1968, which is superseded by the powers conferred by ss. 52 to 54 and by the Level Crossings Act 1983, is repealed by TAWA, except in its application to Scotland.

10.3.3 Offences relating to signs or gates

Under s. 55, a person who fails to comply with any requirement, restriction or prohibition conveyed by a crossing sign placed at a private crossing in accordance with ss. 52 to 54 is guilty of a summary offence and liable to a fine not exceeding level 3 on the standard scale. There is a presumption under s. 55(2) that a crossing sign on or near a private crossing has been placed there in accordance with ss. 52 to 54 unless the contrary is proved. Proceedings for an offence under s. 55 can only be instituted in England and Wales by or with the consent of the Secretary of State or the Director of Public Prosecutions (s. 58). Where an offence is committed by a body corporate, any director, manager or other officer of the body is also guilty of the offence if it is committed with his consent or connivance or is attributable to any neglect on his part (s. 59).

Consistently with the new offence under s. 55, the penalty for an offence under s. 75 of the Railways Clauses Consolidation Act 1845 or s. 68 of the Railways Clauses Consolidation (Scotland) Act 1845 is increased to level 3 on the standard scale (s. 49). These provisions make it an offence to omit to shut and fasten gates at accommodation crossings.

ELEVEN
SAFETY ON TRANSPORT SYSTEMS

11.1 INTRODUCTION

Before the passing of TAWA, the safety of passenger railway services was governed by the Regulation of Railways Act 1871 and the Road and Rail Traffic Act 1933. The regime provided by these Acts included the appointment of railway inspectors, the reporting of railway accidents and the holding of inquiries into accidents. Under s. 41 of the 1933 Act, the Minister's approval was required for the opening of a railway for the public conveyance of passengers, the opening of additional railway lines, deviation lines, stations, junctions or level-crossings forming part of, or directly connected with, a railway used for the public conveyance of passengers and for a railway to be adapted for electric traction. As their titles suggest, these Acts were concerned only with regulating railways. For tramways, the relevant statutory provision was s. 25 of the Tramways Act 1870, which provided that a tramway could not be opened for public traffic until it had been inspected.

These powers, which were inadequate to deal with modern conditions, were supplemented in a piecemeal way by provisions in private Acts dealing with specific railway or tramway systems. One such example is s. 19 of the South Yorkshire Light Rail Transit Act 1988.

The Fennell and Hidden Reports on the King's Cross and Clapham Junction accidents drew attention to the fact that the existing legislation was inconsistent and had not kept pace with the many technological changes that had taken place since 1933. They recommended that the Secretary of State should have wider powers of approval, extending not only to transport works but also to equipment used on transport systems. Consequently, ss. 41 to 46 of TAWA give the Secretary of State a wide power to make regulations about the approval of new works and equipment to be used on transport systems, enlarge the powers of inspectors and extend the provisions about the reporting of accidents to cover also the reporting of incidents, such as signal failure, which could well have led to accidents. Powers are taken to limit speeds and loads on transport systems and to ensure that they carry proper third-party insurance.

11.2   APPROVAL OF WORKS, PLANT AND EQUIPMENT

Section 41 of TAWA gives power to the Secretary of State to make regulations for the purpose of securing the safe operation of railways, tramways, trolley vehicle systems and systems using prescribed modes of guided transport. These terms, which are defined in s. 67(1), have been discussed in 3.1 above. The regulations will require the approval of the Secretary of State to be obtained before new works, plant or equipment (including vehicles) are first brought into use or are first brought into use after alterations have been made to them.

It should be noted that the regulations will not be limited to the approval of new railways and tramways but will extend to the approval of items such as buildings, level-crossings, electrical traction equipment, signalling equipment, locomotives and rolling stock. New works, plant and equipment will require to be inspected before they are permitted to be brought into use. If major modifications are made to them, they will have to be inspected before they are permitted to be brought into use after the modifications are made.

It is expected that the regulations will apply to new works, plant and equipment of all the transport undertakings in question, including those in existence before the passing of TAWA, whether the undertakings were authorised by private Act, by light railway order or by an order under s. 1 of TAWA. The regulations will prescribe modes of guided transport other than railways, tramways and trolley vehicle systems to which the regulations will apply. These modes of transport need not necessarily be the same as those to which s. 1 of TAWA will apply by virtue of an order under s. 2 of TAWA (see 3.1.5). Before making the regulations, the Secretary of State is under a duty to consult such organisations as he considers to be representative of persons affected by the regulations (s. 57).

To ensure a smooth interface between the s. 41 regulations and other safety legislation such as the Construction and Use Regulations and approval systems of road vehicles under ss. 54 to 65 of the Road Traffic Act 1988, the s. 41 regulations may authorise the Secretary of State to issue exemptions or waivers, or to require compliance with regulations that would not otherwise apply. The non-electrical aspects of tramway or trolley bus systems are likely to be dealt with under the safety systems applying to buses rather than under the s. 41 regulations. The authorisation may allow exceptions or waivers to be granted or compliance to be required generally or on a case by case basis, and either conditionally or unconditionally.

The regulations will prescribe the cases in which approval is required and the procedure for obtaining it. They will also contain provision for determining when works, plant or equipment are to be treated for the purposes of the regulations as first having been brought into use. Periods of testing may be disregarded so as to enable equipment to be sanctioned provisionally for a period of testing, final approval being deferred until the test period has been satisfactorily completed.

The regulations will provide that it is to be a summary offence punishable with a maximum fine of level 5 on the standard scale (under s. 37 of the Criminal Justice Act 1982) for a person to contravene any specified provision of the regulations without reasonable excuse. Where the commission by a person of an offence is due to the act or default of some other person, that other person will be liable to be charged and convicted of the offence, whether or not proceedings are taken against the first person (s. 41(5)). Where an offence is committed by a body corporate with the consent or connivance of, or attributable to any neglect on the part of, a director, manager or similar officer of the body, the officer as well as the body will be guilty of an offence (s. 59). Proceedings for an offence under the regulations cannot be instituted in England and Wales except by or with the consent of the Secretary of State or the Director of Public Prosecutions (s. 58).

The regulations to be made under s. 41 of TAWA will replace s. 41 of the Road and Rail Traffic Act 1933 and s. 25 of the Tramways Act 1870 (referred to in 11.1 above), both of which are therefore repealed.

11.3   EXTENSION OF POWERS OF HM RAILWAY INSPECTORS

Section 3 of the Regulation of Railways Act 1871 provides for the appointment of railway inspectors. Their functions are contained in ss. 4 to 7 of the 1871 Act, s. 13 of the Railway Employment (Prevention of Accidents) Act 1900, s. 41(2) of the Road and Rail Traffic Act 1933 and s. 125 of the Transport Act 1968. Railway inspectors may, if directed by the Secretary of State, make inquiries into the cause of railway accidents, and for this purpose and to enforce statutory requirements relating to railways may enter and inspect railways, stations, plant and machinery. In general their functions are limited to railways authorised by Act of Parliament, though the powers in the 1871 Act extend also to tramways so authorised.

By s. 42 of TAWA, these functions are extended to all railways (whether or not authorised by Act of Parliament), and also to all tramways and trolley vehicle systems and to any system using a mode of guided transport prescribed by regulations under s. 41 of TAWA. The enactments relating to those functions are consequentially amended: references to railways are to be construed so as to include all transport systems to which the inspector's functions now relate by virtue of s. 41, and references to a company working a railway are to be construed as references to the operator of any such system. The terms 'railway', 'tramway', 'trolley vehicle system', 'system using a mode of guided transport' and 'operator', are defined in s. 67(1). (See further 3.1.) The prescription of a mode of guided transport under s. 41 regulations is discussed at 11.2 above.

Railway inspectors will have power to inspect all the modes of transport covered by the new safety regulations to be made under s. 41 of TAWA and to inquire into all transport accidents required to be reported under s. 43. Under the Regulation of Railways Act 1871, the powers of railway inspectors are exercisable in accordance with directions given by the Secretary of State. When a railway accident takes place the Secretary of State has discretion either to direct HM Railway Inspectorate to inquire into the cause of the accident or to determine that a more formal investigation should be held (see s. 7 of the 1871 Act). That will continue to be the case. Where an accident is more similar to a road traffic accident than a railway accident, as, for instance, where a motor vehicle collides with a tramcar, the Secretary of State may decide that it would be inappropriate to hold a Railway Act inquiry.

Section 41(2) repeals the proviso to s. 3 of the Regulation of Railways Act 1871 which prohibited an inspector from exercising 'any powers of interference in the affairs of any company'. This proviso, with its splendidly Victorian ring, is at odds with the power conferred by the 1871 Act to hold inquiries into railway accidents. Happily there is no evidence to suggest that HM Railway Inspectors have, at least in recent times, felt themselves inhibited by the proviso, and this modest relic of nineteenth-century non-interventionism is now consigned to history.

11.4 REPORTING OF ACCIDENTS

Before the passing of TAWA the requirements to report railway accidents causing death and personal injuries were contained in s. 6 of the Regulation of Railways Act 1871, as amended by s. 13(2) of the Railway Employment (Prevention of Accidents) Act 1900 and s. 43(1) of the Road and Rail Traffic Act 1933, and the Railways (Notice of Accidents) Order 1986 (SI 1986/2187). These provisions are now repealed and will be replaced by regulations to be made under s. 43 of TAWA.

Regulations under s. 43 will extend not only to railways and tramways authorised by Act of Parliament but also to all railways and tramways, trolley vehicle systems and modes of guided transport prescribed by regulations. These expressions, which are defined in s. 67(1), are discussed at 3.1. The systems of guided transport to be prescribed for this purpose will probably be the same as those prescribed by regulations under s. 41 (see 11.2 above).

The regulations may require the reporting not only of accidents involving death or personal injury but also 'circumstances involving a danger of death or personal injury' which have not led to accidents (s. 43(1)(b)). This implements the recommendations of the Fennell and the Hidden Reports into the King's Cross and Clapham Junction accidents, which pointed out that incidents constituting a serious risk to passengers should be investigated even if no accident has in fact taken place. Such incidents would include severe passenger congestion at stations and unprotected wrong side failures of signalling (a failure affecting a signalling system which is not automatically detected and prevented from having dangerous consequences by another part of the signalling system).

The detailed requirements of the reporting system will be set out in the regulations. Before making the regulations, the Secretary of State is under a duty to consult such organisations as he considers to be representative of persons who will be affected by them (see s. 57). As in the case of regulations under s. 41 (see 11.2 above), the regulations may authorise the Secretary of State to dispense with the requirements of the regulations generally or in particular cases. The Secretary of State might, for instance, decide that the reporting regulations should not apply in the case of an accident involving a tramcar which was essentially a road traffic accident as opposed to a tramway accident. It is likely that the regulations will not apply to very small undertakings.

Failure, without reasonable excuse, to make a report as required by the regulations is punishable on summary conviction by a fine not exceeding level 2 on the standard scale (s. 43(4) and (5)). An offence committed by a body corporate with the consent or connivance of, or attributable to any neglect on the part of, a director, manager or other officer of the body will render the officer as well as the body corporate guilty of the offence (s. 59). Proceedings may not be instituted in England and Wales for an offence under s. 43 except by or with the consent of the Secretary of State or the Director of Public Prosecutions (s. 58).

11.5   INSURANCE AND LIMITS ON SPEED AND LOADS

Section 45 of TAWA confers on the Secretary of State power to give directions imposing speed restrictions for vehicles in use on railways, tramways or systems using any other mode of guided transport, and imposing the maximum weights that may be transmitted by such vehicles to the rails or other support structure. Trolley vehicle systems are not covered by s. 45 because they, being more akin to buses, are more appropriately subject to the speed limits imposed by road traffic legislation and to the weight restrictions imposed by the Construction and Use Regulations. Directions under s. 45 are to be given to the person carrying on the undertaking which includes the provision of services on the system in question.

Similarly, under s. 46, directions may be given by the Secretary of State requiring the operator of a railway, tramway, trolley vehicle system or system using any other mode of guided transport to take out and hold such insurance policies in respect of death and personal injury as comply with the requirements of the direction. The Secretary of State may specify the minimum insurance cover and the insurer or class of insurer by whom the policy is to be issued.

Previously there was no generally applicable power to impose speed and weight limits. Section 46 of the Tramways Act 1870 (repealed by TAWA) conferred on local authorities power to prescribe speed limits, while s. 28 of the Regulation of Railways Act 1868 enabled the Board of Trade to regulate the weight and speed of light railways. Nor was there any general requirement for railway operators to hold public liability insurance policies. The gap was filled on an *ad hoc* basis by provisions included in private Acts and light railway orders. The current minimum level of insurance required in light railway orders is one million pounds, operators being required to keep the adequacy of insurance cover under consideration. The Department of Transport's policy on insurance on light railways is currently under review.

Directions under ss. 45 and 46 are intended to be made in the case of small independent railways which are chiefly used for pleasure purposes, some of which have not been required to be authorised by light railway order because they are situated on private land. It is not envisaged that directions will be used to impose restrictions on statutorily authorised undertakings run by the British Railways Board or London Regional Transport. The power is, however, intended to be a catch-all provision, and is therefore drafted in wide enough terms to enable speed restrictions, weight limits or insurance requirements to be imposed on any transport system, whether authorised by statute or not, including systems in existence before the coming into force of TAWA.

Directions could be used to impose more stringent restrictions or more stringent insurance requirements on an undertaking than those currently imposed by private Acts or light railway orders. However, statutory restrictions or requirements cannot be lifted or relaxed by direction. For that, further statutory authority would be required such as an order under s. 1 of TAWA. Before giving a direction under s. 45 or s. 46, the Secretary of State is required to consult with the transport operator in question (see s. 45(4) and s. 46(3)). Any limits imposed by a direction under s. 45 would be additional to, and not in substitution for, a speed restriction applicable under another enactment such as the Road Traffic Regulation Act 1984.

The contravention of a direction under s. 45 or s. 46 constitutes a summary offence carrying a fine not exceeding level 5 on the standard scale. Proceedings for such an offence cannot be instituted in England and Wales except by and with the consent of the Secretary of State or the Director of Public Prosecutions (see s. 58). Such an offence is also subject to s. 59, under which a director, manager or similar officer of a body corporate who participates in an offence committed by the body is also guilty of an offence.

TWELVE
CONTROL OF DRINK AND DRUGS ON
TRANSPORT SYSTEMS

12.1 INTRODUCTION

For nearly 150 years it has been an offence to work on a railway while drunk. But up to now there has been no comprehensive system of enforcement equivalent to the 'breathalyser' provisions introduced for drivers of motor vehicles by the Road Safety Act 1967 and now contained in ss. 4 to 11 of the Road Traffic Act 1988.

The former offence relating to railways was contained in s. 17 of the Railway Regulation Act 1842, which prohibited any engine driver, wagon driver, guard, porter, servant or other person employed in conducting traffic upon a railway or in repairing or maintaining the works of a railway from being drunk while so employed. Further provision was made by the railway companies themselves in byelaws made under their statutory powers. The driving of tramcars and trolley vehicles was covered by the provisions of the Road Traffic Act 1988 (by virtue of the Road Traffic Act 1991, sch. 4, para. 79) but only when the vehicle was being operated on a road or other public place. The legislation regulating the use of drink and drugs was therefore defective in a number of respects. On railways, persons concerned with servicing (as opposed to driving or operating) locomotives and rolling stock were not covered; there was no provision for testing for alcohol and drugs were not covered at all. So far as tramways and other systems of guided transport were concerned, only the drivers of the vehicles were covered, and then only when the vehicle was being operated on a road or public place.

After a railway accident at Morpeth in 1984, and in the light of the inspector's subsequent report, the Government undertook to modernise drink offences relating to railway employees and to extend them to drugs. Their intention was reinforced by a further accident in 1990 at Cannon Street Station in London. After the inquest the coroner wrote to the Secretary of State for Transport emphasising the need for statutory powers to enable the police to carry out tests on railway employees for drink and drugs. This gap is now filled by chapter I of Part II of TAWA (ss. 26 to 40), which contains comprehensive provisions to control the use of alcohol and drugs by those who work on railways, tramways and other guided transport systems. These provisions come into force on 7 December 1992 (Transport and Works Act 1992 (Commencement No. 2) Order 1992 (SI 1992/2043)). The regime introduced by chapter I is very similar to that applicable to motor vehicles under the Road Traffic Act 1988 and the Road Traffic Offenders Act 1988.

The new powers are intended to back up the strict policy of the British Railways Board and London Regional Transport on alcohol and drug abuse. It is the rule of both organisations that no one may report for duty while under the influence of, nor take while on duty, alcohol or any other substance which might impair his safety, efficiency or vigilance. Contraventions of that rule are viewed very seriously under the codes of practice issued by each organisation and normally lead to dismissal. They have a policy of pre-employment testing for drugs of recruits to safety posts. They also have voluntary in-service and post-incident testing. (House of Commons, H.C. Debate, *Hansard*, Standing Committee A, Transport and Works Bill, Eighth sitting, col. 263.)

Section 27 of TAWA, the key provision in chapter I, makes it an offence for a person to work on a railway, tramway or specified system of public transport in various activities which directly affect public safety while unfit through drink or drugs, or when his alcohol level is over the prescribed limit. The limit is the same as that laid down in the Road Traffic Act 1988. The police are given similar powers of testing and arrest as those in the Road Traffic Act 1988. Operators of transport systems are rendered accountable by s. 28, which makes the operator liable where an offence under s. 27 has been committed unless the operator has exercised all due diligence to prevent the commission of the offence. Under s. 59, where the operator is a body corporate individual directors, managers and other officers can be prosecuted under s. 27 as well as the body itself.

12.2 TRANSPORT SYSTEMS TO WHICH THE NEW CONTROLS APPLY

The new controls in chapter I of Part II of TAWA apply to all railway or tramway systems which are used, or are intended to be used, wholly or partly for the carriage of members of the public (s. 26(1)(a), (b) and (2)). In addition, the Secretary of State may by order apply the provisions of chapter I to any system specified in the order which uses another mode of guided transport (s. 26(1)(c)). The Secretary of State's power to make such an order is exercisable by statutory instrument subject to negative resolution procedure (s. 26(3)). The power is subject to s. 26(2) discussed below.

This power to specify *systems* may be contrasted with the power to prescribe modes of guided transport under s. 2 so as to extend the provisions of Part I to systems using those modes and the power under s. 41 or s. 43 to enable safety and reporting regulations to be made covering systems using the prescribed modes. Under ss. 2, 41 and 43, once the mode of guided transport has been prescribed, all systems using that mode will be covered. Section 26 requires each system to be specified separately because of the particular need for certainty in applying a criminal code, as is demonstrated by the Transport (Guided Systems) Order 1992 (SI 1992/2044) which specifies five particular systems, including those at Birmingham, Gatwick and Stanstead Airports.

The expressions 'railway', 'tramway' and 'guided transport', which are defined in s. 67(1), are discussed at 3.1.

Under s. 26(2), the provisions of chapter I do not apply to a transport system unless it is used, or is intended to be used, wholly or partly for the carriage of members of the public. Heritage lines such as the tramways at the Beamish and Crich Museums will therefore be covered. Provided part of a system is used for the carriage of members of the public, the provisions of chapter I will apply to every part of the system. So the new controls apply to freight-only lines which form part of a wider system carrying members of the public. They do not, however, apply to lines used wholly for industrial purposes, such as lines within steel works and collieries. Very small railways running on track of a gauge of less than 350mm are not included (unless they cross a carriageway) since such railways are excluded from the definition of 'railway' in s. 67(1).

12.3   PRINCIPAL OFFENCES

12.3.1   Offences by employees

Section 27 of TAWA makes it an offence for a transport employee to work in a specified capacity directly affecting the safety of the public or other employees when he is unfit to carry out that work through drink or drugs, or after he has consumed so much alcohol that the proportion of it in his breath, blood or urine exceeds the prescribed limit. 'Drug' includes any intoxicant other than alcohol (s. 38(1)).

For that purpose, a person is taken to be unfit to carry out any work if his ability to carry out the work properly is for the time being impaired (s. 27(4)). The onus of proving that a person's ability to carry out work was impaired is on the prosecution. Impairment includes both doing things unsatisfactorily and not doing things at all. The expressions 'unfit through drink or drugs' and 'for the time being impaired' are also used in s. 4(3) and (5) of the Road Traffic Act 1988, which make it an offence to drive a motor vehicle when under the influence of drink or drugs. These provisions have generated a great deal of case law, full consideration of which would be outside the scope of this work. The reader is referred to *Halsbury's Laws*, 4th edn, London: Butterworths, 1983, vol. 40, paras. 481 to 496 and specialist works.

The provisions of s. 27 apply to an employee who works as a driver, guard, conductor or signalman or in any other capacity in which he can control or affect the movement of a vehicle (s. 27(1)(a) and (2)(a)). This includes railway station staff who despatch trains, train captains on the Docklands Light Railway, level-crossing keepers and persons performing traffic functions.

The offences also cover a person working on a transport system in a maintenance capacity or as a supervisor of, or look-out for, persons working in a maintenance capacity (s. 27(1)(b) and (2)(b)). What is meant by 'working on a transport system in a maintenance capacity' is further explained in s. 27(3) as work on the system which involves:

. . . maintenance, repair or alteration of—
    (a)   the permanent way or other means of guiding or supporting vehicles,

(b) signals or other means of controlling the movement of vehicles, or
(c) any means of supplying electricity to vehicles or to the means of guiding or supporting vehicles,
or involves coupling or uncoupling vehicles or checking that they are working properly before they are used on any occasion.

The provisions are intended to cover maintenance work to the railway system while it is in operation and to vehicles while, or shortly before, they are in motion. The criminal offences are not aimed at persons who undertake the sort of maintenance or repair work to vehicles which could be done in depots or factories, even if the work is on occasion done while the vehicles are on the track. The test is whether the maintenance work is sufficiently proximate to the use of the system for the carriage of members of the public.

For the purpose of s. 27 and the ancillary provisions in chapter I of Part II of TAWA, it is immaterial whether a person who works on a transport system does so in the course of his employment, under a contract for services, voluntarily or otherwise (s. 38(3)). Accordingly, the drink and drugs provisions apply to persons who work part time on a voluntary basis on heritage lines in the same way as they apply to employees of a railway operator and employees of contractors undertaking relevant maintenance work.

An offence under s. 27 is punishable on summary conviction with imprisonment for a maximum term of six months, or a fine not exceeding level 5 on the standard scale or both (s. 36(1)). As in the case of other offences under chapter I of Part II, proceedings for an offence under s. 27 cannot be instituted in England and Wales except by or with the consent of the Secretary of State or the Director of Public Prosecutions (s. 58).

Section 27 replaces the former offence under s. 17 of the Railway Regulation Act 1842 of being found drunk while employed on a railway, and s. 17 (so far as it provides for that offence) is repealed by s. 40 of TAWA.

12.3.2 Offences by operators of transport systems

If a s. 27 offence is committed, the 'responsible operator' is by virtue of s. 28 also guilty of an offence unless he exercised all due diligence to prevent the commission on the transport system of any offence under s. 27 (s. 28(1) and (3)). Where the transport system on which the primary offence was committed only has one operator, that operator is 'the responsible operator'. Where the system has more than one operator, the 'responsible operator' is whichever of them is responsible for the work giving rise to the s. 27 offence (s. 28(2)). If the person who committed the s. 27 offence did so in the course of his employment with a person other than the responsible operator, then, without prejudice to the operator's liability, his employer is also guilty of an offence unless he exercised all due diligence to prevent the commission on the transport system by any of his employees of any offence under s. 27 (s. 28(4) and (5)).

The burden of proof is on the operator or employer to show, on the balance of probabilities, that he exercised all due diligence (see s. 101 of the Magistrates' Courts Act 1980). The defences in s. 28(3) or (5) require the operator or employer to show, not that he exercised all due diligence to avoid the commission of the particular s. 27 offence which has been committed, but that he exercised all due diligence to prevent the commission on the transport system of *any* s. 27 offence or, in the case of an employer, the commission of *any* s. 27 offence by *any* of his employees. To set up the defence it is therefore necessary for the operator or employer to prove to the court that an adequate method has been introduced and is being properly monitored to prevent alcohol/drug abuse by employees which would affect safety. It is probable that a method will not be considered adequate unless it includes systematic steps to ascertain whether any employee is prone to alcohol/drug abuse, to supervise employees when signing on or while on duty so that signs of drunkenness or drug abuse are detected, and to discipline any cases which are discovered.

The defence of exercising all due diligence is to be found in other enactments, for example s. 67 of the Offices, Shops and Railway Premises Act 1963 and s. 24(1)(b) of the Trade Descriptions Act 1968. It is probably sufficient for the defendant to show that all reasonable steps were taken to avoid the commission of an offence under s. 27 on the transport system even if not all possible steps were taken. (See Lord Diplock's judgment in *Tesco Supermarkets Ltd* v *Nattrass* [1971] 2 All ER 127, at p. 158.) What is not clear is how far costs considerations would be taken into account by the courts in determining what steps it is reasonable for an operator or employer to take. But it is, for example, unlikely that an operator or employer would be required routinely to breathalyse all employees reporting on duty.

In most cases the operator or employer will be a body corporate, in which case the directors and other officers of the body may be personally liable under s. 59 of TAWA. Under that provision, where an offence committed by a body corporate is committed with the consent or connivance of, or is attributable to any neglect on the part of, a director, manager or other similar officer, or a person purporting to act in such a capacity, he as well as the body is guilty of the offence. Where the affairs of the body in question are managed by its members, a member may be made personally liable under that provision. Section 59(3) makes similar provision for Scotland.

The maximum penalty for an offence under s. 28 is the same as that for an offence under s. 27, namely, on summary conviction, six months' imprisonment and/or a fine of level 5 on the standard scale (s. 36(1)). In this case too, proceedings cannot be instituted in England and Wales in respect of an offence except by or with the consent of the Secretary of State or the Director of Public Prosecutions (s. 58).

12.3.3 The prescribed limits

The prescribed limits (which are identical to those in s. 11 of the Road Traffic Act 1988) are set out in s. 38(2) of TAWA and are:

    (a)   35 microgrammes of alcohol in 100 millilitres of breath;
    (b)   80 milligrammes of alcohol in 100 millilitres of blood; or
    (c)   107 milligrammes of alcohol in 100 millilitres of urine.

The Secretary of State is given power, similar to that in s. 11 of the 1988 Act, to alter these limits by regulations. At the Standing Committee stage of the Bill in the House of Commons a case was made out on behalf of the British Railways Board that the prescribed limits for railway employees (in particular train drivers) should be lower than the road traffic limits in the light of medical evidence suggesting that a train driver's ability is significantly impaired if he has consumed any alcohol whatsoever, even when the concentration of alcohol in his blood is less than the Road Traffic Act limits. These arguments were resisted on the basis that in the context of imposing criminal sanctions there should be consistency between different methods of transport. It would, perhaps, be unreasonable to impose on the driver of a tramcar driving on a road a duty different from that imposed on drivers of buses. However, the specification of these particular alcohol levels for the purposes of criminal sanctions does not, of course, prevent the British Railways Board, London Regional Transport and other transport operators continuing to take disciplinary proceedings against staff found to have consumed alcohol while on duty but to have levels of alcohol which are lower than the prescribed levels.

12.3.4 Interaction with road traffic legislation

It has already been mentioned (in 12.1 above) that, before TAWA, the drivers of tramcars and other vehicles on guided transport which constitute motor vehicles or mechanically propelled vehicles came within the ambit of the drink-driving provisions in ss. 4 to 11 of the Road Traffic Act 1988 while the vehicles were operated on roads and other public places. Because drivers of tramcars and vehicles on other specified systems of guided transport are now, with other key employees, regulated by chapter I of Part II of TAWA, it is unnecessary for them to be covered by the parallel provisions in the 1988 Act.

Section 192A of the Road Traffic Act 1988, inserted into that Act by s. 39 of TAWA, disapplies the provisions of ss. 4 to 11 of the 1988 Act in the case of vehicles on transport systems regulated by chapter I of Part II of TAWA. Trolley buses, which are not covered by chapter I, remain within the Road Traffic Act 1988.

There is power under s. 192A(2) for the Secretary of State to apply ss. 4 to 11 to vehicles on specified systems of guided transport (which expressions have the same meaning here as in s. 67(1) of TAWA). This power, taken with the power under s. 26(1)(c) to specify transport systems to which chapter I is to apply, gives the Secretary of State the flexibility to determine, in the case of each system using a new mode of guided transport, whether it is more appropriate that the vehicles should be regulated by the road traffic legislation (as in the case of trolley buses) or by chapter I (as in the case of trains and tramcars).

12.4 POLICE POWERS

Sections 29 to 33 of TAWA give the police powers to administer breath tests, to arrest persons reasonably suspected to be committing offences and to require them to provide specimens of breath, blood or urine for analysis. The powers are exercisable by British Transport Police Force (appointed under the British Transport Commission Act 1949) as well as by ordinary police officers. The powers, which are briefly set out below, are modelled on the powers contained in ss. 4 and 6 to 9 of the Road Traffic Act 1988. Detailed commentary on these provisions, which have been the subject of considerable judicial scrutiny, is outside the scope of this work. The reader is referred to *Halsbury's Laws*, 4th edn, London: Butterworths, 1983, vol. 40, paras. 481–96 and specialist works.

Section 29 (modelled on s. 6 of the 1988 Act) enables a constable in uniform to require a person to provide a specimen of breath for a breath test if he is working on a transport system in a relevant capacity and the constable has reasonable cause to suspect that he has alcohol in his body. The power also applies where the constable reasonably suspects that person has been working on a transport system in such a capacity with alcohol in his body and that he still has alcohol in his body.

Section 29(2) deals with the powers of constables to breathalyse persons where an accident has occurred on a transport system or an incident has occurred which, in the constable's opinion, involved a danger of death or personal injury. The constable may require a specimen of breath from any person if he has reasonable cause to suspect that he was working in a relevant capacity at the time of the accident or incident, and that his act or omission may have been the cause of the accident or incident.

Persons should be breathalysed either at or near the place where the requirement is made, except in a case where an accident or incident has occurred when the constable may require the sample of breath to be given at a police station (s. 29(4)). Failure or refusal, without reasonable excuse, to comply with the request or to give a specimen of breath such that the test can be carried out, constitutes an offence punishable on summary conviction with a maximum fine of level 3 on the standard scale (ss. 29(5), 36(2) and 38(1) and (4)).

Section 30 (modelled on ss. 4 and 6 of the 1988 Act) enables a constable (whether or not in uniform) to arrest a person without warrant if he has reasonable cause to suspect that that person is or has been committing a s. 27 offence, or if, having breathalysed him, he has reasonable cause to suspect that the person is over the limit or if the person has refused to be breathalysed and the constable has reasonable cause to suspect that he has alcohol in his body. In the case of England and Wales, but not Scotland, powers of entry are conferred on the constable to enable arrests to be effected or breath tests to be carried out (ss. 30(3), (4) and 37(1)).

Section 31 (based on s. 7 of the 1988 Act) enables a constable to require a person who is under investigation for a s. 27 offence to provide two specimens of breath for analysis, or one specimen of blood or urine for laboratory testing. Requirements to provide a specimen of breath may only be made at a police station. A requirement to provide a specimen of blood or urine may be made at a hospital or, in specified circumstances, at a police station. Where a specimen other than a specimen of breath is required by a constable, he may decide whether it is to be blood or urine unless a medical practitioner decides that, for medical reasons, a specimen of blood should not be taken.

Failure or refusal, without reasonable excuse, to provide a specimen under s. 31 (including an adequate specimen of breath) constitutes an offence punishable on summary conviction with a maximum of six months' imprisonment and/or a fine on level 5 of the standard scale (ss. 31(8), 36(1) and 38(1) and (4)).

Where two specimens of breath are provided under s. 31, the one with the higher proportion of alcohol is disregarded (s. 32(1)). In a case where the breath test produces a level of 50 microgrammes of alcohol in 100 millilitres of breath or less, the suspect has the right to require that a specimen of urine or blood should be tested instead (s. 32(2)). These provisions are the same as those contained in s. 8 of the 1988 Act. Suspects who are patients in hospitals are afforded protection under s. 33 equivalent to that provided by s. 9 of the 1988 Act.

12.5 EVIDENCE IN PROCEEDINGS FOR OFFENCES UNDER S. 27

Sections 34 and 35 of TAWA make provision which enables the result of any test of a specimen of breath, blood or urine provided by an accused to be admitted as evidence of the presence of alcohol or drugs in his body in criminal proceedings under s. 27. Corresponding provisions are contained in ss. 15 and 16 of the Road Traffic Offenders Act 1988. Special provisions apply in relation to proceedings for offences in Scotland (see s. 37(2)).

Section 34 provides that in proceedings for an offence under s. 27, account shall be taken of evidence of the proportion of alcohol or any drug in a specimen provided by the accused. Under that provision it is presumed that the proportion of alcohol in the accused's breath, blood or urine at the time of the alleged offence was not less than that in the specimen, unless the accused proved that he consumed alcohol after stopping work and before providing a specimen and that, had he not done so, he would have been under the limit or (as the case may be) fit to work. When the accused provides a specimen of blood or urine he has the right to ask for that specimen to be divided into two parts and to take one of those parts away (s. 34(3)).

Provision is made by s. 35 to enable the prosecution to adduce evidence in proceedings of the result of a breath test or of the analysis of a specimen by the production of documents certified by the constable who carried out the breath test or the person who carried out the analysis. Copies of the certificates are required to be served on the accused who, by serving notice on the prosecution, may require the attendance at the hearing of the person by whom the certificate purports to be signed.

THIRTEEN
PRIVATE BILLS AFTER THE TRANSPORT AND
WORKS ACT 1992

TAWA represents a significant further step in the process, described in chapter 1, whereby matters previously the subject of private Bills have progressively been transferred to the Executive, to be dealt with by means of ministerial order, with little or no parliamentary involvement. The process is, however, largely reactive, as is demonstrated by TAWA itself, which is a response both to the increased number of infrastructure projects coming before Parliament in the 1980s, and to the growing tendency of such projects to be politically and environmentally controversial. Where parliamentary processes are not considered to be under strain, there is a tendency to let them continue to operate. A good example of this can be found in the treatment of Scottish provisional orders and private Bills. As described in chapter 6, the new s. 1 and s. 3 orders introduced by TAWA are confined to England and Wales because the Scottish system of private legislation is perceived to be operating smoothly and does not place any undue demands upon legislators.

None of the other types of private Bill which come before Parliament raises issues similar to those raised by recent works Bills. Local authorities frequently require to go to Parliament to seek additional powers, based upon special (but necessarily unique) local need, and the Joint Committee on Private Bill Procedure recommended no change to this practice. Many statutory companies promote private Bills to amend their powers (and duties) in the light of changing circumstances. Private residential estates often require parliamentary powers to ensure the upkeep of roads and other facilities. Registered companies can obtain parliamentary sanction to change their domicile to other countries without the need to disrupt their affairs, while bodies such as banks, other financial institutions and university colleges find that Parliament can, at a single stroke, merge several major bodies without the usual attendant problems, such as a multiplicity of property transactions and the novation of an enormous number of contracts with customers and other third parties.

While these and other types of private Bills will continue to raise interesting matters, it is unlikely that Parliamentary Committees considering such Bills will find themselves faced with the sort of specialist technical detail which is an inherent part of works Bills. Nor do any of these types of Bill raise the spectre of conflict with the town and country planning system, and the local inquiry process in particular. Thanks to TAWA, however, Parliament will no longer be the backdrop to such spectacles as Isambard Kingdom Brunel and the promoters of the Great Western Railway Bill having to contend with such an argument as that which predicted the company's passengers would all be suffocated when their train passed through a tunnel. Pleasures of that kind are henceforth to be reserved solely for the long-suffering Departmental inspector.

Transport and Works Act 1992

CHAPTER 42

ARRANGEMENT OF SECTIONS

PART I   ORDERS AUTHORISING WORKS ETC

Power to make orders

Section
1. Orders as to railways, tramways etc.
2. Extension of section 1 to other guided transport systems.
3. Orders as to inland waterways etc.
4. Description of works for purposes of section 3.
5. Subject-matter of orders under sections 1 and 3.

Procedure for making orders

6. Applications for orders under sections 1 and 3.
7. Orders under sections 1 and 3 made otherwise than on application.
8. Model clauses.
9. Schemes of national significance.
10. Objections.
11. Inquiries and hearings.
12. Special parliamentary procedure.
13. Making or refusal of orders under section 1 or 3.
14. Publicity for making or refusal of orders.

Consents etc under other enactments

15. Assimilation of procedures.
16. Town and country planning.
17. Listed buildings and conservation areas.
18. Hazardous substances.
19. Coast Protection Act 1949.
20. Power to apply for, or object to, orders.
21. Transport Consultative Committees.

Miscellaneous

22. Validity of orders under section 1 or 3.
23. Exercise of Secretary of State's functions by appointed person.
24. Private legislation procedure in Scotland.
25. Crown land.

PART II   SAFETY OF RAILWAYS ETC

CHAPTER I   OFFENCES INVOLVING DRINK OR DRUGS

Preliminary

26.   Transport systems to which Chapter I applies.

Principal offences

27.   Offences involving drink or drugs on transport systems.
28.   Offences by operators of transport systems.

Police powers etc

29.   Breath tests.
30.   Powers of arrest and entry.
31.   Provision of specimens for analysis.
32.   Choice of specimens of breath.
33.   Protection for hospital patients.

Evidence in proceedings for offences under section 27

34.   Use of specimens in proceedings.
35.   Documentary evidence as to specimens.

Penalties

36.   Penalties.

Miscellaneous and supplementary

37.   Special provision for Scotland.
38.   Interpretation of Chapter I.
39.   Amendment of scope of offences involving drink or drugs under Road Traffic Act 1988.
40.   Consequential amendment.

CHAPTER II   OTHER SAFETY PROVISIONS

General

41.   Approval of works, plant and equipment.
42.   Inspectors.
43.   Accidents etc.
44.   Accidents etc: consequential amendments.
45.   Directions limiting speeds and loads.
46.   Directions requiring insurance.

Rail crossings

47.   Stopping up and diversion of crossings.
48.   Footpaths and bridleways over railways.
49.   Securing of gates and barriers.
50.   Orders under Transport Act 1968.
51.   Amendment of Level Crossings Act 1983.

Signs and barriers at private crossings

52. Placing of signs and barriers.
53. Rights to enter land.
54. Default powers of Secretary of State.
55. Offence of failing to comply with sign.
56. Interpretation of sections 52 to 55.

CHAPTER III   SUPPLEMENTARY

57. Duty to consult.
58. Prosecutions.
59. Offences by bodies corporate etc.

PART III   MISCELLANEOUS AND GENERAL

Tramways

60. Powers of leasing.
61. Amendment of Public Passenger Vehicles Act 1981.
62. Exclusion of hackney carriage legislation.

Harbours

63. Harbours.

Miscellaneous

64. Maintenance of footpaths and bridleways.
65. Certain enactments to cease to have effect.

General

66. Service of notices.
67. Interpretation.
68. Repeals.
69. Expenses.
70. Commencement.
71. Extent.
72. Short title.

SCHEDULES

Schedule 1 — Matters within sections 1 and 3.
Schedule 2 — Stopping up and diversion of rail crossings.
Schedule 3 — Amendment of Harbours Act 1964.
Schedule 4 — Repeals.
       Part I — Railways and tramways.
       Part II — Harbours.

Transport and Works Act 1992

1992 CHAPTER 42   An Act to provide for the making of orders relating to, or to matters ancillary to, the construction or operation of railways, tramways, trolley vehicle systems, other guided transport systems and inland waterways, and orders relating to, or to matters ancillary to, works interfering with rights of navigation; to make further provision in relation to railways, tramways, trolley vehicle systems and other guided transport systems; to amend certain enactments relating to harbours; and for connected purposes.   [16th March 1992]

BE IT ENACTED by the Queen's most Excellent Majesty, by and with the advice and consent of the Lords Spiritual and Temporal, and Commons, in this present Parliament assembled, and by the authority of the same, as follows:—

PART I   ORDERS AUTHORISING WORKS ETC

Power to make orders

1. Orders as to railways, tramways etc

(1) The Secretary of State may make an order relating to, or to matters ancillary to, the construction or operation of a transport system of any of the following kinds, so far as it is in England and Wales—

    (a) a railway;

    (b) a tramway;

    (c) a trolley vehicle system;

    (d) a system using a mode of guided transport prescribed by order made under section 2 below.

(2) The power to make orders under this section shall be exercisable by statutory instrument.

2. Extension of section 1 to other guided transport systems

(1) The Secretary of State may by order prescribe modes of guided transport for the purposes of section 1(1)(d) above.

(2) The power to make orders under this section shall be exercisable by statutory instrument; but no order shall be made unless a draft of it has been laid before, and approved by a resolution of, each House of Parliament.

3. Orders as to inland waterways etc

(1) The Secretary of State may make an order relating to, or to matters ancillary to—

(a)   the construction or operation of an inland waterway in England and Wales;

(b)   the carrying out of works which—

(i)   interfere with rights of navigation in waters within or adjacent to England and Wales, up to the seaward limits of the territorial sea, and

(ii)   are of a description prescribed by order made under section 4 below.

(2)   The Secretary of State shall not make an order under this section if in his opinion the primary object of the order could be achieved by means of an order under the Harbours Act 1964.

(3)   The power to make orders under this section shall be exercisable by statutory instrument.

4.   Description of works for purposes of section 3

(1)   The Secretary of State may by order prescribe descriptions of works for the purposes of section 3(1)(b) above.

(2)   The power to make orders under this section shall be exercisable by statutory instrument; but no order shall be made unless a draft of it has been laid before, and approved by a resolution of, each House of Parliament.

5.   Subject-matter of orders under sections 1 and 3

(1)   Without prejudice to the generality of sections 1 and 3 above, the matters as to which provision may be made by an order under either of those sections include those set out in Schedule 1 to this Act.

(2)   An order under section 1 or 3 above may make provision in relation to more than one scheme, system or mode of transport.

(3)   An order under section 1 or 3 above may—

(a)   apply, modify or exclude any statutory provision which relates to any matter as to which an order could be made under section 1 or, as the case may be, 3, and

(b)   make such amendments, repeals and revocations of statutory provisions of local application as appear to the Secretary of State to be necessary or expedient in consequence of any provision of the order or otherwise in connection with the order; and for the purposes of this subsection "statutory provision" means provision of an Act of Parliament or of an instrument made under an Act of Parliament.

(4)   The provisions that may be made by an order under section 1 or 3 above include—

(a)   any provision that appears to the Secretary of State to be necessary or expedient for giving full effect to—

(i)   any other provision of the order,

(ii)   any provision of an earlier order under the section concerned, or

(iii)   any provision which is contained in an Act of Parliament passed before the time when this Part of this Act is first wholly in force, or in an instrument made under an Act of Parliament before that time, and which is of a kind which could be included in an order under section 1 or 3 above;

(b)   such supplemental and transitional provisions as appear to him to be necessary or expedient in connection with the order.

(5)   A provision of an order under section 1 or 3 above relating to offences shall not authorise the imposition on persons convicted of an offence of a term of imprisonment or of a fine exceeding level 3 on the standard scale.

(6)   An order under section 1 or 3 above shall not extinguish any public right of way over land unless the Secretary of State is satisfied—
(a)   that an alternative right of way has been or will be provided, or
(b)   that the provision of an alternative right of way is not required.

(7)   Where an order under sections 104(3), 105(3) or 112 of the Transport Act 1968 (classification and maintenance of the British Waterways Board's waterways, and maintenance and use of other waterways) is required so as to give effect to any proposal, no provision shall be included in an order under section 1 or 3 above which would—
(a)   remove that requirement, or
(b)   alter the requirements of sections 104, 105 or 112 of, or Schedule 13 to, that Act relating to orders under those sections.

Procedure for making orders

6. Applications for orders under sections 1 and 3

(1)   Subject to section 7 below, the Secretary of State shall not make an order under section 1 or 3 above except on an application made to him in accordance with rules made under this section.

(2)   The Secretary of State may make rules as to—
(a)   the form of an application under this section;
(b)   the documents and information that must be submitted with it;
(c)   the giving and publication of notices of an application;
(d)   any other steps that must be taken before an application is made or in connection with the making of an application.

(3)   Any provision made by rules as to the consultation that must be carried out before an application is made may include provision requiring compliance with general or special directions given by the Secretary of State.

(4)   Rules under this section may make different provision for different cases, and may include provision authorising the Secretary of State—
(a)   to dispense with compliance with rules that would otherwise apply, or
(b)   to require compliance with rules that would not otherwise apply, in any case where he considers it appropriate to do so.

(5)   Rules may provide for fees of such amounts as may be determined by or in accordance with the rules to be payable to the Secretary of State on the making of applications under this section.

(6)   The power to make rules under this section shall be exercisable by statutory instrument which shall be subject to annulment in pursuance of a resolution of either House of Parliament.

7.   Orders under sections 1 and 3 made otherwise than on application

(1)   The Secretary of State may without any application being made to him make—
(a)   an order under section 1 above which relates to, or to matters ancillary to, the construction for naval, military, air force or other defence purposes of a railway, tramway or other system within section 1(1), or the operation of a railway, tramway or other system constructed for those purposes;
(b)   an order under section 1 or 3 above making any provision which appears to the Secretary of State to be necessary or expedient, in the interests of safety,—

(i)   for the purpose of suspending or discontinuing any operations, or

(ii) in consequence of the abandonment or neglect of any works;

(c)   an order under section 1 or 3 above repealing or revoking provisions which appear to the Secretary of State to be spent.

(2)   An order made by virtue of subsection (1)(b) above may include provision for the recovery by the Secretary of State of the costs of making the order and of carrying its provisions into effect.

(3)   Where the Secretary of State proposes to make an order by virtue of this section, he shall—

(a)   prepare a draft of the order,

(b)   publish a notice of the proposal, containing such particulars as may be prescribed, in the London Gazette and in a local newspaper circulating in the area (or each of the areas) in which any proposed works are to be carried out, and

(c)   give such further notices of the proposal as may be prescribed.

(4)   The power to make provision by rules under section 6 above in relation to applications shall include power to make such corresponding provision as the Secretary of State considers appropriate in relation to proposals to make orders by virtue of this section; and in subsection (3) above "prescribed" means prescribed by rules under section 6.

8.   Model clauses

(1)   The Secretary of State may by order prescribe model provisions for incorporation in any draft orders which, in accordance with rules made under section 6 above, may be required to be submitted with applications under that section.

(2)   Different provisions may be prescribed under this section for different cases.

(3)   The prescribing under this section of a model provision shall not of itself make it mandatory for a provision in the terms of the model to be incorporated in a draft order or in any order eventually made by the Secretary of State under section 1 or 3 above.

(4)   The power to make orders under this section shall be exercisable by statutory instrument.

9.   Schemes of national significance

(1)   This section applies where an application made under section 6 above relates (wholly or in part) to proposals which in the opinion of the Secretary of State are of national significance.

(2)   Before the end of the period of 56 days beginning with the day on which he receives the application, the Secretary of State shall publish in the London Gazette a notice identifying the application and the proposals which in his opinion are of national significance.

(3)   On, or as soon as practicable after, the day on which the notice required by subsection (2) above is published, the Secretary of State shall—

(a)   publish a like notice in a local newspaper circulating in the area (or each of the areas) in which any proposed works are to be carried out, and

(b)   send a copy of the notice to the applicant and to every person within section 11(4) below who objected to the application in accordance with rules made under section 10 below.

(4)　The Secretary of State shall not make an order on the application unless each House of Parliament, on a motion moved by a Minister of the Crown which identifies the proposals referred to above, passes a resolution approving them at some time later than 56 days after the day of publication of the notice required by subsection (2) above.

(5)　An order made on the application shall not include any provision that is inconsistent with a proposal approved by a resolution in accordance with this section unless that provision gives effect to modifications of the proposal which have themselves been approved by a resolution of each House of Parliament passed on a motion moved by a Minister of the Crown.

(6)　This section shall apply in relation to an order which the Secretary of State makes or proposes to make by virtue of section 7 above as it applies in relation to an order for which an application is made to him, except that in such a case—

　　(a)　subsections (2) and (3) above shall not apply, and

　　(b)　subsection (4) above shall apply as if the reference to the notice required by subsection (2) above were a reference to the notice required by section 7(3) above to be published in the London Gazette;

and any proposals which in the opinion of the Secretary of State are of national significance shall be identified as such in any notice required by or under section 7(3) above.

10.　Objections

　(1)　The Secretary of State may make rules as to—

　　(a)　the making of objections to an application under section 6 above or to a proposal to make an order by virtue of section 7 above;

　　(b)　the information to be comprised within or submitted with an objection;

　　(c)　the submission by the person making the application of written representations or information in relation to objections;

　　(d)　the submission of further written representations or information;

　　(e)　such other matters relating to the consideration of objections as appear to the Secretary of State to be appropriate.

　(2)　Subject to the following provisions of this section, the Secretary of State shall not make a determination under section 13(1) below to make an order without first taking into consideration the grounds of any objection in respect of which rules under this section have been complied with.

　(3)　If an objection is withdrawn or appears to the Secretary of State—

　　(a)　to be frivolous or trivial, or

　　(b)　to relate to matters which fall to be determined by a tribunal concerned with the assessment of compensation,

he may make a determination under section 13(1) below without further consideration of the objection.

　(4)　Subsection (2) above shall not apply where the Secretary of State causes an inquiry to be held under section 11(1) below or causes an objection to be dealt with in accordance with section 11(2) below, but the Secretary of State shall not make a determination under section 13(1) below without first taking into consideration the report of the person holding the inquiry, or as the case may be of the person appointed under section 11(2).

(5)   Rules under this section may make different provision for different cases, and may include provision authorising the Secretary of State—

(a)   to dispense with compliance with rules that would otherwise apply, or

(b)   to require compliance with rules that would not otherwise apply,

in any case where he considers it appropriate to do so.

(6)   The power to make rules under this section shall be exercisable by statutory instrument which shall be subject to annulment in pursuance of a resolution of either House of Parliament.

11.   Inquiries and hearings

(1)   The Secretary of State may cause a public local inquiry to be held for the purposes of an application under section 6 above or a proposal by the Secretary of State to make an order by virtue of section 7 above.

(2)   The Secretary of State may give to a person who makes an objection in accordance with rules under section 10 above an opportunity of appearing before and being heard by a person appointed by the Secretary of State for the purpose.

(3)   Where an objection is made by a person within subsection (4) below who informs the Secretary of State in writing that he wishes the objection to be referred to an inquiry or dealt with in accordance with subsection (2) above, then, unless section 10(3) above applies, the Secretary of State shall either cause an inquiry to be held or, if he so determines, cause the objection to be dealt with in accordance with subsection (2).

(4)   The persons within this subsection are—

(a)   any local authority for an area in which any works authorised by the proposed order are to be carried out, and

(b)   where the proposals include the compulsory acquisition of land, any person who, if Part II of the Acquisition of Land Act 1981 (notice to owners, lessees and occupiers) applied to the acquisition, would be entitled to a notice under section 12 of that Act;

and for the purposes of paragraph (a) above "local authority" means a county council, a district council, a London borough council, the Common Council of the City of London, the Council of the Isles of Scilly and a Passenger Transport Executive.

(5)   Subsections (2) to (5) of section 250 of the Local Government Act 1972 (attendance and evidence at, and costs of, inquiries) shall apply to an inquiry held under subsection (1) above; but—

(a)   in its application by virtue of this subsection, section 250(4) shall have effect with the omission of the words "and any amount" onwards, and

(b)   the power to make an order as to costs under section 250(5) as applied by this subsection shall be exercisable not only where the inquiry takes place but also where arrangements are made for it but it does not take place.

(6)   Subsections (4) and (5) of section 250 of the Local Government Act 1972 (costs) shall apply in relation to proceedings under subsection (2) above as they apply in relation to an inquiry under subsection (1) above.

12.   Special parliamentary procedure

(1)   An order under section 1 or 3 above authorising a compulsory purchase shall be subject to special parliamentary procedure to the same extent as it would be, by virtue of section 18 or 19 of the Acquisition of Land Act 1981 (or by virtue

of paragraph 5 or 6 of Schedule 3 to that Act) (National Trust land, commons etc), if the purchase were authorised by an order under section 2(1) of that Act.

(2)   In section 3 of the Statutory Orders (Special Procedure) Act 1945 (petitions against orders subject to special parliamentary procedure) after subsection (4) there shall be inserted—

"(4A)   The Chairmen shall not certify that a petition is proper to be received if the order to which it relates is made under section 1 or 3 of the Transport and Works Act 1992 and either—

(a)   the petition is a petition of general objection and the order relates to proposals which have been approved by each House of Parliament in accordance with section 9 of that Act, or

(b)   the petition is a petition for amendment and any of the amendments asked for would in the opinion of the Chairmen be inconsistent with such proposals."

(3)   In relation to an order under section 1 or 3 above which is subject to special parliamentary procedure—

(a)   section 13(5) below shall not apply,

(b)   section 22 below shall not apply if the order is confirmed by Act of Parliament under section 6 of the Statutory Orders (Special Procedure) Act 1945, and

(c)   in any other case, section 22(1) below shall have effect as if for the reference to the day on which the notice required by section 14(1)(b) is published there were substituted a reference to the day on which the order comes into operation under the Statutory Orders (Special Procedure) Act 1945.

13.   Making or refusal of orders under section 1 or 3

(1)   Where an application has been made to the Secretary of State under section 6 above, or he proposes to make an order by virtue of section 7 above, and (in either case) the requirements of the preceding provisions of this Act in relation to any objections have been satisfied, he shall determine—

(a)   to make an order under section 1 or 3 above which gives effect to the proposals concerned without modifications, or

(b)   to make an order which gives effect to those proposals with modifications, or

(c)   not to make an order.

(2)   Where an application has been made to the Secretary of State under section 6 above and he considers that any of the objects of the order applied for could be achieved by other means, he may on that ground determine not to make the order (but this subsection is without prejudice to subsection (3) below).

(3)   The power of the Secretary of State to make a determination under subsection (1) above includes power to make a determination in respect of some only of the proposals concerned, while making a separate determination in respect of, or deferring consideration of, others (and accordingly the power to make an order under section 1 or 3 above includes power to make two or more orders on the same application).

(4)   Where the Secretary of State proposes to make an order which gives effect to the proposals concerned with modifications which will in his opinion make a substantial change in the proposals—

(a) he shall notify any person who appears to him to be likely to be affected by the modifications,

(b) he shall give that person an opportunity of making representations to him about the modifications within such period as he may specify in the notice, and

(c) he shall before making the order consider any representations duly made to him.

(5) An order under section 1 or 3 above shall come into operation on the date on which the notice required by subsection (1)(b) of section 14 below is first published, or on such later date, if any, as may be specified in the order.

14. Publicity for making or refusal of orders

(1) As soon as practicable after making a determination under section 13(1) above, the Secretary of State shall—

(a) give notice of the determination to the person (if any) who applied for the order and to every person who made an objection which was referred to an inquiry or hearing in accordance with section 11(3) above, and

(b) publish a notice of the determination in the London Gazette.

(2) A notice under subsection (1)(a) above shall state the reasons for the determination.

(3) A notice under subsection (1) above of a determination to make an order shall give such particulars of the terms of the order as the Secretary of State considers appropriate, and in particular shall (except where the order is made by virtue of section 7 above) state the name and address of the person who applied for the order.

(4) Where the Secretary of State determines to make an order, the person who applied for the order (or, where the order is made by virtue of section 7 above, the Secretary of State) shall publish a copy of the notice given to him under subsection (1) above in a local newspaper circulating in the area (or each of the areas) in which any works authorised by the order are to be carried out.

(5) As soon as practicable after the making of an order under section 1 or 3 above, the person who applied for the order (or, where the order is made by virtue of section 7 above, the Secretary of State) shall—

(a) deposit in the office of the Clerk of the Parliaments a copy of the order, and of any plan or book of reference prepared in connection with the application (or proposed order), and

(b) deposit with each of the councils mentioned in subsection (7) below in whose area works authorised by the order are to be carried out a copy of each of those documents, or of so much of them as is relevant to those works.

(6) Where a plan or book of reference is revised before the order is made, the reference in subsection (5)(a) above is to the latest version.

(7) The councils referred to in subsection (5) above are district councils, London borough councils and the Common Council of the City of London.

(8) A council with which documents are deposited in accordance with subsection (5) above shall make them available for inspection free of charge at all reasonable hours.

Consents etc under other enactments

15. Assimilation of procedures

(1) This section applies to applications made under section 6 above relating to proposals for the purposes of which the giving of a consent, permission or licence under any enactment, or the making or confirmation of an order under any enactment, is required.

(2) The Secretary of State may make regulations for securing that, where the requirement referred to in subsection (1) above would not be removed by the order to which the application relates—

(a) the procedure for obtaining, or otherwise relating to, the consent, permission, licence, order or confirmation, and

(b) the procedure relating to the application made under section 6 above, are wholly or partly assimilated (and in particular that proceedings relating to the one may be held concurrently with proceedings relating to the other).

(3) Regulations under this section may include provision—

(a) excluding or modifying the application of any enactment;

(b) authorising the Secretary of State to give directions or take such other steps as may be appropriate for the purpose of securing the object mentioned in subsection (2) above.

(4) The power to make regulations under this section shall be exercisable by statutory instrument, which shall be subject to annulment in pursuance of a resolution of either House of Parliament.

(5) This section shall apply to proposals by the Secretary of State to make orders by virtue of section 7 above as it applies to applications under section 6 above.

16. Town and country planning

(1) In section 90 of the Town and Country Planning Act 1990 (which gives power to deem planning permission to be granted in certain cases where development is authorised by a government department) after subsection (2) there shall be inserted—

"(2A) On making an order under section 1 or 3 of the Transport and Works Act 1992 which includes provision for development, the Secretary of State may direct that planning permission for that development shall be deemed to be granted, subject to such conditions (if any) as may be specified in the direction."

(2) In Schedule 13 to the Town and Country Planning Act 1990 (blighted land) after paragraph 22 there shall be added—

"23. Land—

(a) the compulsory acquisition of which is authorised by an order under section 1 or 3 of the Transport and Works Act 1992, or

(b) which falls within the limits of deviation within which powers of compulsory acquisition conferred by such an order are exercisable, or

(c) which is the subject of a proposal, contained in an application made in accordance with rules under section 6 of that Act or in a draft order prepared under section 7(3) of that Act, that it should be such land."

17. Listed buildings and conservation areas

In section 12 of the Planning (Listed Buildings and Conservation Areas Act 1990, after subsection (3) there shall be inserted—

"(3A) An application for listed building consent shall, without any direction by the Secretary of State, be referred to the Secretary of State instead of being dealt with by the local planning authority in any case where the consent is required in consequence of proposals included in an application for an order under section 1 or 3 of the Transport and Works Act 1992."

18. Hazardous substances

In section 12 of the Planning (Hazardous Substances) Act 1990 (which gives power to deem hazardous substances consent to be granted in certain cases) after subsection (2) there shall be inserted—

"(2A) On making an order under section 1 or 3 of the Transport and Works Act 1992 which includes any provision that would involve the presence of a hazardous substance in circumstances requiring hazardous substances consent, the Secretary of State may direct that hazardous substances consent shall be deemed to be granted, subject to such conditions (if any) as may be specified in the direction."

19. Coast Protection Act 1949

In section 35 of the Coast Protection Act 1949 (which excepts certain operations from the requirement to obtain the Secretary of State's consent under section 34) in subsection (1) there shall be added after paragraph (g)—

"(h) any operations authorised by an order under section 1 or 3 of the Transport and Works Act 1992."

20. Power to apply for, or object to, orders

(1) A body which has power to promote or power to oppose Bills in Parliament shall also have power to apply for, or as the case may be power to object to, orders under sections 1 and 3 above.

(2) Where the power of a body to promote or to oppose Bills is subject to any condition, then, except as provided by subsection (3) below, the corresponding power conferred on the body by subsection (1) above shall be subject to the like condition.

(3) The powers conferred by subsection (1) above on—

    (a) the British Railways Board,

    (b) the British Waterways Board, and

    (c) London Regional Transport,

shall be exercisable without the consent of the Secretary of State.

21. Transport Consultative Committees

(1) In section 56 of the Transport Act 1962 (which establishes a Central Transport Consultative Committee and Area Transport Users Consultative Committees) after subsection (6) there shall be inserted—

"(6A) An Area Committee may consider, and if they think fit object to, any proposal for the discontinuance of railway services made in an application for an order under section 1 of the Transport and Works Act 1992 or made by the Secretary of State by virtue of section 7 of that Act."

(2)   In section 41 of the London Regional Transport Act 1984 (which provides for the London Regional Passenger Committee to be treated as an Area Transport Users Consultative Committee for certain purposes) in subsection (2)(c) for "(7)" there shall be substituted "(6A)".

Miscellaneous

22.   Validity of orders under section 1 or 3

(1)   If a person aggrieved by an order under section 1 or 3 above desires to question the validity of it, or of any provision contained in it, on the ground—

(a)   that it is not within the powers of this Act, or

(b)   that any requirement imposed by or under this Act or the Tribunals and Inquiries Act 1971 has not been complied with,

he may, within the period of 42 days beginning with the day on which the notice required by section 14(1)(b) above is published, make an application for the purpose to the High Court.

(2)   On any such application, the court—

(a)   may by interim order suspend the operation of the order, or of any provision contained in it, either generally or in so far as it affects any property of the applicant, until the final determination of the proceedings, and

(b)   if satisfied that the order or any provision contained in it is not within the powers of this Act, or that the interests of the applicant have been substantially prejudiced by a failure to comply with any requirement imposed by or under this Act or the Tribunals and Inquiries Act 1971, may quash the order or any provision contained in it, either generally or in so far as it affects any property of the applicant.

(3)   Subject to subsections (1) and (2) above, an order under section 1 or 3 above shall not, either before or after it has been made, be questioned in any legal proceedings whatever.

23.   Exercise of Secretary of State's functions by appointed person

(1)   The Secretary of State may by regulations prescribe classes of application which are to be dealt with by a person appointed by the Secretary of State for the purpose instead of by the Secretary of State.

(2)   The Secretary of State may if he thinks fit direct that an application which would otherwise fall to be determined by an appointed person shall be determined by the Secretary of State.

(3)   Subject to subsection (4) below, a person appointed under this section shall have in relation to the application—

(a)   the same powers and duties as the Secretary of State has under sections 1 and 3 above, and

(b)   such other powers and duties conferred on the Secretary of State under or by virtue of this Part of this Act as may be specified in the regulations; and for that purpose any reference in any Act or instrument (including this Act and any instrument made under it) to the Secretary of State, or to anything done or authorised or required to be done by or to the Secretary of State, shall be construed, so far as the context permits and subject to regulations under this section, as a reference to that person.

(4)   An order made on an application dealt with by a person appointed under this section shall not authorise the compulsory acquisition of land, or the compulsory creation or extinguishment of rights over land (including rights of navigation over water).

(5)   Where an application has been dealt with by a person appointed under this section, any order made by him under section 1 or 3 shall be treated as made by the Secretary of State.

(6)   At any time before the appointed person has determined the application the Secretary of State may—

(a)   revoke his appointment, and

(b)   appoint another person under subsection (1) above to deal with the application instead;

and where such a new appointment is made the consideration of the application shall begin afresh, except to the extent that regulations under this section provide otherwise.

(7)   If the Secretary of State exercises the power conferred on him by subsection (6)(a) above, he shall give reasons to the appointed person for revoking his appointment.

(8)   Regulations under this section may provide for the giving of publicity to any directions given by the Secretary of State under subsection (2) above and to any appointment made by virtue of subsection (6) above.

(9)   The Tribunals and Inquiries Act 1971 shall apply to a local inquiry or other hearing by a person appointed under this section as it applies to a statutory inquiry held by the Secretary of State, but as if in section 12(1) of that Act (statement of reasons for decisions) the reference to any decision taken by the Secretary of State were a reference to a decision taken by an appointed person.

(10)   Where a person appointed under this section is an officer of the Department of Transport, the Department of the Environment, the Department of Energy or the Welsh Office, his functions shall be treated for the purposes of the Parliamentary Commissioner Act 1967—

(a)   if he was appointed by the Secretary of State for the time being having general responsibility in transport matters, as functions of the Department of Transport;

(b)   if he was appointed by the Secretary of State for the time being having general responsibility in planning matters in relation to England, as functions of the Department of the Environment;

(c)   if he was appointed by the Secretary of State for the time being having general responsibility in energy matters, as functions of the Department of Energy;

(d)   if he was appointed by the Secretary of State for the time being having general responsibility in planning matters in relation to Wales, as functions of the Welsh Office.

(11)   The power to make regulations under this section shall be exercisable by statutory instrument, which shall be subject to annulment in pursuance of a resolution of either House of Parliament.

24.   Private legislation procedure in Scotland

In section 1 of the Private Legislation Procedure (Scotland) Act 1936 (which requires the promotion of Provisional Orders rather than Private Bills in connection with powers relating to Scotland), in subsection (4) (which provides an exception from the requirement in certain cases relating to Scotland and elsewhere if the promotion of a Private Bill would be more appropriate than the promotion of a Private Bill and a Provisional Order) after the words "Provisional Order" there shall be inserted the words "(or a Provisional Order and an order under section 1 or 3 of the Transport and Works Act 1992)".

25. Crown land

(1) If the appropriate authority agrees—

    (a) an interest which—

        (i) subsists in land in which there is a Crown or Duchy interest, but

        (ii) is not itself a Crown or Duchy interest,

may be acquired compulsorily by virtue of an order under section 1 or 3 above, and

    (b) any provision of this Act or of such an order (other than a provision by virtue of which an interest in land is compulsorily acquired) may apply in relation to land in which there is a Crown or Duchy interest.

(2) In this section "Crown or Duchy interest" means an interest belonging to Her Majesty in right of the Crown or of the Duchy of Lancaster, or belonging to the Duchy of Cornwall, or belonging to a government department, or held in trust for Her Majesty for the purposes of a government department.

(3) In this section "the appropriate authority" means—

    (a) in the case of land belonging to Her Majesty in right of the Crown and forming part of the Crown Estate, the Crown Estate Commissioners;

    (b) in the case of other land belonging to Her Majesty in right of the Crown, the government department having the management of the land;

    (c) in the case of land belonging to Her Majesty in right of the Duchy of Lancaster, the Chancellor of the Duchy;

    (d) in the case of land belonging to the Duchy of Cornwall, such person as the Duke of Cornwall, or the possessor for the time being of the Duchy of Cornwall, appoints;

    (e) in the case of land belonging to a government department or held in trust for Her Majesty for the purposes of a government department, that department.

(4) If any question arises as to what authority is the appropriate authority in relation to any land, that question shall be referred to the Treasury, whose decision shall be final.

PART II   SAFETY OF RAILWAYS ETC

CHAPTER I   OFFENCES INVOLVING DRINK OR DRUGS

Preliminary

26. Transport systems to which Chapter I applies

(1) This Chapter applies to transport systems of any of the following kinds—

    (a) a railway;

    (b) a tramway;

    (c)   a system which uses another mode of guided transport and is specified for the purposes of this Chapter by an order made by the Secretary of State.

    (2)   This Chapter shall not apply to a transport system unless it is used, or is intended to be used, wholly or partly for the carriage of members of the public.

    (3)   The power to make orders under this section shall be exercisable by statutory instrument, which shall be subject to annulment in pursuance of a resolution of either House of Parliament.

Principal offences

27.   Offences involving drink or drugs on transport systems

    (1)   If a person works on a transport system to which this Chapter applies—

    (a)   as a driver, guard, conductor or signalman or in any other capacity in which he can control or affect the movement of a vehicle, or

    (b)   in a maintenance capacity or as a supervisor of, or look-out for, persons working in a maintenance capacity,

when he is unfit to carry out that work through drink or drugs, he shall be guilty of an offence.

    (2)   If a person works on a transport system to which this Chapter applies—

    (a)   as a driver, guard, conductor or signalman or in any other capacity in which he can control or affect the movement of a vehicle, or

    (b)   in a maintenance capacity or as a supervisor of, or look-out for, persons working in a maintenance capacity,

after consuming so much alcohol that the proportion of it in his breath, blood or urine exceeds the prescribed limit, he shall be guilty of an offence.

    (3)   For the purposes of this section, a person works on a transport system in a maintenance capacity if his work on the system involves maintenance, repair or alteration of—

    (a)   the permanent way or other means of guiding or supporting vehicles,

    (b)   signals or any other means of controlling the movement of vehicles, or

    (c)   any means of supplying electricity to vehicles or to the means of guiding or supporting vehicles,

or involves coupling or uncoupling vehicles or checking that they are working properly before they are used on any occasion.

    (4)   For the purposes of subsection (1) above, a person shall be taken to be unfit to carry out any work if his ability to carry out that work properly is for the time being impaired.

28.   Offences by operators of transport systems

    (1)   If a person commits an offence under section 27 above, the responsible operator shall also be guilty of an offence.

    (2)   In this section "the responsible operator" means—

    (a)   in a case where the transport system on which the offence under section 27 above is committed has only one operator, that operator;

    (b)   in a case where the transport system on which the offence under section 27 above is committed has more than one operator, whichever of them is responsible for the work giving rise to the offence.

    (3)   No offence is committed under subsection (1) above if the responsible

operator has exercised all due diligence to prevent the commission on the transport system of any offence under section 27 above.

(4)   If a person commits an offence under section 27 above in the course of his employment with a person other than the responsible operator, his employer shall (without prejudice to any liability of that operator under subsection (1) above) also be guilty of an offence.

(5)   No offence is committed under subsection (4) above if the employer has exercised all due diligence to prevent the commission on the transport system by any of his employees of any offence under section 27 above.

Police powers etc

29.   Breath tests

(1)   Where a constable in uniform has reasonable cause to suspect—

(a)   that a person working on a transport system to which this Chapter applies in any capacity mentioned in section 27(1) and (2) above has alcohol in his body, or

(b)   that a person has been working on a transport system to which this Chapter applies in any capacity mentioned in section 27(1) and (2) above with alcohol in his body and still has alcohol in his body,
he may require that person to provide a specimen of breath for a breath test.

(2)   Where an accident or dangerous incident occurs on a transport system to which this Chapter applies, a constable in uniform may require a person to provide a specimen of breath for a breath test if he has reasonable cause to suspect that—

(a)   at the time of the accident or incident that person was working on the transport system in a capacity mentioned in section 27(1) and (2) above, and

(b)   an act or omission of that person while he was so working may have been a cause of the accident or incident.

(3)   In subsection (2) above "dangerous incident" means an incident which in the constable's opinion involved a danger of death or personal injury.

(4)   A person may be required under subsection (1) or subsection (2) above to provide a specimen either at or near the place where the requirement is made or, if the requirement is made under subsection (2) above and the constable making the requirement thinks fit, at a police station specified by the constable.

(5)   A person who, without reasonable excuse, fails to provide a specimen of breath when required to do so in pursuance of this section shall be guilty of an offence.

30.   Powers of arrest and entry

(1)   A constable may arrest a person without warrant if he has reasonable cause to suspect that that person is or has been committing an offence under section 27(1) above.

(2)   A constable may arrest a person without warrant if—

(a)   as a result of a breath test under section 29 above he has reasonable cause to suspect that the proportion of alcohol in that person's breath or blood exceeds the prescribed limit, or

(b)   that person has failed to provide a specimen of breath for a breath test when required to do so in pursuance of section 29 above and the constable has reasonable cause to suspect that he has alcohol in his body.

(3)   For the purpose of arresting a person under subsection (1) above, a constable may enter (if need be by force) any place where that person is or where the constable, with reasonable cause, suspects him to be.

(4)   A constable may, for the purpose of—

(a)   requiring a person to provide a specimen of breath under section 29(2) above in the case of an accident which the constable has reasonable cause to suspect involved the death of, or injury to, another person, or

(b)   arresting a person in such a case under subsection (2) above,

enter (if need be by force) any place where that person is or where the constable, with reasonable cause, suspects him to be.

31.   Provision of specimens for analysis

(1)   In the course of an investigation into whether a person has committed an offence under section 27 above, a constable may require him—

(a)   to provide two specimens of breath for analysis by means of a device of a type approved by the Secretary of State, or

(b)   to provide a specimen of blood or urine for a laboratory test.

(2)   A requirement under this section to provide specimens of breath shall only be made at a police station.

(3)   A requirement under this section to provide a specimen of blood or urine shall only be made at a police station or at a hospital; and it shall not be made at a police station unless subsection (4) below applies.

(4)   This subsection applies if—

(a)   the constable making the requirement has reasonable cause to believe that for medical reasons a specimen of breath cannot be provided or should not be required,

(b)   at the time the requirement is made, either a device (or reliable device) of the type mentioned in subsection (1)(a) above is not available at the police station or it is for any other reason not practicable to use such a device there, or

(c)   the suspected offence is one under section 27(1) above and the constable making the requirement has been advised by a medical practitioner that the condition of the person required to provide the specimen might be due to a drug.

(5)   A person may be required to provide a specimen of blood or urine in pursuance of this section notwithstanding that he has already provided or been required to provide two specimens of breath.

(6)   If the provision of a specimen other than a specimen of breath may be required in pursuance of this section, the question whether it is to be a specimen of blood or a specimen of urine shall be decided by the constable making the requirement; but if a medical practitioner is of the opinion that for medical reasons a specimen of blood cannot or should not be taken, the specimen shall be a specimen of urine.

(7)   A specimen of urine shall be provided within one hour of the requirement for its provision being made and after the provision of a previous specimen of urine.

(8)   A person who, without reasonable excuse, fails to provide a specimen when required to do so in pursuance of this section shall be guilty of an offence.

(9)   A constable shall, on requiring a person to provide a specimen in

pursuance of this section, warn him that a failure to provide it may render him liable to prosecution.

32. Choice of specimens of breath

(1)   Of any two specimens of breath provided by a person in pursuance of section 31 above, the one with the lower proportion of alcohol in the breath shall be used and the other shall be disregarded.

(2)   But if the specimen with the lower proportion of alcohol contains no more than 50 microgrammes of alcohol in 100 millilitres of breath, the person who provided it may claim that it should be replaced by such specimen as may be required under section 31(6) above and, if he then provides such a specimen, neither specimen of breath shall be used.

(3)   The Secretary of State may by regulations substitute another proportion of alcohol in the breath for that specified in subsection (2) above.

(4)   The power to make regulations under this section shall be exercisable by statutory instrument; and no such regulations shall be made unless a draft of the instrument containing them has been laid before, and approved by a resolution of, each House of Parliament.

33. Protection for hospital patients

(1)   While a person is at a hospital as a patient, he shall not be required to provide a specimen of breath for a breath test or to provide a specimen for a laboratory test unless the medical practitioner in immediate charge of his case has been notified of the proposal to make the requirement; and—

(a)   if the requirement is then made, it shall be for the provision of a specimen at the hospital, but

(b)   if the medical practitioner objects on the ground specified in subsection (2) below, the requirement shall not be made.

(2)   The ground on which the medical practitioner may object is that the requirement or the provision of a specimen or (in the case of a specimen of blood or urine) the warning required under section 31(9) above would be prejudicial to the proper care and treatment of the patient.

(3)   A person shall not be arrested under section 30(2) above while he is at a hospital as a patient.

Evidence in proceedings for offences under section 27

34. Use of specimens in proceedings

(1)   In proceedings for any offence under section 27 above—

(a)   evidence of the proportion of alcohol or any drug in a specimen of breath, blood or urine provided by the accused shall be taken into account, and

(b)   it shall be assumed that the proportion of alcohol in the accused's breath, blood or urine at the time of the alleged offence was not less than in the specimen.

(2)   That assumption shall not be made if the accused proves—

(a)   that he consumed alcohol before he provided the specimen and after he had stopped work on the occasion of the alleged offence, and

(b)   that, had he not done so, the proportion of alcohol in his breath, blood or urine would not have exceeded the prescribed limit and, where the offence alleged is an offence of being unfit to carry out the work in question through drink, would not have been such as to impair his ability to carry out that work properly.

(3) Where, at the time a specimen of blood or urine was provided by the accused, he asked to be provided with such a specimen, evidence of the proportion of alcohol or any drug found in the specimen shall not be admissible in the proceedings on behalf of the prosecution unless—

(a) the specimen in which the alcohol or drug was found is one of two parts into which the specimen provided by the accused was divided at the time it was provided, and

(b) the other part was supplied to the accused.

35. Documentary evidence as to specimens

(1) In proceedings for any offence under section 27 above, evidence of the proportion of alcohol in a specimen of breath may be given by the production of a document (or documents) purporting to be—

(a) a statement automatically produced by the device by which the proportion of alcohol in the specimen was measured, and

(b) a certificate signed by a constable (which may but need not be contained in the same document as the statement) that the specimen was provided by the accused at the date and time shown in the statement.

(2) In such proceedings, evidence of the proportion of alcohol or a drug in a specimen of blood or urine may be given by the production of a document purporting to be a certificate signed by an authorised analyst identifying the specimen and stating the proportion of alcohol or drug found in it.

(3) In such proceedings, evidence that a specimen of blood was taken from the accused with his consent by a medical practitioner may be given by the production of a document purporting to be a certificate to that effect signed by the practitioner.

(4) A document such as is mentioned in subsection (1) above shall be admissible in evidence on behalf of the prosecution in pursuance of this section only if a copy of it either was handed to the accused when the document was produced or was served on him not later than seven days before the hearing.

(5) A document such as is mentioned in subsection (2) or (3) above shall be admissible in evidence on behalf of the prosecution in pursuance of this section only if a copy of it was served on the accused not later than seven days before the hearing.

(6) A document purporting to be a certificate (or so much of a document as purports to be a certificate) shall not be admissible in evidence on behalf of the prosecution in pursuance of this section if the accused, not later than three days before the hearing or within such further time as the court may in special circumstances allow, has served notice on the prosecutor requiring the attendance at the hearing of the person by whom the document purports to be signed.

(7) In this section "served" means served personally or sent by registered post or recorded delivery service.

(8) In subsection (2) above "authorised analyst" means—

(a) any person possessing the qualifications prescribed by regulations made under section 76 of the Food Act 1984 or section 27 of the Food and Drugs (Scotland) Act 1956 as qualifying persons for appointment as public analysts under those Acts, or

(b)   any other person authorised by the Secretary of State to make analyses for the purposes of this section.

Penalties

36.   Penalties

(1)   A person guilty of any offence under this Chapter other than an offence under section 29(5) above shall be liable on summary conviction to imprisonment for a term not exceeding six months, to a fine not exceeding level 5 on the standard scale or to both.

(2)   A person guilty of an offence under section 29(5) above shall be liable on summary conviction to a fine not exceeding level 3 on the standard scale.

Miscellaneous and supplementary

37.   Special provision for Scotland

(1)   Section 30(3) and (4) above shall not extend to Scotland, and nothing in those subsections shall affect any rule of law in Scotland concerning the right of a constable to enter any premises for any purpose.

(2)   In proceedings for any offence under section 27 above in Scotland—

(a)   a document produced in evidence on behalf of the prosecution in pursuance of section 35 above and, where the person by whom the document was signed is called as a witness, the evidence of that person, shall be sufficient evidence of the facts stated in the document, and

(b)   a written execution purporting to be signed by the person who handed to or served on the accused or the prosecutor a copy document or notice under section 35 above, together with, where appropriate, a post office receipt for the relevant registered or recorded delivery letter, shall be sufficient evidence of the handing or service of the copy document or notice.

38.   Interpretation of Chapter I

(1)   In this Chapter—

"breath test" means a preliminary test for the purpose of obtaining, by means of a device of a type approved by the Secretary of State, an indication whether the proportion of alcohol in a person's breath or blood is likely to exceed the prescribed limit;

"drug" includes any intoxicant other than alcohol;

"fail" includes refuse; "hospital" means an institution which provides medical or surgical treatment for in-patients or out-patients.

(2)   In this Chapter "the prescribed limit" means, as the case may require—

(a)   35 microgrammes of alcohol in 100 millilitres of breath,

(b)   80 milligrammes of alcohol in 100 millilitres of blood, or

(c)   107 milligrammes of alcohol in 100 millilitres of urine,

or such other proportion as may be prescribed by regulations made by the Secretary of State.

(3)   For the purposes of this Chapter, it is immaterial whether a person who works on a transport system does so in the course of his employment, under a contract for services, voluntarily or otherwise.

(4)   For the purposes of this Chapter, a person does not provide a specimen of breath for a breath test or for analysis unless the specimen—

(a)   is sufficient to enable the test or the analysis to be carried out, and

(b)   is provided in such a way as to enable the objective of the test or analysis to be satisfactorily achieved.

(5)   For the purposes of this Chapter, a person provides a specimen of blood if and only if he consents to its being taken by a medical practitioner and it is so taken.

(6)   The power to make regulations under subsection (2) above shall be exercisable by statutory instrument; and no such regulations shall be made unless a draft of the instrument containing them has been laid before, and approved by a resolution of, each House of Parliament.

39.   Amendment of scope of offences involving drink or drugs under Road Traffic Act 1988

The following section shall be inserted in the Road Traffic Act 1988 after section 192—

"192A.   Tramcars and other guided vehicles: drink and drugs

(1)   Sections 4 to 11 of this Act shall not apply (to the extent that apart from this subsection they would) to vehicles on any transport system to which Chapter I of Part II of the Transport and Works Act 1992 (offences involving drink or drugs on railways, tramways and certain other guided transport systems) applies.

(2)   Subject to subsection (1) above, the Secretary of State may by regulations provide that sections 4 to 11 of this Act shall apply to vehicles on a system of guided transport specified in the regulations with such modifications as he considers necessary or expedient.

(3)   Regulations under subsection (2) above may make different provision for different cases.

(4)   In this section—

"guided transport" means transport by vehicles guided by means external to the vehicles (whether or not the vehicles are also capable of being operated in some other way), and

"vehicle" includes mobile traction unit."

40.   Consequential amendment

In section 17 of the Railway Regulation Act 1842 (punishment of persons employed on railways guilty of misconduct) the words "who shall be found drunk while so employed upon the said railway" shall be omitted.

CHAPTER II   OTHER SAFETY PROVISIONS

General

41.   Approval of works, plant and equipment

(1)   For the purpose of securing the safe operation of railways, tramways, trolley vehicle systems and prescribed systems of guided transport, the Secretary of State may make regulations requiring that his approval be obtained before—

(a)   new works, plant or equipment are first brought into use, or

(b)   works, plant or equipment are first brought into use after alterations have been made to them.

(2)   Regulations under this section—

(a) shall prescribe the cases in which approval is required and the procedure for obtaining it;

(b) may include provision as to the time when works, plant or equipment are to be treated as first brought into use, including provision for disregarding periods of testing and other periods of use before sufficient information is available for a decision to be made on an application for approval;

(c) may include provision prohibiting the giving of false information to the Secretary of State.

(3) Regulations under this section may make different provision for different cases, and may include provision authorising the Secretary of State—

(a) to dispense (conditionally or unconditionally) with compliance with regulations that would otherwise apply, or

(b) to require compliance with regulations that would not otherwise apply, either in the case of any particular works, plant, equipment or alterations, or in the case of works, plant, equipment or alterations of such descriptions as he may determine.

(4) Regulations under this section may provide that any person who without reasonable cause contravenes any specified provision of the regulations, or does so in specified circumstances, shall be guilty of an offence under this section.

(5) Where the commission by any person of an offence under this section is due to the act or default of some other person, that other person shall be guilty of the offence, and a person may be charged with and convicted of the offence by virtue of this subsection whether or not proceedings are taken against the first-mentioned person.

(6) A person guilty of an offence under this section shall be liable on summary conviction to a fine not exceeding level 5 on the standard scale.

(7) In this section—

"equipment" includes vehicles;

"prescribed systems of guided transport" means systems using a mode of guided transport prescribed by regulations under this section.

(8) The power to make regulations under this section shall be exercisable by statutory instrument, which shall be subject to annulment in pursuance of a resolution of either House of Parliament.

42. Inspectors

(1) The functions of inspectors appointed under section 3 of the Regulation of Railways Act 1871 shall extend not only to railways (as defined by section 2 of that Act) but also to other railways and tramways, to trolley vehicle systems and to any system using a mode of guided transport prescribed by regulations under section 41 above; and in any enactment relating to those functions—

(a) references to railways or matters relating to railways shall be construed accordingly, and

(b) references to a company working a railway shall have effect as references to an operator of a railway, tramway, trolley vehicle system or system using a mode of guided transport prescribed by such regulations.

(2) In section 3 of the Regulation of Railways Act 1871, the proviso (which prohibits an inspector from interfering in the affairs of a company) shall cease to have effect.

43. Accidents etc

(1) The Secretary of State may make regulations requiring the reporting to him of—

(a) accidents involving death or personal injury, and

(b) circumstances involving a danger of death or personal injury,

which occur in the operation of railways, tramways, trolley vehicle systems and systems using a mode of guided transport prescribed by the regulations.

(2) Regulations under this section shall prescribe the cases in which reports are required, the persons required to make them, the time and manner in which they are to be made, and the particulars to be included in them.

(3) Regulations under this section may make different provision for different cases, and may include provision authorising the Secretary of State—

(a) to dispense with compliance with any provision of the regulations that would otherwise apply, or

(b) to require compliance with any provision that would not otherwise apply,

in any case where he considers it appropriate to do so.

(4) A person who, without reasonable excuse, fails to make a report as required by regulations under this section shall be guilty of an offence.

(5) A person guilty of an offence under this section shall be liable on summary conviction to a fine not exceeding level 2 on the standard scale.

(6) The power to make regulations under this section shall be exercisable by statutory instrument, which shall be subject to annulment in pursuance of a resolution of either House of Parliament.

44. Accidents etc: consequential amendments

(1) Section 6 of the Regulation of Railways Act 1871 (which is superseded by section 43 above) shall cease to have effect.

(2) In section 7 of that Act (inquiries into accidents etc)—

(a) for the words "this Act" (in the words preceding the paragraphs) there shall be substituted the words "regulations under section 43 of the Transport and Works Act 1992";

(b) after paragraph (4) there shall be added—

"In this section any reference to an accident includes a reference to circumstances involving a danger of death or personal injury."

(3) In section 8 of that Act (appointment of assessor to coroner) for the words "of this Act" there shall be substituted the words "of regulations under section 43 of the Transport and Works Act 1992".

45. Directions limiting speeds and loads

(1) The Secretary of State may give a direction under this section to any person carrying on an undertaking which includes the provision of transport services on a railway, tramway or system using any other mode of guided transport.

(2) A direction under this section may impose—

(a) maximum speeds at which vehicles in use on the system may travel, and

(b) maximum weights that may be transmitted to the rails (or other structures which support vehicles in use on the system) by any one pair of wheels, or by such other parts of the vehicles as may be specified in the direction.

(3)   Directions under this section may make different provision for different vehicles, different parts of the system, or otherwise for different circumstances.

(4)   Before giving a direction under this section, the Secretary of State shall consult the person to whom he proposes to give it.

(5)   If a direction under this section is contravened in the course of the provision of transport services by the person to whom the direction was given, that person shall be guilty of an offence.

(6)   A person guilty of an offence under this section shall be liable on summary conviction to a fine not exceeding level 5 on the standard scale.

46.   Directions requiring insurance

(1)   The Secretary of State may give a direction under this section to an operator of a railway, tramway, trolley vehicle system or system using any other mode of guided transport.

(2)   A direction under this section may require the person to whom it is given to ensure that there are at all times in force such policies of insurance against liability in respect of death or personal injury as comply with the requirements of the direction.

(3)   Before giving a direction under this section, the Secretary of State shall consult the person to whom he proposes to give it.

(4)   If a direction under this section is contravened, the person to whom the direction was given shall be guilty of an offence.

(5)   A person guilty of an offence under this section shall be liable on summary conviction to a fine not exceeding level 5 on the standard scale.

Rail crossings

47.   Stopping up and diversion of crossings

(1)   Schedule 2 to this Act (which amends the Highways Act 1980 so as to provide for the stopping up or diversion of footpaths and bridleways crossing railways and tramways) shall have effect.

(2)   Where a public right of way over a footpath or bridleway where it crosses a railway or tramway is extinguished by an order under sections 118 to 119A of the Highways Act 1980, any obligation (however imposed) to maintain the crossing for the benefit of the public shall cease to have effect.

48.   Footpaths and bridleways over railways

(1)   This section applies where—

(a)   a public right of way over a footpath or bridleway crosses a railway or tramway otherwise than by a tunnel or bridge,

(b)   the operator of the railway or tramway has made a closure or diversion application in respect of the crossing, and

(c)   in the opinion of the Secretary of State the crossing constitutes a danger to members of the public using it or likely to use it.

(2)   The Secretary of State may by order require the operator to provide a tunnel or a bridge, or to improve an existing tunnel or bridge, to carry the path or way over or under the railway or tramway at or reasonably near to the crossing to which the closure or diversion application relates.

(3)   An order under this section may include particulars as to the tunnel or bridge which is to be provided or as to the improvements which are to be made.

(4) The Secretary of State shall not make an order under this section after the end of the period of two years beginning with the day on which the closure or diversion application is made, and not less than two months before making an order he shall give written notice of his proposal to make the order to the operator and to each local authority in whose area the crossing (or any proposed new crossing) is situated.

(5) A notice given under subsection (4) above must be accompanied by a draft of the proposed order under this section; and any order eventually made may include modifications of the draft.

(6) An operator shall not be regarded as in breach of a duty imposed by an order under this section if he has used his best endeavours to comply with the order.

(7) Where an operator is required by an order under this section to provide or improve a bridge or tunnel, but is unable to do so because he does not have the powers or rights (including rights over land) needed for the purpose, he shall not be taken to have used his best endeavours to comply with the order unless he has used his best endeavours to obtain those powers or rights (whether by means of an order under section 1 above or otherwise).

(8) In this section—

"bridleway" has the same meaning as in the Highways Act 1980;

"closure or diversion application" means—

    (a) an application made under section 6 above, or

    (b) a request made in accordance with section 120(3A)(b) of the Highways Act 1980,

for an order by virtue of which a public right of way would be extinguished or diverted;

"footpath" has the same meaning as in the Highways Act 1980;

"local authority" means a county council, a district council, a London borough council, the Common Council of the City of London, a parish or community council and a parish meeting of a parish not having a separate parish council;

"operator", in relation to a railway or tramway, means any person carrying on an undertaking which includes maintaining the permanent way.

49. Securing of gates and barriers

(1) Section 75 of the Railways Clauses Consolidation Act 1845 and section 68 of the Railways Clauses Consolidation (Scotland) Act 1845 (which make it an offence for any person to fail to fasten gates) shall be amended as follows.

(2) After the word "gate" there shall be inserted the words "or to lower any barrier".

(3) For the words "not exceeding" onwards there shall be substituted the words "not exceeding level 3 on the standard scale."

50. Orders under Transport Act 1968

Section 124 of the Transport Act 1968 (which gives the Secretary of State power to impose obligations in respect of level crossings), in its application in England and Wales, shall cease to have effect.

51. Amendment of Level Crossings Act 1983

In section 1 of the Level Crossings Act 1983 (safety arrangements at level crossings) in subsection (11), for the definition of "operator" there shall be substituted—

"   "operator", in relation to a crossing, means any person carrying on an undertaking which includes maintaining the permanent way;".

Signs and barriers at private crossings

52. Placing of signs and barriers

(1)   Subject to any directions under subsection (2) below, the operator of a railway or tramway which is crossed in any place by a private road or path may cause or permit crossing signs or barriers of a character—

(a)   prescribed in regulations made by the Secretary of State, or

(b)   otherwise authorised by him,

to be placed on or near the road or path near the crossing.

(2)   The Secretary of State may give directions to the operator of a railway or tramway which is crossed in any place by a private road or path for the placing of crossing signs or barriers of a character specified in the directions on or near the road or path near the crossing.

(3)   For the purposes of this section—

(a)   the size and colour of a crossing sign and whether or not it is illuminated (by lighting or the use of reflectors or reflecting material), and

(b)   the nature of the warnings, information, requirements, restrictions or prohibitions conveyed by it,

shall be regarded as part of the sign's character.

(4)   The power to make regulations under this section shall be exercisable by statutory instrument, which shall be subject to annulment in pursuance of a resolution of either House of Parliament.

(5)   Regulations under this section may make different provision for different cases.

53. Rights to enter land

(1)   The operator of a railway or tramway shall not enter or do anything on any land for the purpose of exercising his powers under section 52(1) above except—

(a)   with the consent of every owner of the land, or

(b)   in accordance with an authorisation given by the Secretary of State under subsection (4) below.

(2)   Where the operator of a railway or tramway proposes to enter or do anything on any land for the purpose of exercising his powers under section 52(1) above but has not obtained the consent of every owner of the land to his proposals (after making reasonable efforts to do so), he shall serve on every owner whose consent he has not obtained a notice giving details of the proposals and stating that—

(a)   he is referring the proposals to the Secretary of State for a decision as to whether or not they should be carried out, and

(b)   in making that decision, the Secretary of State will consider any written representations made to him by the owner within the period of forty-two days beginning with the date of the notice.

(3)   Where subsection (2) above applies, the operator shall—

(a)   submit a copy of every notice served by him under that subsection to the Secretary of State, and

(b)   provide the Secretary of State with such further information about the proposals as he may require.

(4)   Where proposals are referred to the Secretary of State under this section, he shall after the expiry of the period of forty-two days beginning with the date of the latest notice served under subsection (2) above and after considering any representations made to him in accordance with that subsection—

(a)   authorise the operator to carry out the proposals (either without modifications or with such modifications as the Secretary of State may specify), or

(b)   direct him not to carry out the proposals,

and shall serve notice of his decision on every owner served with a notice under subsection (2) above.

(5)   Any authorisation under subsection (4) above may be given subject to such conditions as the Secretary of State may specify, including conditions that compensation shall be payable by the operator.

(6)   Any dispute as to the amount of any compensation payable by virtue of subsection (5) above shall be referred to and determined by the Lands Tribunal or, in relation to land in Scotland, the Lands Tribunal for Scotland.

(7)   The operator of a railway or tramway may enter any land and do anything necessary on it (without the consent of the owners of the land) for the purpose of—

(a)   complying with any directions given under section 52(2) above, or

(b)   maintaining a crossing sign or barrier lawfully placed on or near a private road or path near a place where it crosses the railway or tramway.

(8)   The Secretary of State may enter any land and do anything necessary on it (without the consent of the owners of the land) for the purpose of exercising his powers under section 54(1) below.

(9)   In this section "owner"—

(a)   in relation to any land in England and Wales, means a person, other than a mortgagee not in possession, who is for the time being entitled to dispose of the fee simple (whether in possession or reversion) and includes also a person holding, or entitled to the rents and profits of, the land under a tenancy, other than a tenancy for a month or any period less than a month;

(b)   in relation to any land in Scotland, means a person who, under the Land Clauses Acts, would be entitled to sell and convey land to the promoters of an undertaking and includes also a person who is or would be entitled to receive the rent of the land under a tenancy, other than a tenancy for a month or any period less than a month.

54.   Default powers of Secretary of State

(1)   If the operator of a railway or tramway fails—

(a)   to comply with a direction given under section 52(2) above, or

(b)   to maintain a crossing sign or barrier lawfully placed on or near a private road or path near a place where it crosses the railway or tramway,

the Secretary of State may himself carry out the work required by the direction or necessary to maintain the crossing sign or barrier.

(2) Any expenses incurred by the Secretary of State in doing so shall be recoverable by him from the operator.

(3) A direction given under section 52(2) above—

(a) if relating to a private road or path in England and Wales, shall be enforceable on the application of the Secretary of State by an order of mandamus;

(b) if relating to a private road or path in Scotland, shall be enforceable by order of the Court of Session on an application by the Lord Advocate under section 45 of the Court of Session Act 1988.

55. Offence of failing to comply with sign

(1) A person who fails to comply with any requirement, restriction or prohibition conveyed by a crossing sign lawfully placed on or near a private road or path near a place where it crosses a railway or tramway shall be guilty of an offence.

(2) In any proceedings for an offence under this section, a crossing sign on or near a private road or path near a place where it crosses a railway or tramway shall be taken to have been lawfully placed there unless the contrary is proved.

(3) A person guilty of an offence under this section shall be liable on summary conviction to a fine not exceeding level 3 on the standard scale.

56. Interpretation of sections 52 to 55

(1) In sections 52 to 55 above (and this section)—

"barrier" includes gate;

"cross" means cross otherwise than by tunnel or bridge;

"crossing sign", in relation to a private road or path and any place where it crosses a railway or tramway, means—

(a) any object or device (whether fixed or portable), or

(b) any line or mark on the road or path,

for conveying to users of the road or path warnings, information, requirements, restrictions or prohibitions relating to the crossing;

"fail" includes refuse;

"lawfully placed" means placed in accordance with sections 52 to 54 above;

"maintain" includes repair and replace;

"place" includes erect and (in relation to a sign) display;

"private road or path" means any length of road or path to which the public does not have access.

(2) In the case of a railway or tramway which has more than one operator, the powers conferred by sections 52 to 54 above shall only be exercisable by or in relation to the operator carrying on the undertaking which includes maintaining the permanent way.

CHAPTER III   SUPPLEMENTARY

57. Duty to consult

It shall be the duty of the Secretary of State, before he makes regulations under section 32, 38(2), 41 or 43 above, to consult such organisations as he considers to be representative of persons who will be affected by the regulations.

58. Prosecutions

No proceedings shall be instituted in England and Wales in respect of an offence under this Part except by or with the consent of the Secretary of State or the Director of Public Prosecutions.

59. Offences by bodies corporate etc.

(1) Where an offence under this Part committed by a body corporate is committed with the consent or connivance of, or is attributable to any neglect on the part of, a director, manager, secretary or other similar officer of the body, or a person purporting to act in such a capacity, he as well as the body corporate shall be guilty of the offence.

(2) In subsection (1) above "director", in relation to a body corporate whose affairs are managed by its members, means a member of the body corporate.

(3) Where, in Scotland, an offence under this Part committed by a partnership or by an unincorporated association other than a partnership is committed with the consent or connivance of, or is attributable to any neglect on the part of, a partner in the partnership or (as the case may be) a person concerned in the management or control of the association, he, as well as the partership or association, shall be guilty of the offence.

PART III   MISCELLANEOUS AND GENERAL

Tramways

60. Powers of leasing

(1) A person authorised by or under an enactment to operate a tramway ("the lessor") may with the consent of the Secretary of State grant to another person ("the lessee"), for a period agreed between the lessor and the lessee, the right to operate the tramway (or any part of it) and such related statutory rights as may be so agreed.

(2) The terms of any agreement made by virtue of subsection (1) above shall be subject to the approval of the Secretary of State.

(3) Where an agreement is made by virtue of subsection (1) above, references in any enactment to the lessor shall, if and to the extent that the agreement so provides, have effect as references to the lessee.

(4) This section shall apply only to tramways in operation at the passing of this Act.

61. Amendment of Public Passenger Vehicle Act 1981

(1) The Public Passenger Vehicles Act 1981 shall be amended as follows.

(2) In section 24 (regulation of conduct of drivers, inspectors and conductors)—

    (a)   at the end of subsection (1) there shall be added the words "and

          (c)   drivers, inspectors and conductors of tramcars";

    (b)   in subsection (2), after the word "driver" there shall be inserted the words "of a public service vehicle".

(3) In section 25(1) (regulation of conduct of passengers) after the words "public service vehicles" there shall be inserted the words "or tramcars", and after the words "public service vehicle" wherever they occur there shall be inserted the words "or tramcar".

(4) In section 27(1) (returns to be provided by persons operating public service vehicles) after the words "public service vehicles" there shall be inserted the words "or tramcars".

(5) In section 60(1) (general power to make regulations)—

(a) at the end of paragraph (j) (carriage of luggage and goods on public service vehicles) there shall be added the words "or tramcars";

(b) in paragraph (k) (custody of property left on a public service vehicle) after the word "vehicle" there shall be inserted the words "or tramcar".

(6) After subsection (1A) of section 60 there shall be inserted—

"(1B) Regulations made under any provision of this Act and applying to tramcars may amend or exclude any provision of an Act or instrument of local application whose subject-matter is the same as that of the regulations."

62. Exclusion of hackney carriage legislation

(1) In section 4 of the Metropolitan Public Carriage Act 1869 (interpretation) in the definition of "hackney carriage", for the words "not a stage carriage" there shall be substituted the words "neither a stage carriage nor a tramcar".

(2) In section 4 of the London Cab Act 1968 (display of signs etc) in subsection (5) in the definition of "private hire-car", after the words "public service vehicle" there shall be inserted the words "or tramcar".

(3) In section 80 of the Local Government (Miscellaneous Provisions) Act 1976 (interpretation) in subsection (1) in the definition of "private hire vehicle", after the words "London cab" there shall be inserted the words "or tramcar".

Harbours

63. Harbours

(1) The Harbours Act 1964 shall have effect with the amendment set out in Schedule 3 to this Act.

(2) In section 37 of the Docks and Harbours Act 1966 (which gives to harbour authorities powers to acquire harbour businesses, and to subscribe for or acquire securities of bodies engaged, or to be engaged, in harbour businesses)—

(a) in subsection (1), for the words "harbour operations" and the words "such operations" there shall be substituted the words "activities relating to harbours";

(b) in subsection (2), for the words "harbour operations" there shall be substituted the words "activities relating to harbours";

(c) after subsection (2) there shall be inserted—

"(2A) Nothing in subsection (2) above shall be construed as authorising a harbour authority to delegate to another body any function that it could not delegate apart from that subsection.";

(d) subsection (3) shall be omitted.

(3) In section 35 of the Coast Protection Act 1949 (which excepts certain operations from the requirement to obtain the Secretary of State's consent under section 34) in subsection (1) there shall be added after paragraph (h)—

"(i) any operations authorised by an order under section 14 or 16 of the Harbours Act 1964."

Miscellaneous

64. Maintenance of footpaths and bridleways

(1)   Section 36 of the Highways Act 1980 (highways maintainable at public expense) shall be amended as follows.

(2)   In subsection (2), at the end of paragraph (c), the word "and" shall be omitted.

(3)   After paragraph (d) of subsection (2), there shall be added—

"(e)   a highway, being a footpath or bridleway, created in consequence of a rail crossing diversion order, or of an order made under section 14 or 16 of the Harbours Act 1964, or of an order made under section 1 or 3 of the Transport and Works Act 1992."

(4)   After subsection (3) there shall be inserted—

"(3A)   Paragraph (e) of subsection (2) above shall not apply to a footpath or bridleway, or to any part of a footpath or bridleway, which by virtue of an order of a kind referred to in that subsection is maintainable otherwise than at the public expense."

65. Certain enactments to cease to have effect

(1)   The following enactments shall cease to have effect—

(a)   the General Pier and Harbour Act 1861;

(b)   in the Tramways Act 1870—

section 3 (except as incorporated in, or otherwise applied by, any Act of Parliament or Provisional Order),

sections 4 to 21,

sections 22 to 24 (except as incorporated in, or otherwise applied by, any Act of Parliament or Provisional Order),

in section 25, the words from the beginning to "surface of the road" (except as incorporated in, or otherwise applied by, any Act of Parliament or Provisional Order),

in section 25, the words "and shall not be opened" onwards,

sections 26 to 40 (except as incorporated in, or otherwise applied by, any Act of Parliament or Provisional Order),

sections 41 and 42,

sections 43 to 47 (except as incorporated in, or otherwise applied by, any Act of Parliament or Provisional Order),

section 48,

sections 49 to 64 (except as incorporated in, or otherwise applied by, any Act of Parliament or Provisional Order),

Parts I and II of Schedule A (except as incorporated in, or otherwise applied by, any Act of Parliament or Provisional Order),

Part III of Schedule A,

Schedule B, and

Schedule C (except as incorporated in, or otherwise applied by, any Act of Parliament or Provisional Order);

(c)   the Military Tramways Act 1887;

(d)   the Railways (Electrical Power) Act 1903;

(e)   the Fishery Harbours Act 1915;

(f)   section 220(1)(a) of the Insolvency Act 1986.

(2)   In the Coast Protection Act 1949, in sections 2(8)(a) and 17(8)(b), for the words "to which the Fishery Harbours Act 1915 applies" there shall be substituted the words "which is a fishery harbour for the purposes of section 21 of the Sea Fish Industry Act 1951".

General

66.   Service of notices

(1)   A notice or other document required or authorised to be served for the purposes of this Act may be served by post.

(2)   Where the person on whom a notice or other document to be served for the purposes of this Act is a body corporate, the notice or document is duly served if it is served on the secretary or clerk of that body.

(3)   For the purposes of section 7 of the Interpretation Act 1978 as it applies for the purposes of this section, the proper address of any person in relation to the service on him of a notice or document under subsection (1) above is, if he has given an address for service, that address, and otherwise—

(a)   in the case of the secretary or clerk of a body corporate, the registered or principal office of that body;

(b)   in any other case, his last known address at the time of service.

(4)   Where for the purposes of this Act a notice or other document is required or authorised to be served on a person as having any interest in, or as the occupier of, land and his name or address cannot be ascertained after reasonable inquiry, the notice may be served by—

(a)   addressing it to him by name or by the description of "owner", or as the case may be "occupier", of the land (describing it), and

(b)   either leaving it in the hands of a person who is or appears to be resident or employed on the land or leaving it conspicuously affixed to some building or object on the land.

(5)   This section shall not be taken to exclude the employment of any method of service not expressly provided for by it.

(6)   This section shall not apply to anything required or authorised to be served under section 35 above.

67.   Interpretation

(1)   In this Act, except where the context otherwise requires—

"carriageway" has the same meaning as in the Highways Act 1980, or in Scotland the Roads (Scotland) Act 1984;

"guided transport" means transport by vehicles guided by means external to the vehicles (whether or not the vehicles are also capable of being operated in some other way);

"inland waterway" includes both natural and artificial waterways, and waterways within parts of the sea that are in Great Britain, but not any waterway managed or maintained by a person who is a harbour authority (within the meaning of the Harbours Act 1964) in relation to the waterway;

"operator", in relation to a transport system, means any person carrying on an undertaking which includes the system or any part of it or the provision of transport services on the system;

"railway" means a system of transport employing parallel rails which—

(a)   provide support and guidance for vehicles carried on flanged wheels, and

(b)   form a track which either is of a gauge of at least 350 millimetres or crosses a carriageway (whether or not on the same level),

but does not include a tramway;

"street" means—

(a)   in England and Wales, a street within the meaning of section 48 of the New Roads and Street Works Act 1991, together with land on the verge of a street or between two carriageways;

(b)   in Scotland, a road within the meaning of section 107 of the New Roads and Street Works Act 1991, together with land on the verge of a road or between two carriageways;

"tramway" means a system of transport used wholly or mainly for the carriage of passengers and employing parallel rails which—

(a)   provide support and guidance for vehicles carried on flanged wheels, and

(b)   are laid wholly or mainly along a street or in any other place to which the public has access (including a place to which the public has access only on making a payment);

"trolley vehicle system" means a system of transport by vehicles constructed or adapted for use on roads without rails under electric power transmitted to them by overhead wires (whether or not there is in addition a source of power on board the vehicles);

"vehicle" includes mobile traction unit.

(2)   References in this Act to rights over land include references to rights to do, or to place and maintain, anything in, on or under land or in the air-space above its surface.

68. Repeals

(1)   The enactments mentioned in Schedule 4 to this Act (which include spent enactments) are hereby repealed to the extent specified in the third column of that Schedule.

(2)   The repeal by this Act of the Notice of Accidents Act 1894 shall not affect section 75 of the Civil Aviation Act 1982 (by virtue of which regulations may include provisions applying section 3 of the 1894 Act).

69. Expenses

There shall be paid out of money provided by Parliament—

(a)   any expenses incurred by the Secretary of State under this Act, and

(b)   any increase attributable to this Act in the sums payable out of money so provided under any other enactment.

70. Commencement

(1)   The preceding sections of, and the Schedules to, this Act shall come into force on such day as the Secretary of State may appoint by order made by statutory instrument; and different days may be appointed for different purposes.

(2)   An order under subsection (1) above may include such transitional provisions and savings as appear to the Secretary of State to be necessary or expedient.

71. Extent
This Act shall not extend to Northern Ireland.

72. Short title
This Act may be cited as the Transport and Works Act 1992.

SCHEDULES

Section 5   SCHEDULE 1
MATTERS WITHIN SECTIONS 1 AND 3

1. The construction, alteration, repair, maintenance, demolition and removal of railways, tramways, trolley vehicle systems and other transport systems within section 1(1) of this Act, waterways, roads, watercourses, buildings and other structures.
2. The carrying out of any other civil engineering or other works.
3. The acquisition of land, whether compulsorily or by agreement.
4. The creation and extinguishment of rights over land (including rights of navigation over water), whether compulsorily or by agreement.
5. The abrogation and modification of agreements relating to land.
6. The conferring on persons providing transport services of rights to use systems belonging to others.
7. The protection of the property or interests of any person.
8. The imposition and exclusion of obligations or of liability in respect of any acts or omissions.
9. The making of agreements to secure the provision of police services.
10. The carrying out of surveys and the taking of soil samples.
11. The payment of compensation.
12. The charging of tolls, fares (including penalty fares) and other charges, and the creation of summary offences in connection with non-payment (or in connection with a person's failure to give his name or address in accordance with provisions relating to penalty fares).
13. The making of byelaws by any person and their enforcement, including the creation of summary offences.
14. The payment of rates.
15. The transfer, leasing, discontinuance and revival of undertakings.
16. The submission of disputes to arbitration.
17. The imposition of requirements to obtain the consent of the Secretary of State.

Section 47   SCHEDULE 2
STOPPING UP AND DIVERSION OF RAIL CROSSINGS

1. The Highways Act 1980 shall be amended as follows.

2.—(1) Section 118 (stopping up of footpaths and bridleways) shall be amended as follows.
(2) In subsection (5), for—

(a)   the words "or public path diversion order made under section 119 below", and

(b)   the words "or the public path diversion order",

there shall be substituted the words ", public path diversion order or rail crossing diversion order".

(3)   In subsection (7), for "119" there shall be substituted "118A".

3.   After section 118 there shall be inserted—

"118A.   Stopping up of footpaths and bridleways crossing railways

(1)   This section applies where it appears to a council expedient in the interests of the safety of members of the public using it or likely to use it that a footpath or bridleway in their area which crosses a railway, otherwise than by tunnel or bridge, should be stopped up.

(2)   Where this section applies, the council may by order made by them and submitted to and confirmed by the Secretary of State, or confirmed as an unopposed order, extinguish the public right of way over the path or way—

(a)   on the crossing itself, and

(b)   for so much of its length as they deem expedient from the crossing to its intersection with another highway over which there subsists a like right of way (whether or not other rights of way also subsist over it).

(3)   An order under this section is referred to in this Act as a "rail crossing extinguishment order".

(4)   The Secretary of State shall not confirm a rail crossing extinguishment order, and a council shall not confirm such an order as an unopposed order, unless he or, as the case may be, they are satisfied that it is expedient to do so having regard to all the circumstances, and in particular to—

(a)   whether it is reasonably practicable to make the crossing safe for use by the public, and

(b)   what arrangements have been made for ensuring that, if the order is confirmed, any appropriate barriers and signs are erected and maintained.

(5)   Before determining to make a rail crossing extinguishment order on the representations of the operator of the railway crossed by the path or way, the council may require him to enter into an agreement with them to defray, or to make such contribution as may be specified in the agreement towards, any expenses which the council may incur in connection with the erection or maintenance of barriers and signs.

(6)   A rail crossing extinguishment order shall be in such form as may be prescribed by regulations made by the Secretary of State and shall contain a map, on such scale as may be so prescribed, defining the land over which the public right of way is thereby extinguished.

(7)   Schedule 6 to this Act has effect as to the making, confirmation, validity and date of operation of rail crossing extinguishment orders.

(8)   In this section—

"operator", in relation to a railway, means any person carrying on an undertaking which includes maintaining the permanent way;

"railway" includes tramway but does not include any part of a system where rails are laid along a carriageway."

4.   After section 119 (diversion of footpaths and bridleways) there shall be inserted—

"119A.   Diversion of footpaths and bridleways crossing railways

(1)   This section applies where it appears to a council expedient in the interests of the safety of members of the public using it or likely to use it that a footpath or bridleway in their area which crosses a railway, otherwise than by tunnel or bridge, should be diverted (whether on to land of the same or of another owner, lessee or occupier).

(2)   Where this section applies, the council may by order made by them and submitted to and confirmed by the Secretary of State, or confirmed as an unopposed order—

(a)   create, as from such date as may be specified in the order, any such new path or way as appears to the council requisite for effecting the diversion, and

(b)   extinguish, as from such date as may be so specified, the public right of way over the crossing and over so much of the path or way of which the crossing forms part as appears to the council requisite as aforesaid.

(3)   An order under this section is referred to in this Act as a "rail crossing diversion order".

(4)   The Secretary of State shall not confirm a rail crossing diversion order, and a council shall not confirm such an order as an unopposed order, unless he or, as the case may be, they are satisfied that it is expedient to do so having regard to all the circumstances, and in particular to—

(a)   whether it is reasonably practicable to make the crossing safe for use by the public, and

(b)   what arrangements have been made for ensuring that, if the order is confirmed, any appropriate barriers and signs are erected and maintained.

(5)   A rail crossing diversion order shall not alter a point of termination of a path or way diverted under the order—

(a)   if that point is not on a highway over which there subsists a like right of way (whether or not other rights of way also subsist over it), or

(b)   (where it is on such a highway) otherwise than to another point which is on the same highway, or another such highway connected with it.

(6)   A rail crossing diversion order may make provision requiring the operator of the railway to maintain all or part of the footpath or bridleway created by the order.

(7)   Where it appears to the council that work requires to be done to provide necessary facilities for the convenient exercise of any such new right of way as is mentioned in subsection (2)(a) above, the date specified under subsection (2)(b) shall be later than the date specified under subsection (2)(a) by such time as appears to the council requisite for enabling the work to be carried out.

(8)   Before determining to make a rail crossing diversion order on the representations of the operator of the railway crossed by the path or way, the council may require him to enter into an agreement with them to defray, or to make such contribution as may be specified in the agreement towards,—

(a)   any compensation which may become payable under section 28 above as applied by section 121(2) below;

(b)   any expenses which the council may incur in connection with the erection or maintenance of barriers and signs;

(c)   where the council are the highway authority for the path or way in question, any expenses which they may incur in bringing the new site of the path or way into fit condition for use by the public;

(d)   where the council are not the highway authority, any expenses which may become recoverable from them by the highway authority under the provisions of section 27(2) above as applied by subsection (11) below.

(9)   A rail crossing diversion order shall be in such form as may be prescribed by regulations made by the Secretary of State and shall contain a map, on such scale as may be so prescribed—

(a)   showing the existing site of so much of the line of the path or way as is to be diverted by the order and the new site to which it is to be diverted,

(b)   indicating whether a new right of way is created by the order over the whole of the new site or whether some part of it is already comprised in a footpath or bridleway, and

(c)   where some part of the new site is already so comprised, defining that part.

(10)   Schedule 6 to this Act has effect as to the making, confirmation, validity and date of operation of rail crossing diversion orders.

(11)   Section 27 above (making up of new footpaths and bridleways) applies to a footpath or bridleway created by a rail crossing diversion order with the substitution, for references to a public path creation order, of references to a rail crossing diversion order and, for references to section 26(2) above, of references to section 120(3) below.

(12)   In this section and in section 120 below—

"operator", in relation to a railway, means any person carrying on an undertaking which includes maintaining the permanent way;

"railway" includes tramway but does not include any part of a system where rails are laid along a carriageway."

5.—(1)   Section 120 (exercise of powers of making public path extinguishment and diversion orders) shall be amended as follows.

(2)   In subsection (1), for the words "and 119" there shall be substituted the words "to 119A".

(3)   In subsection (2), for the words from "public path extinguishment" to "and 119" there shall be substituted the words "orders under sections 118 to 119A".

(4)   In subsection (3)—

(a)   after "118(1)" there shall be inserted "or 118A(1) or 119A(1)";

(b)   after the words "stopped up" there shall be inserted the words "or diverted";

(c)   after the words "extinguishment order" there shall be added the words ", a rail crossing extinguishment order, a rail crossing diversion order";

(d)   for the words "and 119" there shall be substituted the words "to 119A";

(e)   after the word "consultation" there shall be inserted the words "(subject to subsection (3A) below)".

(5)   After subsection (3) there shall be inserted—

"(3A)   Where—

(a)   the operator of a railway makes a request to a council to make an order under section 118A or 119A above in respect of a crossing over the railway,

(b)   the request is in such form and gives such particulars as are prescribed by regulations made by the Secretary of State, and

(c)   the council have neither confirmed the order nor submitted it to the Secretary of State within 6 months of receiving the request,

the power conferred on the Secretary of State by subsection (3) above may be exercised without consultation with the council."

(6)   In subsection (4), after the words "public path diversion order" there shall be inserted the words "or a rail crossing diversion order".

(7)   In subsection (5)—

(a)   for the words "he may require the owner, lessee or occupier" there shall be substituted the words "or, on the representations of the operator of the railway concerned, a rail crossing diversion order, he may require the person";

(b)   for the words "for the owner, lessee or occupier" there shall be substituted the words "for that person";

(c)   after "119(5)" there shall be inserted the words ", or as the case may be 119A(8),".

6.—(1)   Section 121 (supplementary provisions) shall be amended as follows.

(2)   In subsection (1)—

(a)   for the words "or a public path diversion order" there shall be substituted the words ", a rail crossing extinguishment order, a public path diversion order or a rail crossing diversion order";

(b)   after the words "and a public path diversion order" there shall be added the words "or a rail crossing diversion order".

(3)   In subsection (2), for the words "and to public path diversion orders" there shall be substituted the words ", rail crossing extinguishment orders, public path diversion orders and rail crossing diversion orders".

(4)   In subsection (3), for the words "and public path diversion orders" there shall be substituted the words ", rail crossing extinguishment orders, public path diversion orders and rail crossing diversion orders".

(5)   In subsection (4), for the words "or a public path diversion order" there shall be substituted the words ", a rail crossing extinguishment order, a public path diversion order or a rail crossing diversion order".

7.   In section 293 (powers of entry for purposes connected with certain orders relating to footpaths and bridleways) in subsection (1) for the words "or a public path diversion order" there shall be substituted the words ", a rail crossing extinguishment order, a public path diversion order or a rail crossing diversion order".

8.   In section 325 (provisions as to regulations, schemes and orders) in subsection (2)(a), after the word "section", there shall be inserted the words "120(3A) or".

9.   In section 329(1) (interpretation) after the definition of "rack rent" there shall be inserted—
"rail crossing diversion order" means an order under section 119A above; "rail crossing extinguishment order" means an order under section 118A above;".

10.—(1)   Schedule 6 shall be amended as follows.
(2)   In paragraph 1—
(a)   in sub-paragraphs (1) and (2) for the words "or a public path diversion order" there shall be substituted the words ", a rail crossing extinguishment order, a public path diversion order or a rail crossing diversion order";
(b)   in sub-paragraph (3A) for the words "and public path diversion orders" there shall be substituted the words ", rail crossing extinguishment orders, public path diversion orders and rail crossing diversion orders";
(c)   in sub-paragraph (3B) for the words "and draft public path diversion orders" there shall be substituted the words ", draft rail crossing extinguishment orders, draft public path diversion orders and draft rail crossing diversion orders".
(3)   In paragraph 2A(1), after the words "shall, except in" there shall be inserted the words "the case of a rail crossing extinguishment order, the case of a rail crossing diversion order and".
(4)   In paragraph 3(2)—
(a)   after the words "public path extinguishment order" there shall be inserted the words "or a rail crossing extinguishment order";
(b)   for the words "or a public path diversion order" there shall be substituted the words ", a public path diversion order or a rail crossing diversion order".

Section 63   **SCHEDULE 3**
AMENDMENT OF HARBOURS ACT 1964

1.—(1)   Section 14 (harbour revision orders) shall be amended as follows.
(2)   In subsection (2)(b) at the end there shall be added the words "or in the interests of the recreational use of sea-going ships".
(3)   After subsection (2A) there shall be inserted—
"(2B)   Nothing in subsection (2)(b) of this section shall prevent the making of an order for facilitating—
(a)   the closing of part of the harbour,
(b)   a reduction in the facilities available in the harbour, or
(c)   the disposal of property not required for the purposes of the harbour,
if the appropriate Minister is satisfied that the making of the order is desirable on grounds other than those specified in that subsection."
(4)   In subsection (3)—
(a)   for the words from "a provision" to "said objects" there shall be substituted the words "any other provision of the order";
(b)   after the words "for the purposes of" there shall be inserted the words ", or in connection with,";

(c)   for the words "repealing and amending" there shall be substituted the words "excluding or modifying any provision of any Act or of any instrument made under any Act (including this Act) and for repealing".

(5)   After subsection (4) there shall be inserted—

"(4A)   Where two or more harbours are being improved, maintained or managed by the same harbour authority or by harbour authorities which are members of the same group, a harbour revision order may relate to more than one of the harbours; and for this purpose two authorities are members of the same group if one is a subsidiary (within the meaning of the Companies Act 1985) of the other or both are subsidiaries of another company (within the meaning of that Act)."

(6)   In subsection (5), for the words "large-scale map" there shall be substituted the words "map of a scale not less than 1:2500".

(7)   After subsection (5) there shall be inserted—

"(5A)   Where a harbour revision order includes provision for extinguishing or diverting a public right of way over a footpath or bridleway, there must be annexed to the order a map of a scale not less than 1:2500 on which the path or way concerned, and in the case of a diversion the new path or way, are plainly delineated."

2.—(1)   Section 16 (harbour empowerment orders) shall be amended as follows.

(2)   At the end of subsection (5) there shall be added the words "or in the interests of the recreational use of sea-going ships".

(3)   In subsection (6), after the words "any other enactment" there shall be inserted the words "and provisions for excluding or modifying any provision of any Act or of any instrument made under any Act (including this Act)".

(4)   In subsection (7), for the words "large-scale map" there shall be substituted the words "map of a scale not less than 1:2500".

(5)   After subsection (7) there shall be inserted—

"(7A)   Where a harbour empowerment order includes provision for extinguishing or diverting a public right of way over a footpath or bridleway, there must be annexed to the order a map of a scale not less than 1:2500 on which the path or way concerned, and in the case of a diversion the new path or way, are plainly delineated."

3.   In section 17 (procedure for making harbour revision and empowerment orders) after subsection (2) there shall be inserted—

"(2A)   Neither the Secretary of State nor the Minister of Agriculture, Fisheries and Food shall make a harbour revision or empowerment order which provides for extinguishing a public right of way over a footpath or bridleway unless he is satisfied—

(a)   that an alternative right of way has been or will be provided, or

(b)   that the provision of an alternative right of way is not required.

(2B)   Neither the Secretary of State nor the Minister of Agriculture, Fisheries and Food shall make a harbour revision or empowerment order which provides for diverting a public right of way over a footpath or bridleway unless he is satisfied that the path or way will not be substantially less convenient to the public in consequence of the diversion."

4.   In section 18 (harbour reorganisation schemes) in subsection (3), for the words "large-scale map" there shall be substituted the words "map of a scale not less than 1:2500".

5.—(1)   Section 47 (provisions as to inquiries and hearings) shall be amended as follows.

(2)   After subsection (1) there shall be inserted—

"(1A)   The power to make an order as to costs under section 250(5) of the Local Government Act 1972 as applied by subsection (1) above shall be exercisable not only where the inquiry or hearing takes place but also where arrangements are made for it but it does not take place."

(3)   After subsection (2) there shall be inserted—

"(2A)   The power to make an award as to expenses under section 210(8) of the Local Government (Scotland) Act 1973 as applied by subsection (2) above shall be exercisable not only where the inquiry or hearing takes place but also where arrangements are made for it but it does not take place."

(4)   In subsection (3), for the words from "required by paragraph 4(3)" to "Schedule 4" there shall be substituted the words "into an order subject to the provisions of paragraph 4B of Schedule 3".

6.   After section 48 (service of documents) there shall be inserted—

"48A.   Environmental duties of harbour authorities

It shall be the duty of a harbour authority in formulating or considering any proposals relating to its functions under any enactment to have regard to—

(a)   the conservation of the natural beauty of the countryside and of flora, fauna and geological or physiographical features of special interest;

(b)   the desirability of preserving for the public any freedom of access to places of natural beauty; and

(c)   the desirability of maintaining the availability to the public of any facility for visiting or inspecting any building, site or object of archaeological, architectural or historic interest;

and to take into account any effect which the proposals may have on the natural beauty of the countryside, flora, fauna or any such feature or facility."

7.—(1)   Section 57 (interpretation) shall be amended as follows.

(2)   After the definition of "the Boards" there shall be inserted—

" "bridleway", in relation to England and Wales, has the same meaning as in the Highways Act 1980 and, in relation to Scotland, has the same meaning as in Part III of the Countryside (Scotland) Act 1967;".

(3)   After the definition of "fishery harbour" there shall be inserted—

" "footpath", in relation to England and Wales, has the same meaning as in the Highways Act 1980 and, in relation to Scotland, has the same meaning as in the Roads (Scotland) Act 1984;".

8.   Section 62 (saving for private Bills etc) shall be omitted.

9.—(1)   Schedule 2 (objects for whose achievement harbour revision orders may be made) shall be amended as follows.

(2)   In paragraph 3(c) for the words from "out" to "others of" there shall be substituted the words "on by others of activities relating to the harbour or of".

(3)   After paragraph 7 there shall be inserted—

"7A.   Extinguishing or diverting public rights of way over footpaths or bridleways for the purposes of works described in the order or works ancillary to such works.

7B.   Extinguishing public rights of navigation for the purposes of works described in the order or works ancillary to such works, or permitting interference with the enjoyment of such rights for the purposes of such works or for the purposes of works carried out by a person authorised by the authority to carry them out."

(4)   After paragraph 8 there shall be inserted—

"8A.   Enabling the authority to close part of the harbour or to reduce the facilities available in the harbour."

(5)   After paragraph 9 there shall be inserted—

"9A.   Empowering the authority (alone or with others) to develop land not required for the purposes of the harbour with a view to disposing of the land or of interests in it, and to acquire land by agreement for the purpose of developing it together with such land.

9B.   Empowering the authority to delegate the performance of any of the functions of the authority except—

(a)   a duty imposed on the authority by or under any enactment;

(b)   the making of byelaws;

(c)   the levying of ship, passenger and goods dues;

(d)   the appointment of harbour, dock and pier masters;

(e)   the nomination of persons to act as constables;

(f)   functions relating to the laying down of buoys, the erection of lighthouses and the exhibition of lights, beacons and sea-marks, so far as those functions are exercisable for the purposes of the safety of navigation."

(6) After paragraph 16 there shall be inserted—

"16A.   Imposing or conferring on the authority duties or powers (including powers to make byelaws) for the conservation of the natural beauty of all or any part of the harbour or of any of the fauna, flora or geological or physiographical features in the harbour and all other natural features."

10.—(1)   Schedule 3 (procedure for making harbour orders) shall be amended follows.

(2)   After paragraph 1 A there shall be inserted—

"1B.   Such fees as may be determined by the Secretary of State shall be payable on the making of an application for a harbour revision order."

(3)   In paragraph 3, after sub-paragraph (b) there shall be inserted—

"(ba)   if provision is proposed to be included in the order extinguishing or diverting a public right of way over a footpath or bridleway, the applicant shall—

(i)   serve on every local authority for the area in which the path or way is situated a notice stating the effect of the provision, naming a place where a copy of the draft of the proposed order (and of any relevant map accompanying the application for the order) may be seen at all reasonable hours and stating that, if the local authority desire to make to the Secretary of State objection to the inclusion of the provision in the order, they should do so in writing (stating the grounds of their objection) before the expiration of the period of forty-two days from the date on which the notice is served on them;

    (ii)   cause a copy of the notice to be displayed in a prominent position at the ends of so much of any path or way as would by virtue of the order cease to be subject to a public right of way;

and for the purposes of this sub-paragraph, "local authority" means, in England and Wales, a county council, a district council, a London borough council, the Common Council of the City of London, the Council of the Isles of Scilly, a parish or community council and a parish meeting of a parish not having a separate parish council and, in Scotland, a regional, islands or district council;".

    (4)   In paragraph 4A, in sub-paragraph (1) for the words "is opposed" there shall be substituted the words "authorises the compulsory purchase of land", and for sub-paragraphs (2) to (4) there shall be substituted—

    "(2)   Where this paragraph has effect in relation to an order, it shall be subject to special parliamentary procedure to the same extent as it would be, by virtue of section 18 or 19 of the Acquisition of Land Act 1981 (or by virtue of paragraph 5 or 6 of Schedule 3 to that Act) (National Trust land, commons etc), if the purchase were authorised by an order under section 2(1) of that Act."

    (5)   For paragraph 4B there shall be substituted—

    "4B.—   (1)   The provisions of this paragraph apply to—

    (a)   a harbour revision order relating to a harbour in Scotland, or

    (b)   a harbour empowerment order relating to a harbour or to works to be carried out in Scotland,

where the order authorises the compulsory purchase of land.

    (2)   Where this paragraph applies to an order, the order shall be subject to special parliamentary procedure to the same extent as it would be, by virtue of section 1(2)(b) of the Acquisition of Land (Authorisation Procedure) (Scotland) Act 1947 (land forming part of a common or open space or held inalienably by the National Trust for Scotland), if the purchase were authorised by an order under section 1(1) of that Act."

    (6)   In paragraph 5(a), for the words from "to which" to "so affected" there shall be substituted the words "which is not subject to special parliamentary procedure,".

    (7)   Paragraphs 8A and 8B shall be omitted.

    (8)   In paragraph 14(3), for the words "(b) and (c)" there shall be substituted the words "(b) to (c)".

Section 68   SCHEDULE 4
                                           REPEALS

                             PART I   RAILWAYS AND TRAMWAYS

Chapter	Short title	Extent of repeal
5 & 6 Vict. c. 55.	The Railway Regulation Act 1842.	In section 17, the words "who shall be found drunk while so employed upon the said railway".
33 & 34 Vict. c. 78.	The Tramways Act 1870.	Section 3 (except as incorporated in, or otherwise applied by, any Act of Parliament or Provisional Order).
		Sections 4 to 21.
		Sections 22 to 24 (except as incorporated in, or otherwise applied by, any Act of Parliament or Provisional Order).
		In section 25, the words from the beginning to "surface of the road" (except as incorporated in, or otherwise applied by, any Act of Parliament or Provisional Order).
		In section 25, the words "and shall not be opened" onwards.
		Sections 26 to 40 (except as incorporated in, or otherwise applied by, any Act of Parliament or Provisional Order).
		Sections 41 and 42.
		Sections 43 to 47 (except as incorporated in, or otherwise applied by, any Act of Parliament or Provisional Order).
		Section 48.
		Sections 49 to 64 (except as incorporated in, or otherwise applied by, any Act of Parliament or Provisional Order).

Chapter	Short title	Extent of repeal
		Parts I and II of Schedule A (except as incorporated in, or otherwise applied by, any Act of Parliament or Provisional Order).
		Part III of Schedule A.
		Schedule B.
		Schedule C (except as incorporated in, or otherwise applied by, any Act of Parliament or Provisional Order).
34 & 35 Vict. c. 78.	The Regulation of Railways Act 1871.	In section 3, the words "Provided that" onwards. Section 6.
45 & 46 Vict. c. 50.	The Municipal Corporations Act 1882.	In Part I of Schedule 9, the entry relating to the Tramways Act 1870 (except as incorporated in, or otherwise applied by, any Act of Parliament or Provisional Order).
50 & 51 Vict. c. 65.	The Military Tramways Act 1887.	The whole Act.
52 & 53 Vict. c. 14.	The Town Police Clauses Act 1889.	In section 3, the words from "duly licensed" to "Act of Parliament."
57 & 58 Vict. c. 28.	The Notice of Accidents Act 1894.	The whole Act, so far as unrepealed.
59 & 60 Vict. c. 48.	The Light Railways Act 1896.	The whole Act, so far as unrepealed (except as it applies in Scotland).
63 & 64 Vict. c. 27.	The Railway Employment (Prevention of Accidents) Act 1900.	Section 13(2).
3 Edw. 7 c. 30.	The Railways (Electrical Power) Act 1903.	The whole Act.
6 Edw. 7 c. 53.	The Notice of Accidents Act 1906.	The whole Act, so far as unrepealed.
2 & 3 Geo. 5 c. 19.	The Light Railways Act 1912.	The whole Act, so far as unrepealed (except as it applies in Scotland).

Chapter	Short title	Extent of repeal
11 & 12 Geo. 5 c. 55.	The Railways Act 1921.	Sections 68 and 69 (except as they apply in Scotland). Section 71 (except as it applies in Scotland). Sections 73 and 74 (except as they apply in Scotland).
24 & 25 Geo. 5 c. 53.	The Road and Rail Traffic Act 1933.	Section 41. Section 43.
2 & 3 Eliz. 2 c. 64.	The Transport Charges &c (Miscellaneous Provisions) Act 1954.	Section 9. In section 13(1)— the definition of "railway of the nature of a tramway"; the definition of "tramcar"; the words "and references to" to "Road Traffic Act 1960". Section 14(5).
8 & 9 Eliz. 2 c. 16.	The Road Traffic Act 1960.	In Schedule 17, the entry relating to the Transport Charges &c (Miscellaneous Provisions) Act 1954.
10 & 11 Eliz. 2 c. 46.	The Transport Act 1962.	In section 83— subsections (1) to (5) (except as they apply in Scotland); subsection (6).
1965 c. 2.	The Administration of Justice Act 1965.	In Schedule 1— the entry relating to the Tramways Act 1870; the entry relating to the Light Railways Act 1896.
1965 c. xxi.	The British Railways Act 1965.	Section 35(3) and (8).
1965 c. xli.	The London Transport Act 1965.	Section 34(3).
1967 c. 80.	The Criminal Justice Act 1967.	In Part I of Schedule 3— the entry relating to section 75 of the Railways Clauses Consolidation Act 1845; the entry relating to section 68 of the Railways Clauses Consolidation (Scotland) Act 1845.

Chapter	Short title	Extent of repeal
1968 c. 73.	The Transport Act 1968.	Section 121(4) (except as it applies in Scotland). In section 121(5), the words "or by virtue of subsection (4) thereof" (except as they apply in Scotland). In section 121(6), the words "or by virtue of subsection (4)" (except as they apply in Scotland). Section 124 (except as it applies in Scotland). Section 125(4).
1972 c. 70.	The Local Government Act 1972.	Section 131(2)(c).
1975 c. 9.	The Supply Powers Act 1975.	In Schedule 1, the entry relating to the Military Tramways Act 1887.
1975 c. 53.	The Public Service Vehicles (Arrest of Offenders) Act 1975.	The whole Act, so far as unrepealed.
1977 c. xii.	The London Transport Act 1977.	In the Schedule, the entry relating to section 75 of the Railways Clauses Consolidation Act 1845.
1977 c. xvii.	The British Railways Act 1977.	In Schedule 1— the entry relating to section 75 of the Railways Clauses Consolidation Act 1845; the entry relating to section 68 of the Railways Clauses Consolidation (Scotland) Act 1845.
1980 c. 66.	The Highways Act 1980.	In section 36(2), at the end of paragraph (c), the word "and".
1982 c. 53.	The Administration of Justice Act 1982.	Section 46(2)(b)(i). Section 46(2)(d).
1984 c. 12.	The Telecommunications Act 1984.	In Schedule 4, paragraph 7.

Chapter	Short title	Extent of repeal
1984 c. 54.	The Roads (Scotland) Act 1984.	In Schedule 9— paragraph 6 (except as incorporated in, or otherwise applied by, any Act of Parliament or Provisional Order); paragraph 12.
1986 c. 45.	The Insolvency Act 1986.	Section 220(1)(a).
1987 c. 53.	The Channel Tunnel Act 1987.	In paragraph 3 of Schedule 6— in the entry relating to the Regulation of Railways Act 1871, the words "and 6" and the words "returns of and"; the entry relating to the Road and Rail Traffic Act 1933.

PART II

HARBOURS

Chapter	Short title	Extent of repeal
24 & 25 Vict. c. 45.	The General Pier and Harbour Act 1861.	The whole Act, so far as unrepealed.
25 & 26 Vict. c. 19.	The General Pier and Harbour Act 1861, Amendment Act.	The whole Act, so far as unrepealed.
25 & 26 Vict. c. 69.	The Harbours Transfer Act 1862.	Sections 13 and 14.
5 & 6 Geo. 5 c. 48.	The Fishery Harbours Act 1915.	The whole Act, so far as unrepealed.
1 Edw. 8 & 1 Geo. 6 c. 28.	The Harbours, Piers and Ferries (Scotland) Act 1937.	Sections 4 and 5.
14 & 15 Geo. 6 c. 30.	The Sea Fish Industry Act 1951.	Section 21(4). In section 21(5), the words "in section two of the said Act of 1915 or". In section 21(8), the word "either" and the words from "or of the Fishery Harbours Act 1915" to "the Minister of Transport)".

Chapter	Short title	Extent of repeal
1964 c. 40.	The Harbours Act 1964.	Section 17(3) and (4). In section 57(1), the definition of "large-scale". Section 62. In Schedule 3— paragraph 5A; paragraph 8A; paragraph 8B; in paragraph 9, the words from "and further stating" to "or will come into operation"; paragraph 9A.
1966 c. 28.	The Docks and Harbours Act 1966.	Section 37(3).
1973 c. 65.	The Local Government (Scotland) Act 1973.	In Schedule 19— paragraph 5; paragraph 8.
1981 c. 56.	The Transport Act 1981.	In Schedule 6, paragraph 4(4) to (7).

Index

Abrogation of agreements relating to
    land 26
Accident reporting 115–16
Acquisition of land 26
    see also Compulsory purchase
Aerial cableways 23
Alcohol *see* Drink and drugs control
Amenity groups 34
Application for orders 29–31
    alterations 31
    commencement of orders 18–19, 38
    decisions *see* Decisions on applications
    estimate of cost 30–1
    objections *see* Objections to orders
    powers to apply 44–5
    procedure 29–30
Appointed persons
    delegation of functions to 47
    limitation on power 47
Arbitration for disputes 28
Area Transport Users Consultative
    Committees 45
Authorising system
    application for orders *see* Application for
      orders
    challenging validity *see* Challenging validity
      of orders
    commencement 18–19, 38
    intention of promoters 23
    multi-purpose orders 23
    national significance *see* Schemes of
      national significance
    objections *see* Objections to orders
    Scottish transport systems 17
    Secretary of State initiated orders
      defence transport systems 16–17
      interest of safety orders 17
    Section 1 orders 23–9
    Section 3 orders 23–9
    supplementary provisions 24–5
    transport systems to which applies
      forms yet to be invented 23

Authorising system – *continued*
    other guided transport 22–3
    railways *see* Railways
    tramways *see* Tramways
    trolley vehicle systems 22
    vehicles 22
    validity of orders *see* Challenging validity of
      orders

Blight notices 74–5
Bridleways
    stopping up or diversion for rail crossings
      agriculture or forestry needs 108
      compensation payment 108
      default powers of Secretary of State 107
      diversion orders 105–6
      extinguishment orders 104–5
      maintenance of alternate route 108
      outline 103–4
      partly within and partly outside council
        area 107
      procedure for making orders 106–7
      rail crossing extinguishment orders
        104–5
      right of entry to survey 108
      tunnel or bridge rail crossings 108–9
      time limit for order 109
      written notice of proposed order 109
British Railways Board 11, 27, 44, 45, 46
British Waterways Board 44

Cable guidance, road based 23
Central Transport Consultative Committee
    45
Challenging validity of orders 38–40
    grounds 38–9
    interim order 39
    jurisdiction of court 39–40
    time limit 39
Charging of tolls or fares 27–8
Closure of stations or services 46
Coast protection consent 71–2, 88

Commencement of orders   18–19, 38
Community councils   45
Compulsory purchase   2
  compensation payment   26
  Crown land   48
  special parliamentary procedure   40–3
  see also Acquisition of land
Conservation areas
  planning permission   60, 66–71
    private Bills   66–8
    section 17   68–9
      consequences   69–71
    TAWA approach   68–71
Conservation and harbours   90–2
Construction or operation of inland waterway
  system   23–9
Construction or operation of transport
  system   23–9
Costs
  estimate in application   30–1
  harbours   94
  public hearings or inquiries   35
County councils   45
Crown Estates Commission   48
Crown land   48

Decisions on applications
  general power   36–7
  modification of proposals   37
  publicity for decisions   37–8
Defence transport systems orders   16–17
Discontinuance of undertaking   28
Dispute settlement   28
District councils   45
Drink and drugs control   118–25
  due diligence defence   121–2
  evidence in proceedings   125
  maintenance workers   120–1
  offences by employees   120–1
  offences by operators   121–2
  operator liability   119
  police powers
    failure to provide specimen   124–5
    testing   119, 123–4
  prescribed limits   122–3
  road traffic legislation and   123
  supervisors   120–1
  TAWA provisions   118–19
  transport systems to which control
    applies   119–20
  volunteers   120, 121
Drugs see Drink and drugs control
Duchy of Cornwall   48
Duchy of Lancaster   48

English Heritage   34, 45
Environmental matters in harbours   90–2

Fares   27–8
Fees   93–4
Fennell Report   112, 115
Footpaths
  harbours   85–6
  stopping up or diversion for rail crossings
    agriculture or forestry needs   107
    compensation payment   107
    diversion orders   105–6
    extinguishment orders   105–6
    maintenance of alternate route   108
    outline   103–4
    partly within and partly outside council
      area   107
    procedure for making orders   106–7
    rail crossing extinguishment orders
      104–5
    right of entry to survey   107
    tunnel or bridge rail crossings   108–9
    time limit for order   109
    written notice of proposed order   109

General Development Order   64
Guided transport system
  definition   22
  forms yet to be invented   23

Hackney carriage legislation   101–2
Harbours   14
  businesses   88–9
  conservation   90–2
  costs   94
  delegation of functions   90
  development of land   88, 89–90
  empowerment orders   82, 86
  environmental matters   90–2
  fees   93–4
  footpaths   85–6
  Harbour Authorities
    several harbours   85
    types   80–1
  'harbour' meaning   81
  Joint Committee on Private Bill procedure
    recommendations   12–13
  marinas and recreational facilities   83–4
  need for statutory authorisation   3
  private Acts   82–3
  reduction of facilities   84
  revision orders   81–2, 86
  rights of way   85–6
  Scottish orders   79, 92–3
  special parliamentary procedure   92–3
  technical changes   94–5
  works in
    coast protection consent   88
    licensing powers   86–7
    navigation rights and   87–8

Harbours – *continued*
    types of works licensed 88
    see also Inland waterways
Hazardous substances 71
'Henry VIII clause' 24
Heritage lines 120, 121
Hidden Report 112, 115
Hybrid Acts 2, 57–8
    procedural advantages over private
        Bills 58
    schemes of national significance 57–9

Immunity from nuisance claims 2, 3
Inland waterways 96–8
    changing maintenance requirement 25
    classification changing 25
    construction or operation 23–9, 97–8
    section 3 orders 23–9, 97–8
    see also Harbours
Insurance 116–17
Interest of safety orders 17

Joint Committee on Private Bill procedure
        10–13
    constitutional questions 12
    Government response 13–14
    planning permission 61–2, 73
    ports and harbours recommendations
        12–13
    railways recommendations 11
    schemes of national significance 49–50
    Scotland 77–8
    tramways 99

Land
    abrogation or modification of
        agreements 26
    acquisition *see* Acquisition of land;
        Compulsory purchase
    meaning 34
Leasing of undertaking 28, 100
Legislation
    'clauses' Acts 3
    hackney carriage legislation 101–2
    hybrid Acts 2, 57–9
    private Acts *see* Private Acts
    public Act 1
    public service vehicles legislation 100–1
    safety on transport systems 112
    Scottish procedure 76–7
Liability
    for acts or omissions 27
    nuisance immunity 2, 3
Light rail rapid transit systems *see* Tramways
Listed buildings
    planning permission 60, 66–71
        private Bills 66–8
        section 17 68–9

Listed buildings – *continued*
        consequences 69–71
        TAWA approach 68–71
Load limits 16
Local planning authorities
    consultation by applicant 30
London borough councils 45
London Gazette
    application, publication in 30
    commencement of orders 38
    publicity for decisions on applications 37
    schemes of national significance
        notification 53, 56–7
    special parliamentary procedure 43
London Regional Passengers' Committee 45
London Regional Transport
        11, 27, 44, 45, 46

Magnetic levitation monorail 23
Marinas 83–4
Ministerial orders 8–10
    provisional 8–9
    special parliamentary procedure 9–10
Model clauses 43–4
Modification of agreements relating to
        land 26
Multi-purpose orders 23

National Rivers Authority 30
National Trust 41
Nationally significant schemes *see* Schemes of
        national significance
Nature Conservancy Council 11
Navigation
    harbour works and rights of 87–8
    inland waterways 96–8
    section 3 orders 97–8
Nuisance immunity 2, 3

Objections to orders
    amenity groups 34
    persons objecting 31–2
    powers to object 44–5
    procedure 32–3
    public hearings 33–5
    public local inquiries 33–5
    written representations 35–6
Obligations 27
Omissions, liability in respect of 27
Open Spaces Society 11
'Opposed' Committees 4–5
    advantages of 6–7
    comparison with inquiries 6
    increase in number and length 4–5
Orders *see* Authorising system
'Owner' 34

Parish councils 45

Permitted development 63
Planning authorities consultation 30
Planning inquiries *see* Public local inquiries
Planning permission 60, 61–6
  assimilation of procedures 72–4
  automatic 64
  blight notices 74–5
  coast protection 71–2
  conservation areas *see* listed buildings and
    conservation areas
  deemed grant 65–6
  General Development Order 64
  hazardous substances 71
  Joint Committee recommendations
    61–2, 73
  listed buildings and conservation areas
    60, 66–71
    private Bills 66–8
    TAWA approach 68–71
  need for regulation-making power 73
  Parliamentary debates 63–4
  permitted development 63
  scheduled monument consent 74
  Secretary of State, section 15 power 73–4
  section 15 power 73–4
  section 16 effect 65–6
  section 17 68–9
    consequences 69–71
  TAWA approach 62–3, 68–71
Ports
  Joint Committee recommendations 12–13
  need for statutory authorisation 3
  see also Harbours
Private Acts 1–2
  harbour orders and 82–3
  importance of 2
  intention of promoters 23
  movement to ministerial orders 8–10
    provisional orders 8–9
    special parliamentary procedure 9–10
  'Opposed' Committees
    advantages of 6–7
    comparison with inquiries 6
    increase in number and length 4–5
  opposition on floor of House 5
  planning inquiries 5–6
  Scottish procedure 76–7
Private Bills
  Joint Committee *see* Joint Committee on
    Private Bill procedure
  listed buildings and conservation areas
    planning permission 66–8
  planning system and 7–8
  problems with 4–5
  TAWA and 126–7
Promoters intention 23
Protection of property or interests 27
Public footpaths *see* Footpaths; Rights of way

Public hearings 33–5
  costs 35
Public local inquiries 33–5
  costs 35
  private Bills and 5–6
  schemes of national significance 50–1
Public rights of way *see* Footpaths; Rights
  of way
Public service vehicles
  legislation 100–1
  meaning 100–1

Rail crossings
  safety signs and barriers
    offences 111
    power to place 110
    Secretary of State's powers 111
  stopping up and diversion of footpaths and
    bridleways 103–8
    agriculture or forestry needs 108
    compensation payment 108
    default powers of Secretary of State 107
    diversion orders 105–6
    extinguishment orders 104–5
    maintenance of alternate route 108
    outline 103–4
    partly within and partly outside council
      area 107
    procedure for making orders 106–7
    right of entry to survey 108
  tunnels and bridges for footpaths and
    bridleways 108–9
  time limit for order 109
  written notice of proposed order 109
  see also Railways
Rail guidance, road-based 23
Railways
  accident reporting 115–16
  approval of works, plant and equipment
    113–14
  closure of stations or services 46
  compulsory purchase 3
  definition 20–1
  heritage lines 120, 121
  immunity from nuisance claims 3
  insurance 16–17
  Joint Committee on Private Bill procedure
    recommendations 11
  load limits 16
  narrow gauge 21
  need for statutory authorisation 2, 3
  powers of HM Railway Inspectors 114–15
  Scottish authorisations 78–9
  speed limits 16
  see also Drink and drugs control; Rail
    crossings
Ramblers' Association 11, 109
Rapid transit systems *see* Tramways

Rates payment 28
Revival of undertaking 28
Rights to use systems belonging to others 26–7
Rights of way
  extinguished 25
  harbours 85–6
  see also Footpaths

Safety 112–17
  accident reporting 115–16
  approval of works, plant and equipment 113–14
    offences 113–14
  existing legislation 112
  Fennell Report 112, 115
  Hidden Report 112, 115
  HM Railway Inspectors powers 114–15
  insurance 116–17
  limits on speed and loads 116
  rail crossings
    Secretary of State default powers 107
    signs and barriers
      offences 111
      power to place 110
      Secretary of State's powers 111
  Secretary of State initiated orders 16–17
  see also Drink and drugs control
Scheduled monument consent 74
Schemes of national significance 17–18, 49–51
  commissions 51
  discretion of Secretary of State 51–2
  division of responsibilities 54–6
  hybrid Bills 57–9
  initiated by Secretary of State 56–7
  Joint Committee on Private Bill procedure 49–50
  judicial review 52
  London Gazette notice 53, 56–7
  Parliamentary approval 49
    effect 54–6
    modifications 54
  procedure 53–4
  public inquiries 50–1
  schemes 51–3
Scotland 17
  Government response to Joint Committee 78
  harbours 79, 92–3
  Joint Committee's recommendations 77–8
  petitions for provisional order 76
  private Acts procedure 76–7
  railway authorisations 78–9
  scope of orders 76
Secretary of State
  compulsory purchase certificate 41, 42

Secretary of State – *continued*
  delegation of functions to appointed persons 47
  imposition of requirements to obtain consent of 28–9
  model clauses 43–4
  planning permission
    deemed grant 65–6
    listed buildings and conservation areas 70–1
    section 15 power 73–4
  rail crossing safety 107
  schemes of national significance
    decision 51–2
    initiation 56–7
Section 1 orders 23–9
Section 3 orders 23–9, 97–8
Side guidance
  road-based 23
  track-based 23
Soil sample taking 27
Special parliamentary procedure 9–10
  certificate from Secretary of State 41, 42
  compulsory purchase 40–3
  harbours 92–3
  London Gazette notification 43
  problems with 10
Speed limits 16
Subordinate legislation 18–19
Survey provisions 27
Systems belonging to others 26–7

Tidal barrages 14
Toll charging provisions 27–8
Tramways 99–102
  accident reporting 15–16
  approval of works, plant and equipment 113–14
  crossings *see* Rail crossings
  definition 21
  hackney carriage legislation 101–2
  insurance 16–17
  Joint Committee on Private Bill procedure 99
  leasing 100
  load limits 16
  narrow gauge 21–2
  public service vehicles legislation 100–1
  speed limits 16
  see also Drink and drugs control
Transfer of undertaking 28
Transport Consultative Committees 45–6
Transport systems
  belonging to others 26–7
  construction or operation 23–9
  see also individual forms e.g. Railways
Transport and Works Act 1992
  orders *see* Authorising system

Transport and Works Act 1992 – *continued*
   outline   15
   planning permission   62–3
   restriction of provisions in orders   25
   schedule 1 matters   25–9
   section 1 orders   23–9
   section 3 orders   23–9, 97–8
   supplementary provisions   24–5

Transport and Works Act 1992 – *continued*
   text   128–78
Transport and Works Bill   14–15
'Trolley vehicle system'   22

Validity of order *see* Challenging validity
   of orders
'Vehicles'   22